Fooling
Some of the People
All of the Time

Fooling *Some* of the People *All* of the Time

A Long Short Story

David Einhorn
Foreword by Joel Greenblatt

WILEY

John Wiley & Sons, Inc.

Published by John Wiley & Sons, Inc., Hoboken, New Jersey
Published simultaneously in Canada

For general information on our other products and services or for technical
support, please contact our Customer Care Department within the United States
at (800) 762-2974, outside the United States at (317) 572-3993 or fax (317)
572-4002.

Wiley also publishes its books in a variety of electronic formats. Some content that
appears in print may not be available in electronic books. For more information
about Wiley products, visit our Web site at www.wiley.com.

ISBN-13 978-0-470-07394-0
Printed in the United States of America

10 9 8 7 6 5 4 3 2

In honor of my parents,
Stephen and Nancy Einhorn,
who demonstrated business success
while maintaining high standards of
personal integrity and good humor.

Contents

Foreword

You don't have to be a financial expert to read a great detective novel. But since this story involves billions of dollars and an elaborate plan, it does help to have one of the world's greatest investors around to lead you through all the twists and turns. In the end, the story is simple. It's also thrilling and scary—even more so because, sadly, this isn't a novel. It all actually happened, and as I write, the story continues.

I read this book in two sittings. If eating and sleeping hadn't gotten in the way, it would have been one. I was drawn into a world that few of us have experienced other than at the movies. It really is hard to believe how the legal system, government regulators, and the financial press can all come together and fail so miserably. Most great stories have good guys and bad guys. In simplest form, there are black hats and white hats, and you can tell which side the players are on. Not so in *Fooling Some of the People All of the Time*. Our hero is never quite sure whom he can trust.

But that's okay. As long as you can experience the excitement and intrigue vicariously in the comfort of a bed or couch, it doesn't seem so bad. It's also not so bad to lose some innocence about how the world sometimes works. In the short run, the good guys may get dragged through the mud and the bad guys may get away with millions. But in the long run, the good guys may get dragged through the mud and the bad guys may get away with millions. In the meantime, I will have to give the movie version of the book an R rating. I just don't want my kids to lose their innocence too soon.

JOEL GREENBLATT

Acknowledgments

I am sure that many books benefit from help beyond the author's own ability. *Fooling Some of the People All of the Time* is an extreme example. I have had so much help from so many people, it is impossible to remember who did what. This book is truly a group effort.

First, I want to thank my family. My wife, Cheryl, has been a tremendous helper and supporter both in a literary and an emotional sense. My parents, Nancy and Stephen; brother, Danny; uncle Robbie; mother-in-law, Judie; and sister-in-law Marcy have all helped out on many iterations and made many fantastic suggestions. Finally, I want to thank my children, Rachel, Naomi, and Mitchell, who have allowed me to spend some of our precious family time to work on this book. I hope that when they are older, they will appreciate why I felt telling this story is so important.

Next, I want to thank the entire Greenlight Capital team. My partner, James Lin, has done an incredible job helping me research, follow, and catalog the story. My other partners, Vinit Sethi, Daniel Roitman, Bruce Gutkin, and Harry Brandler, have each made enormous contributions that include everything from suggesting language, improving my memory, helping control the tone, and hunting for typos. Justin Lepone helped with a lot of suggestions and in educating our investors to keep them informed and supportive of this project. Andy Weinfeld coordinated the legal and fact-checking effort. Helen Gorgoni kept track of the various drafts and collated the comments from the many readers. Thank you all.

Thank you, James Schembari for all your hard work and writing. I really appreciate your sharp eye and help in capturing my voice. David Breskin's efforts to polish the manuscript have been truly heroic. Thank you for playing through pain and even putting your his book aside to help mine. I want to thank Rich Zabel, Hyongsoon Kim, Mike Kenny, and Rex Heinke for your excellent advice. I owe thanks to Kelly O'Connor and David Pugh at John Wiley & Sons and from Sandy Dijkstra, my literary agent. Joel Greenblatt has my enormous gratitude—first for introducing me to John Wiley & Sons and second for writing a three-hundred-word Foreword that so perfectly encapsulates the point of this hundred-thousand-word book.

One of the best parts of this experience has been meeting Jim Brickman. I am inspired by his incredible dedication, persistence, research capabilities, and discoveries. Also, thanks to my friend Curtis Schenker. You really had nothing to do with this book, but you got so little credit for building Scoggin in *Hedge Hunters* that I thought you should get a shout out here.

Finally, I need to thank my personal and business friends who took time to read various drafts and give me feedback: Bill Ackman, Steve Bruce, Jim Carruthers, Claire Davis, Lenny Goldberg, Brian Goldman, Adam Goldsmith, Mary Beth Grover, Ian and Neil Isaacs, Daniel Loeb, Robert Medway, Mark Roberts, Jerome Simon, Leonard Tannenbaum, Whitney Tilson, Glenn Tongue, and Rob Usdan. I have taken many of your suggestions, and I hope you smile when you see them in the final book.

SEC lawyer: "At the time that you made the speech, did you anticipate that your position on Allied would become so public, or was it your thought that you would give this speech, say what you thought about the company, and then that would sort of be it, and what would happen to the stock would happen to the stock?"

David Einhorn: "If what you're asking is did I feel that the reaction was much, much greater than I would have anticipated? The answer is *yes*."

Allied Capital Stock Price 2002–2004

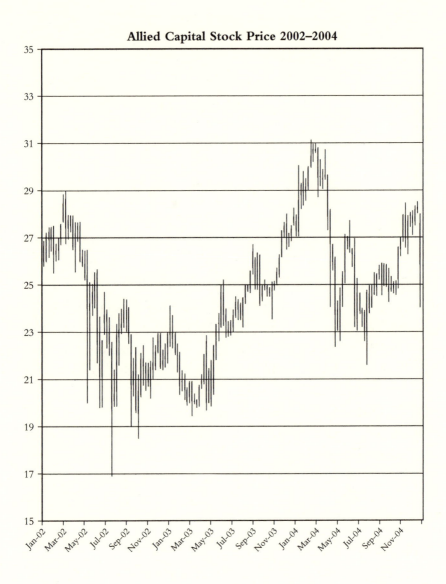

Allied Capital Stock Price 2005–2007

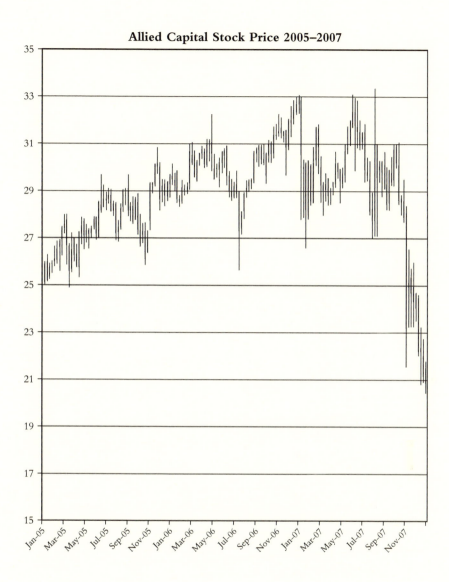

Who's Who

GREENLIGHT & ADVISERS

Steve Bruce Outside PR adviser for Greenlight

Jock Ferguson An investigator with Kroll

Bruce Gutkin Greenlight head trader

Bruce Hiler Outside lawyer for Greenlight

Alexandra Jennings Greenlight analyst

Jeff Keswin Greenlight co-founder

James Lin Greenlight analyst

Daniel Roitman Greenlight COO

Ed Rowley Outside PR adviser for Greenlight

Richard Zabel Outside lawyer for Greenlight

ALLIED & ADVISERS

Steve Auerbach Former BLX workout specialist

Allison Beane Member of Allied's Investor Relations department

Lanny Davis Outside PR adviser for Allied

Seth Faison Outside PR adviser for Allied at Sitrick and Co.

David Gladstone CEO of Gladstone Capital and former CEO of Allied

Patrick Harrington Former executive vice president of Allied and BLX

Robert D. Long Allied managing director

Dale Lynch Head of Allied's Investor Relations department

Matthew McGee Head of the Richmond, Virginia, office of BLX

Penni Roll Allied CFO

Marc Racicot Director of Allied, former governor of Montana and head of Republican National Committee

Deryl Schuster BLX executive

Suzanne Sparrow Former head of Allied's Investor Relations department

Joan Sweeney Allied COO

Robert Tannenhauser BLX CEO

William Walton Allied CEO

George C. Williams Allied Capital founder and chairman emeritus

Tim Williams Former BLX workout specialist

GOVERNMENT OFFICIALS & REGULATORS

Jonathan Barr Federal prosecutor

Mark Braswell SEC lawyer, Allied lobbyist

Christopher Cox chairman of the SEC

William Donaldson Former chairman of the SEC

David R. Gray Counsel to OIG of the SBA and later to the OIG of the USDA

Keith Hohimer Investigator, SBA's Office of Inspector General

Senator John Kerry Chairman of the Senate Committee on Small Business and Entrepeneurship

Kelly Kilroy SEC lawyer

Kevin Kupperbusch Investigator, SBA Office of Inspector General

Tedd Lindsey FBI agent

Steven Preston SBA administrator

Doug Scheidt Associate director of the SEC's Division of Investment Management

Janet Tasker SBA associate administrator for Lender Oversight

Eric Thorson SBA inspector general

Congresswoman Nydia Velázquez Chairwoman of the House Small Business Committee

Senator Olympia Snowe Ranking member of the Senate Committee on Small Business and Entrepeneurship

Eliot Spitzer New York attorney general

WALL STREET ANALYSTS

Mark Alpert Deutsche Bank analyst

Ken Bruce Merrill Lynch analyst

Henry Coffey Ferris Baker Watts analyst

Meghan Crowe Fitch analyst who covers BLX

Don Destino Bank of America and later JMP Securities analyst

Charles Gunther Farmhouse Securities analyst

Joel Houck Wachovia analyst

Michael Hughes Merrill Lynch analyst

Robert Lacoursiere Bank of America analyst

JOURNALISTS

Jenny Anderson Reporter for *The New York Times*

David Armstrong Reporter for *The Wall Street Journal*

Julie Creswell Reporter for *The New York Times*

Kurt Eichenwald Reporter for *The New York Times* and author of *Conspiracy of Fools*

Jesse Eisinger Reporter for *The Wall Street Journal*

Herb Greenberg Columnist for *TheStreet.com* and *CBS Marketwatch.com*

Holman W. Jenkins Jr. Columnist for *The Wall Street Journal*

Jerry Knight Columnist for the *Washington Post*

Floyd Norris Columnist for *The New York Times*

Terrence O'Hara Reporter for the *Washington Post*

Steven Pearlstein Columnist for the *Washington Post*

Carol Remond Reporter for *Dow Jones Newswire*

Thor Valdmanis Reporter for *USA Today*

PROFESSIONAL INVESTORS

Bill Ackman Manager of Gotham Partners

David Berkowitz Manager of Gotham Partners

Warren Buffett Berkshire Hathaway CEO

Jim Carruthers Partner at Eastbourne Capital Management

Peter Collery Manager of Siegler, Collery

Dan Loeb Manager of Third Point Partners

Bill Miller Chief investment officer at Legg Mason Funds

Mark Roberts Founder of *Off Wall Street*

Larry Robbins Manager of Glenview Capital Management

Gary Siegler Manager of Siegler, Collery

Dr. Sam Stewart Founder of Wasatch Advisors
Whitney Tilson Manager of Tilson Capital Partners

ALLIED & BLX CUSTOMERS
Abdulla Al-Jufairi Loan broker on defaulted BLX SBA loans
Hussein Charour Defaulted on SBA loans made through BLX
Amer Farran Defaulted on SBA loans made through BLX
Mangu Patel Defaulted on SBA loans made through BLX
Holly Hawley Defaulted on SBA loans made through BLX
Todd Wichmann Former Redox Brands CEO

NONE OF THE ABOVE
Jim Brickman Retired real-estate developer
Patrick Byrne Overstock.com CEO
André Perold Professor at Harvard Business School

INTRODUCTION

The Spark of a Speech

My father, Stephen, wanted to write a book before he turned forty, and at thirty-eight realized he better get started. Since he wasn't yet ready to delve into a serious issue or share a grand vision of the future, he wrote a joke book.

On his fortieth birthday, our entire extended family from around the country joined us in Milwaukee to celebrate. The party was held at a Chinese restaurant. Each member of the family had to give a "review" of the book. The catch: The books weren't to be handed out until the end of the night.

I remember Grandpa Ben getting up with his notes. As he stood there, he allowed the paper to unwind like a roll of toilet paper until it extended to the floor. He proceeded to review the book. "On page 11 it says . . ." and he told a funny story. "On page 49 the joke goes . . ." and he told a funnier story. "On page 361 Steve wrote . . ." and we were falling off our seats. "On page 12,329 the joke begins . . ."

That evening is one of my best childhood memories.

After the party, Dad gave me the very first copy of his book *If You Try to Please Everyone, You Will Lose Your A** . . . and 89 Other Philosophical Thoughts*. My parents sold about a thousand copies. I think there are probably a few hundred left in the basement. Dad has updated it for his sixty-fifth birthday in June 2008.

Though I had no intention of writing a book by the time I turned forty, extraordinary circumstances have caused me to beat the deadline. I wish it were a joke book. It's not.

This is the story of a dishonest company called Allied Capital. If you play with the name it isn't hard to conjure ALL LIED CAPITAL. Think of it as *The Firm* in John Grisham's book without the sexual tension and chase scenes. This is a company that is not only fooling its shareholders by paying lofty "dividends" partly based on new capital contributions in a classic pyramid scheme format, but is also robbing taxpayers.

I may be a "whistle-blower," but I'm no Erin Brockovich. I am one of the luckiest people in the world. I have terrific parents who raised me well. I have a smart and wonderful wife and three good-spirited, healthy children. I have had success in business that I never dreamed I could achieve. I work with intelligent, good people. To me, it isn't even really work. Compared to hard work like manual labor or dealing with a difficult boss, my work is fun.

Not many people have heard of Allied. I have been asked repeatedly: "Who cares about Allied Capital? What are you trying to accomplish? Who is the audience?"

There are a few possible audiences for this book. The first is members of the Greenlight Capital "family." Greenlight is the investment company I run. Our core products are commonly known as hedge funds. I believe we have an excellent reputation—not just for good results, but for thorough analysis and integrity. We are a firm that is not shy about self-criticism when we make mistakes, and we make plenty.

For those of you who are part of the Greenlight family, I am happy you are reading this story, but you are not the target audience. As you may already know, Greenlight has held a "short" position in Allied Capital for six years; that is, we have allocated a portion of the fund to profit if Allied's stock declines in value. Most of you have heard me describe Allied's misconduct for years. As a result, you may already agree with me and share my frustration.

A second possible audience is the tens of thousands of holders of Allied stock. If you have invested in this business development company (BDC), you have done consistently well for up to forty-five years. As a large group of mostly individual investors, you appear not to care about what I have to say. Judging by some of the nasty e-mails I have received, some of you vociferously resent Greenlight's efforts. You do care about Allied's quarterly cash distributions. As long as they keep coming, most of you are in for the ride. Many of you will probably think this book is a desperate attempt to persuade you to dump your Allied stock so Greenlight can make money as the stock falls. Management has repeatedly said I am on a "campaign of misinformation for personal profit." You probably believe them. If so, nothing I write will change your view.

What you may not understand is that in the scheme of things, Greenlight's bet against Allied Capital is not that significant. While there may be a lot of dollars at stake, Allied is not our largest or most important investment. Over the last six years, our firm has had 3 percent to 8 percent of its capital invested in selling short Allied.

Also, in 2002 Greenlight's principals pledged to donate half of anything we personally made on Allied to a pediatric cancer hospital. When the investment didn't pan out as quickly as we hoped, Greenlight donated $1 million to the hospital in 2005. As I said at the time, "I have been waiting, but the children should not have to wait." With the publication of this book, we are now pledging to give the other half of our potential personal profit (including our share of book royalties), to two worthy organizations: the Center for Public Integrity and the Project On Government Oversight, both in Washington, D.C. This book shows, if nothing else, that we need better investigative journalism and government watch-dogs. This should make clear that my interest in the story now extends well beyond money, because no matter how far Allied's stock price eventually falls, I personally don't stand to make a dime. Nonetheless, Allied shareholders are not the target audience for this book, either. Frankly, I'm surprised if many of you have read this far.

Of course, Allied management doesn't want you to read this book, either. In fact, they don't want anyone to read this book. They have had their lawyers send at least five letters to the publisher to discourage this book's publication. They have offered to make Allied's senior management available to the publisher to make sure the book is "accurate, responsible and fair." The publisher advised Allied that it would be more appropriate to have management direct its concerns to the author of the book, and I offered to meet with them to give management that opportunity and to ask some questions of my own. Of course, this same management, which has refused opportunities to meet with us for years, declined again. In fact, as I will describe later, Allied management has a standing policy of avoiding meeting with *any* hedge funds. Allied's lawyers say, "There may well be a book that a long-short hedge fund manager like Mr. Einhorn should write that tells the story of how the 'shorts do well' by 'doing good,' i.e., how they make millions while also helping the SEC and other regulators." They just don't think Allied is the right example. I think readers of this book will be the judge of that.

My desired audience is much broader than these small groups. I hope this book is ideal for those who know something about investing and care about the stock market, business, ethics, and government itself, which is supposed to keep the playing field flat and fair. As you read this book, at some point you will say to yourself, "Enough! Enough! I get it, already! This is a bad company! You've made your point!"

But have I? The reason for writing this story is to document via a "case study" the wrongdoing of Allied Capital, and as important, to unveil the indifferent attitude of regulators—our government representatives—toward that wrongdoing.

As you read, you may ask the same questions I ask myself: Where are the regulators? Where is the Securities and Exchange Commission (SEC)? Who works at these government agencies that are so uncaring about misuse of taxpayer money? What is Congress doing? What are the prosecutors doing? What are the auditors and the board of directors doing? And, finally, where are the investigative reporters and their editors who are capable of digging into a tough story and blowing the whistle?

Many believe that Enron and WorldCom exposed corporate fraud. The lawbreakers, after all, were prosecuted and Congress came in and passed new, tough antifraud laws. It's true that many public companies are now more careful and have better financial controls. The problem is that not all the bad guys have been prosecuted, the authorities do not seem to care and investors will get hurt, again.

As bizarre as this seems, in retrospect, this all began as a charity case—a charity called the Tomorrows Children's Fund. The fund supports a hospital, based in Hackensack, New Jersey, that treats kids with cancer.

The charity raises money by hosting an annual investment research conference, where well-known investors share a few stock picks and pans with an audience that pays to attend the event. All proceeds go to the hospital. Though I didn't consider myself to be well known, I was honored to speak at the 2002 conference. After I learned about the cancer center and the services that it provides to sick children and their families, I immediately knew that this was a cause worth supporting. I would be in special company, and I wanted to do a good job.

I had never given a public speech to a large group of strangers. I really wanted to discuss an idea that would hold the audience's attention. At that moment, the most compelling idea in our portfolio was to sell short the shares of Allied. Short selling is the opposite of owning, or being *long*, a stock. When you are long, the idea is to buy low and sell high. In a short sale, you still want to buy low and sell high, but in this case the sale comes before the purchase. It works this way: Your broker borrows shares from a shareholder who lends them to you, and you sell them in the market to a new buyer, thus establishing a short position. To close out the position at a later date, you buy shares in the market and return them to your broker to "cover" your short, and the broker returns them to the owner. Your profit or loss is the difference between the price you receive when you sell the shares short and the price you pay to buy them back. The more the stock falls, the more money you make—and vice versa.

At a conference of eleven speakers, I spoke third to last. A number of the speakers before me had superb ideas. Larry Robbins of Glenview Capital explained how General Motors' long-term pension and health liabilities would become a large problem for the company—this was two years before the subject became front-page news. Bill Miller of Legg Mason recommended Nextel, while Morris Smith, the former manager of the Fidelity Magellan mutual fund, talked about Candies, the shoe company.

By the time I gave my speech about Allied Capital, it was late in the afternoon. The market had closed for trading. After I detailed Allied's problems, word spread about the speech, and the next morning the company's stock was unable to open when the market did because there were too many sell orders for the New York Stock Exchange specialist to balance them on time. When the shares did trade, they opened down 20 percent. But the steep decline that day was nothing compared to the plunge I was about to take, spending years uncovering what I view as a fathomless fraud.

This book details the company's fraud; the regulatory agencies that are failing to do their jobs to stop it; and the stock analysts and reporters who mostly fail to print the truth because they are biased, intimidated, lazy or just not interested. As I wrote to the SEC about Allied in October 2003, allowing Allied to persist in this behavior harms investors and other honest companies that follow the rules.

Allied's management has had unending opportunities to answer my allegations, and I have not seen them once address the actual facts that form the basis of my allegations. They can't. Instead, they have cried manipulation. Rather than have me tell you about the speech, you can see it for yourself at www.foolingsomepeople.com.

PART ONE

A Charity Case and Greenlight Capital

CHAPTER 1

Before Greenlight

My father and grandfather were businessmen. The family business was Adelphi Paints in New Jersey. When the first energy crisis came in the early 1970s, the business suffered. My grandparents decided to sell. Though my father was a chemist, he worked on the sale of the company. When it was over, he enjoyed the work so much he decided that his future would be in mergers and acquisitions (M&A). He tried to get a job on Wall Street but did not have the right background.

My dad decided to open his own M&A shop in the basement of our house in Demarest, New Jersey. After a year with little success, my mom convinced him to move us back to Milwaukee, where she grew up and where her family remained. We moved in 1976, when I was seven. My father started his business again by working out of a converted bedroom in our house in the suburb of Fox Point.

Suburban Milwaukee was a great place to grow up. I rooted for the Milwaukee Brewers and its stars, Robin Yount and Paul Molitor. I went to a lot of games, including the World Series in 1982. The Brewers may have been a bad team for most of my life, but to have your team at its peak when you are thirteen years old is an experience I wish for every fan.

I was a pretty good student, especially in math. I spent most of high school working on the debate team, probably at some expense to my grades. Being a member of the team was great training in critical analysis, organization, and logic. I was very excited when my wife, Cheryl, announced that in honor of the tenth anniversary of Greenlight Capital, she had sponsored the creation of an Urban Debate League in Milwaukee, where hundreds of high school students will get debate training and experience. Apparently, debate raises test scores, literacy, and graduation rates. I am not surprised—I benefited enormously from the experience.

My parents often discussed business at the dinner table. Like his father, my dad has an enormous reservoir of patience and persistence. My mom is much more demanding. The M&A business was tough. My dad was paid mostly on contingency. This means that he would often work hard for a deal that did not close and would get paid little, if anything, for his effort. Other times, the deal would go so smoothly that the client would look at Dad's work and conclude that it was so easy that the fee was not fair. Because the fee was not due until after the closing, many of the clients would take the opportunity to renegotiate. Mom always thought Dad was soft in these negotiations. Dad tended to take a longer-term view. Eventually, he moved the business out of the house. As it grew, it became successful and enabled Dad to provide well for our family. On my best days, I fancy myself a combination of Dad's persistence/patience and Mom's toughness/skepticism.

I majored in government at Cornell University, but became more interested in economics after I interned during my junior year at the Office of Economic Analysis at the SEC in Washington. I wrote my thesis on the cyclical regulation of the U.S. airline industry. Policy makers balance two competing interests: Airlines want to make money, but consumers want cheap, ubiquitous air transport. In the anticompetitive phase of the cycle, regulators allow airlines to generate generous profits by operating monopolies on routes, capturing cities as hubs, and eliminating competition by merging. This leads to unhappy consumers and politicians, who then require procompetitive measures to provide more and cheaper service, which kills the profitability of the industry. After the airlines suffer through losses or even bankruptcies, policy makers realize that having airlines is a good thing. To induce airlines to buy planes and provide service, there has to be a profit opportunity, so the anti-competitive phase of the cycle returns. This vicious pattern perhaps explains Warren Buffett's quip that investors should have shot the Wright brothers' plane from the sky at Kitty Hawk. This thesis won me highest honors in the Government Department, and Greenlight, not surprisingly, has never owned a U.S. airline stock.

I started to look for a job through on-campus recruiting. I met with a lot of companies, including *The Company*—the Central Intelligence Agency. I received a few offers and decided to take the one as an investment banking analyst at Donaldson, Lufkin & Jenrette (DLJ), even though it offered the lowest salary. I chose it because I liked the people I met during recruiting. I later realized I needed to work on my judgment.

I had two miserable years at DLJ, which provided a different kind of education. Working there felt like pledging a fraternity, except the hazers had no interest in even pretending to be friends. I won't go into the gory details, but a few years ago John Rolfe and Peter Troob wrote *Monkey Business*, a graphic account of life as a junior investment banker at DLJ. Their description is consistent with my memory, including the true-to-life, hysterical description about managing the copying-center personnel. The main difference between their experience and mine: I was one level on the totem pole junior to them, which made life that much worse.

Part of my problem was that I did not have any idea what the job entailed when I started working there. When DLJ recruited its analysts, it sought a mix between finance/economics types and liberal arts types. As a government major, I fell into the latter group. I did not have any friends who had taken junior investment banking jobs, so I did not understand what the company's representatives meant when they asked me during the recruiting process, "Are you willing to work hard?" I gave the right answer, but I didn't realize I had just committed to 100-hour-plus workweeks. When I grew up, Dad made it home for dinner every night, and, I believe, so did all of my friends' dads. I had never heard about jobs that required sitting in the office all day waiting for assignments that were generally passed out around dinner. The work lasted into the wee hours and often overnight. I did not understand the concept of staying in the office until everyone senior to me left—even when I had nothing to do. Further, I did not understand that being an analyst was a rite of passage that required "sacrifice" for its own sake, even when it provided no benefit to the project at hand. But I did it anyway because that was the culture.

I would often sleep on a pillow under my desk while the word-processing department prepared documents or the copy center made them into presentation books. Cheryl, my wife, would bring me a clean shirt in the morning on her way to work. I had certainly never before heard the adage, "If you aren't coming in on Saturday, don't even think about coming in on Sunday!" I started in August 1991 and by Thanksgiving had lost fifteen pounds.

After two years, analysts were expected to need a break that would be provided by business school. I had no intention of continuing my life as an investment banker, so I decided not to go to school. When a headhunter called and asked if I would like to interview at a hedge fund, my first response was, "Yes." Then I asked, "What's a hedge fund?" That is how Siegler, Collery & Company (SC) found me.

Gary Siegler and Peter Collery managed the SC Fundamental Value Fund, a mid-sized hedge fund with about $150 million under management. Today, a similar fund would have a couple of billion dollars. SC grew to about $500 million by the time I left. It was a great place to learn the business.

There, I learned how to invest and perform investment research from Peter, a patient and dedicated mentor. I spent weeks researching a company, reading the SEC filings, building spreadsheets and talking to management and analysts. Then I went into Peter's office to discuss the opportunity with him. He heard me out and then took my file on the train. The next morning he returned to work having read everything and made a detailed list of questions that I *wished* I had asked. When I started working at SC, I would not know the answers to any of them; after a couple of years, I usually could answer about half.

Peter combed through the SEC filings for ambiguities in the description of the business or the discussion of the results. He spotted signs of good or poor corporate behavior, not to mention aggressive or conservative accounting. There were three basic questions to resolve: First, what are the true economics of the business? Second, how do the economics compare to the reported earnings? Third, how are the interests of the decision makers aligned with the investors?

In early 1996, along with an SC colleague, Jeff Keswin, I resigned from the firm to start Greenlight Capital. Cheryl named the firm, giving me the green light. When you leave a good job to go off on your own and don't expect to make money for a while, you name the firm whatever your wife says you should.

CHAPTER 2

Getting the "Green light"

Jeff Keswin and I made our initial business plan on a napkin at a restaurant around the corner from SC's offices. He would be the marketer and business partner, while I would be the portfolio manager. He did not know exactly where he would raise the initial capital, but figured that with his contacts we could start with $10 million. I told my parents about it, and to my surprise, in a vote of support, they volunteered to invest $500,000.

Jeff and I each wrote a $10,000 check to start Greenlight. It was the only check I ever wrote for the business. We printed stationery and bought computers, a TV, and a fax machine. We rented a 130-square-foot space from Spear, Leeds & Kellogg, our custodian or prime broker. It was a tight squeeze getting past the filing cabinet to my desk. We shared a photocopier with the five other small trading outfits in our "suite."

In February 1996, I wrote a brochure outlining our investment program and illustrating sample investments. Though the hedge fund industry is generally known for its secrecy, I saw no reason to be secretive. I felt that if we explained our investment program, how individual investments fit into the program and what happened and why, our investors would have greater confidence in us. They would also understand that even our failures came from reasoned, disciplined decisions.

Either way, I believed this would lead to a more informed, confident, and stable partner base. We refer to our investors as "partners" because that is how we view them.

Part of the reputation hedge funds have for secrecy comes from the SEC's prohibitions against advertising. As a result, many hedge funds make fewer public disclosures than they otherwise would. SEC Commissioner Paul Atkins noted the problem in a speech in January 2007: "We need to stop scaring ourselves and others with rhetoric about hedge funds. Rather than talking about how hedge funds 'operate in the shadows,' let us take a look at the regulatory constraints on hedge fund advisers that stop them from saying anything about their funds publicly. One irony of the SEC's complaints about the secretive nature of the hedge fund industry is that advertising restrictions on hedge funds have been interpreted broadly so that hedge fund advisers do not dare to say anything publicly." Though the outside world may view hedge funds as secretive because the updates are not public, Greenlight communicates openly with our partners except regarding what we are about to buy or sell.

Our investment program employs the skills I learned at SC to analyze the economic value of companies and the alignment of interests between decision makers and investors. Our research process reverses the analytical framework that most traditional value investors use. Many value investors determine whether a security is cheap. If it is, they seek to determine whether it is cheap for a good reason. A typical process to identify opportunities is through computer screens that identify statistical cheapness, such as low multiples of earnings, sales, or book value combined with rising earnings estimates. Then, they evaluate the identified companies as possible investments.

Greenlight takes the opposite approach. We start by asking why a security is likely to be misvalued in the market. Once we have a theory, we analyze the security to determine if it is, in fact, cheap or overvalued. In order to invest, we need to understand why the opportunity exists and believe we have a sizable analytical edge over the person on the other side of the trade. The market is an impersonal place. When we buy something, we generally do not know who is selling. It would be foolish to assume that our counterparty is uninformed or unsophisticated. In most circumstances, today's seller has followed the situation longer and more closely than we have, has previously been a buyer, and has now changed his mind to become a seller. Even worse, the counterparty could be a company insider or an informed industry player working at a key supplier, customer or competitor. Some investors believe they have an advantage trafficking in stocks that have minimal Wall Street analyst coverage. We believe it doesn't matter if a stock is "underfollowed" because the person we are buying from probably *has followed* the stock and we need to have a better grasp on the situation than he does. Given who that may be, our burden is high.

Many traditional long-only managers design their portfolios to perform over the next six to twelve months. Hedge funds attack the resulting inefficiency from both sides. Some believe that horizon is too long. They do not care whether a stock is going to do well in a year. They want to do well today or this week or, at worst, this month. These funds usually hold positions for a short time. Many of them are "black box" funds, where computer programs tell them what to buy. Others are news driven and want to know whether the next piece of news, or "data point," will be positive or negative. Some of these short-term-oriented funds rely on technical analysis, the study of security trading patterns, to decipher the likely near-term future direction, while others rely on the manager's trading instinct, feel, and experience. Many use a combination of insights, and some have been quite successful. These types of funds, though, tend to have little to no transparency. Nobody on the outside really knows much about the portfolio. Even if they were willing to disclose a lot, it would not be so informative because the holdings change so frequently. When the investing is computer driven, the managers of the fund are not interested in sharing the program, because the program *is* the business.

Greenlight believes the traditional investment horizon is too short because equities are long, if not indefinite-duration, assets. When we make an investment, we usually don't have any idea how long we will be invested. If the downside of an opportunity is no short-term return or "dead money," we can live with that. We are happy to hold for more than a year before succeeding. In practice, some "dead money" opportunities work out more quickly than we expect. A portfolio where some investments work quickly, some work slowly, and the rest retain their value generates exciting results. The trick is to avoid losers. Losers are terrible because it takes a success to offset them just to get back to even. We strive to preserve capital on each investment. It does not always work out that way, but that is the goal.

As we generally have long holding periods, there is no reason not to disclose key positions. Some of our peers disclose little because they worry people will gossip over their inevitable errors. Journalists seem increasingly joyful to report stories about hedge fund mistakes. Greenlight experienced that when we were large holders in (and I was a director of) New Century Financial, a subprime mortgage originator, which imploded in early 2007. My view is that actually losing money is much worse than the mere embarrassment of others' seeing we were wrong.

Though our research process relies heavily on my SC training, Greenlight constructs the portfolio differently from SC. The largest investments at SC were "pair trades." A pair trade matches two companies in the same industry trading at widely disparate valuations. SC would buy the cheaper company of the pair and sell short the more expensive one. In the best cases, the long had better prospects or more conservative accounting than the short. Pair trades attempt to hedge a portfolio's investments by eliminating both market risk and industry risk and capturing the valuation convergence over time.

Starting with a good idea and finding a disparately valued industry comparable to match creates a pair trade. Often, the second half of the pair trade is not a worthwhile investment other than as an industry and/or market hedge. If one ranked investments on a scale from one to ten, with one being a perfect long idea and ten being a perfect short idea, a portfolio of pair trades will have a lot of threes and fours paired against sixes and sevens from the same industry. Greenlight generally does not engage in pairs trading. We accept more industry risk, but assemble a portfolio where we believe our longs are ones and twos and our shorts are nines and tens. We do not short to hedge. If we are uncomfortable with the risk in a position, we simply reduce or eliminate it. By having a portfolio of worthwhile longs and worthwhile shorts, we achieve a partial market hedge without having to spend capital on negative-expected-return propositions.

Every time we risk capital long or short, we believe the investment has individual merit. Our goal is to make money, or at least to preserve capital, on every investment. This means securities should be sufficiently mispriced, so that if we are right, we will do well, but if we are mostly wrong, we will roughly break even. Obviously, if we are massively wrong, we will lose money. We do not use indexes to hedge because we can add more value by choosing individual names with poor risk-reward characteristics to short. An index hedge has a negative expected value because the market rises over time and the short pays only in a falling market. Selling short individual names offers two ways to win—either the market declines or the company-specific analysis proves correct. In practice, we have more long exposure than short exposure because our shorts tend to have greater market sensitivity and volatility than our longs. Also, the market tends to rise over time and we wish to participate. It is psychologically challenging to manage a portfolio that outperforms only a falling market. I have no desire to spend my life hoping for a market crash.

Another difference from SC is that we avoid "evolving hypotheses." If our investment rationale proves false, we exit the position rather than create a new justification to hold. We exit when our analysis is wrong or we just can't stand the pain, rather than when the market simply disagrees longer than we had imagined. Everyone is wrong some of the time. At SC, the principals were smart and believed the firm was smart. It is hard for smart people to admit a mistake. As a research analyst at SC, if I recommended a long idea at $10 and the stock fell to $7, there was an enormous institutional bias toward my recommending additional purchase, even if that required inventing a new rationale for the position. If the shares hit $5, it could become one of the largest positions in the fund. This created the risk that SC would put the most money into the ideas where SC was the most wrong.

We consider ourselves to be "absolute-return" investors and do not compare our results to long-only indices. That means that our goal is to try to achieve positive results over time regardless of the environment. I believe the enormous attraction of hedge funds comes from their absolute-return orientation. Most long-only investors, including mutual funds, are relative-return investors; their goal is to outperform a benchmark, generally the S&P 500. In assessing an investment opportunity, a relative-return investor asks, "Will this investment outperform my benchmark?" In contrast, an absolute-return investor asks, "Does the reward of this investment outweigh the risk?" This leads to a completely different analytical framework. As a result, both investors might look at the same situation and come to opposite investment conclusions.

The popular misperception is that investors are attracted to hedge funds for the status, the secrecy, the leverage, and, according to one preposterous magazine account, the high fees. The truth is simpler: Asking the better question of risk-versus-reward gives hedge funds an enormous opportunity to create superior risk-adjusted returns compared to relative-return strategies. While the media do not understand this, hedge fund investors do.

There are other misconceptions about hedge fund performance. It is easy to measure performance, but difficult to assess underlying risks. As a result, it is easy to highlight performance comparisons between hedge funds and the S&P 500. To some, if the S&P is up 20 percent and hedge funds are up 15 percent, then hedge funds have not earned their keep and investors have wasted a lot of money on high fees. Given the different frameworks, comparing the results of an absolute-return strategy to a long-only benchmark is almost meaningless. It is almost like observing that the Dallas Cowboys (football) have a better winning percentage than the New York Yankees (baseball). It is important to judge a strategy compared to its goals and contexts. If the Yankees' goal is to win the World Series and they do, what is the point of comparing their record to the Cowboys' record? Likewise, if a hedge fund seeks to achieve an attractive, risk-adjusted, positive absolute return and does that, then it has accomplished what it set out to do.

Similarly, the media misunderstand the risks in hedge funds. Academic research demonstrates that hedge funds have far less volatility or risk than long-only indices. However, once in a while a hedge fund fails spectacularly. Either the manager made poor or unlucky decisions or, worse, stole the money. Obviously, fraud needs to be prosecuted aggressively.

As a whole, these spectacular blow-ups grab so many headlines that it throws the popular perception of hedge funds out of whack. Just as individual companies implode from time to time due to poor strategy, bad luck, or fraud, so do hedge funds. Even considering the occasional meltdowns and the higher fees, hedge funds generally provide attractive risk-adjusted returns.

I decided to run a concentrated portfolio. As Joel Greenblatt pointed out in *You Can Be a Stock Market Genius Even If You're Not Too Smart: Uncover the Secret Hiding Places of Stock Market Profits*, holding eight stocks eliminates 81 percent of the risk in owning just one stock, and holding thirty-two stocks eliminates 96 percent of the risk. Greenblatt concludes, "After purchasing six or eight stocks in different industries, the benefit of adding even more stocks to your portfolio in an effort to decrease risk is small." This insight struck me as incredibly important. It is hard to find long ideas that are ones and twos or shorts that are nines and tens, so when we find them, it is important to invest enough to be rewarded. Based on this concept, we decided that Greenlight would have a concentrated portfolio with up to 20 percent of capital in a single long idea (so it had better be a one!) and generally would have 30 percent to 60 percent of capital in our five largest longs. We would size the shorts half as large as we would longs of the same quality, because when shorts move against us, they become a bigger portion of the portfolio and to give us the ability to endure initial losses and maintain or even increase the investment. In most successful short sales, we lose money gradually for a period of time until we suddenly make a large gain—often in a single day.

It turned out that raising $10 million to start Greenlight proved too ambitious. As we went through the contact list and took whatever meetings we could get, we soon realized that almost no one would invest with a couple of twenty-seven-year-olds with no track record. We decided that the only way to get a track record would be to get started. In one year we could have a one-year record, and in three years a three-year record. It was not going to happen any faster than that.

We launched in May 1996 with $900,000—more than half from my parents. Our initial investments included MDC Holdings, a homebuilder that we still own, and EMCOR, an electrical and mechanical systems contractor that had recently emerged from bankruptcy. We made a good profit on EMCOR, though it took until 2001 before it really worked.

We made 3.1 percent in May 1996. (Whenever I cite Greenlight fund returns, they are after fees and expenses, that is, the "net" to the partners unless otherwise indicated as "gross." I always discuss the impact of individual investments on the gross return.) At the end of the month, we invested 15 percent of the fund in C. R. Anthony, a small retailer that had recently emerged from bankruptcy and returned to profitability. The market valued the company at $18 million despite its having twice that in net working capital (current assets less all liabilities). Greenlight returned 6.9 percent in June.

In July, the market suffered a correction and the S&P 500 fell 4.5 percent. However, our portfolio enjoyed several good events and generated a 4.8 percent profit. We had bought bonds in the campsite operator U.S. Trails at 77 percent in June, and the bonds got called at 100 percent in July. We made a nice gain when the semiconductor capital equipment manufacturer Tylan General announced it would be sold at a good premium. Finally, our larger short position (we had only two at the time), Microwarehouse, announced terrible results due to systems problems, and the stock collapsed.

After the close of trading on the last day of each month, I stood at the fax machine and sent the statements to the partners one at a time. Most of the people we met before we launched asked to be kept informed, whether they meant it or not. Now, a few began to notice and send money. We got our first million-dollar partner that August.

The year could have gone better only if we had not missed some opportunities. At one point during the summer, I considered an investment in the creditor claims in the bankrupt retailer Best Products. I finished the work, but rather than buy the position, I decided to "sleep on it." I came in the next morning and told Keswin that I wanted to make it a 12 percent position. I called the salesman I had discussed the idea with at a brokerage firm that traded the claims and gave him my order. He asked if I had seen the news. I hadn't. Service Merchandise had agreed to buy the company, and the claims had doubled overnight. Of course, making a mistake on an actual investment is far direr than missing a good opportunity.

Another of our initial partners thanked us for the good results by giving us a list of about a dozen of his "wealthy" friends. Most became partners. One did not invest because he presented me with a brainteaser card puzzle that I couldn't solve. He asked me to take one suit from the deck and arrange it so the cards would appear in sequential order when I turned the top card face up, put the next card on the bottom of the deck, turned the next card face up, put the next card on the bottom of the deck, and so forth. I blew it: I would have to work on my card skills. (The correct order is A, Q, 2, 8, 3, J, 4, 9, 5, K, 6, 10, 7.)

Greenlight returned 37.1 percent in the last two-thirds of 1996 without a down month. Our assets under management hit $13 million. We decided to have a "partners' dinner" to explain our results and rented a small room in an Italian restaurant on the Upper East Side of Manhattan. The partners came on a snowy evening in January. And they weren't just Mom and Dad, but about twenty-five people—almost everyone we invited, including several from outside of New York. We gave a presentation of the business and the results. It was not hard, as both longs and shorts contributed, and we did not have a significant money-losing investment to discuss. The results were led by C. R. Anthony, which had increased 500 percent and generated about one-third of the return.

The next day, Bruce Gutkin, one of our four "Day One" investors, who would eventually become our head trader in 2004—originally our only trader, but this is an age of title inflation—called to say not only how enjoyable the dinner was, but that his wife remarked on the way home that "this is how big things get started."

CHAPTER 3

Greenlight's
Early Successes

We started 1997 strong and returned 13.1 percent in the first quarter. Then, I made my first costly mistake. There are two types of bad outcomes. Sometimes, after analyzing the risk and reward, an investment appears attractive, but the unfortunate or unlikely happens. Such is life. Other times, the analysis is simply flawed: The investment is poor and we deserve the eventual loss. This mistake was the latter. We invested 6 percent of capital into Reliance Acceptance, which charged 18 percent for car loans to people with tarnished credit. The key investment issue: Was that 18 percent enough to cover the losses from loan defaults, which were harder to estimate? I analyzed the car repossession data and determined that Reliance repossessed 20 percent of the cars and lost 40 percent of the loan each time. The loans lasted two years, so I calculated annual losses to be 20 percent × 40 percent ÷ 2, or 4 percent. The high interest rate appeared sufficient to cover the losses and the stock appeared cheap, at a discount to book value.

I erred by not framing the loss analysis properly. The repossession statistics did not include about 10 percent of the loans where the repossessor *could not find the car*. Obviously, these loans were 100 percent losses. This meant the real losses were more than twice what I'd calculated. The 18 percent interest did not cover the cost of funds, the true losses, and the operating expenses. We lost about half our investment before I realized my error. This led to our first down month in April, where we lost 0.3 percent.

The rest of the year was a cakewalk. The biggest winners: insurance company demutualizations, spin-offs, Pinnacle Systems, and some short sales. Demutualizations are good hunting grounds for our type of investing. Many insurance companies have been formed as customer cooperatives, or "mutuals." In a mutual, there is no share ownership, but policyholders, who are considered the "owners," do have some rights, such as electing directors. Management's simple self-interest is to stay solvent. They tend to have conservative accounting policies because there is no stock price or even an organized ownership group to worry about. On the margin, large reported profits generate taxes and raise the possibility that the policyholders might demand some of the money back, either through lower premiums or surplus payments. Reporting profits actually could lead to eventual financial trouble—the one thing management needs to avoid.

From time to time, mutuals convert themselves to stock companies in a transaction called a demutualization. The most attractive deals are 100 percent sales of the stock in an initial public offering (IPO), with the proceeds going to the company. The new investors effectively get the company for free, as ownership of the post-IPO stock includes both the IPO proceeds held at the company and the company itself. Add in a nice dose of stock options for management set at the IPO price, and the incentives and the structure allow new shareholders and management to make a killing with little risk. In many cases, lackluster-performing companies begin to show remarkable profit improvements after the IPO.

Some spin-offs have similar dynamics, though they need to be assessed case by case. A spin-off is when a large company divests a subsidiary by distributing the subsidiary's shares to the parent company's shareholders. Over the years, we have found that carefully selected spin-offs are terrific opportunities.

Pinnacle Systems was a technology company that had reported a couple of disappointing quarters. Its stock traded down to book value, which was mostly cash. Many value investors eschew investing in technology companies because the products are complicated and the field changes rapidly. We take the view that technology companies that are not losing money, are trading at book value, and appear to have a viable product are good investments. It proved to be the case in this instance, and when Pinnacle reported better results, the shares tripled.

Finally, some of our short sales made nice contributions in 1997, including Boston Chicken and Samsonite. Boston Chicken's accounting practices enabled it to recognize up-front revenue and profit when franchisees opened restaurants. Boston Chicken financed the openings and up-front fees and earned interest on loans to the franchisees. The underlying restaurants were not profitable enough to support the payments to the parent. Boston Chicken's shareholders were not concerned, or perhaps were not even aware that franchisees lost money, because Boston Chicken did not consolidate the franchise operations in its financial statements. We believed that if the restaurant economics were not robust enough for the franchisees to satisfy their obligations to Boston Chicken and make a reasonable return for themselves, they would stop opening more restaurants and Boston Chicken's price-to-earnings multiple would fall as it stopped growing. It turned out even worse because the franchisees defaulted on the loans. Eventually, Boston Chicken went bankrupt.

Samsonite also collapsed. We sold its shares short at $28 and watched them soar to $45. I checked and rechecked the thesis and decided to suck it up. Samsonite had raised prices and broadened its distribution network at the same time. It had opened many of its own stores, which aggressively competed against its own wholesale customers, the retailers. We saw a luggage store in Manhattan with a window display sign promoting "Samsonite 40% off." We bought the sign to hang in our office. The clerk gave us a funny look. It turned out that wasn't the only store working off excess Samsonite inventory. When Samsonite acknowledged that consumers didn't accept the price increase and retailers were awash in excess inventory, the shares collapsed to $6.

We hired our first employees in the summer and moved into our own office in the Graybar Building, next to Grand Central Terminal. Our 1,300 square feet felt like a palace. I had my own office and could talk to my wife on the telephone without anyone knowing what we would be having for dinner that night.

We ended 1997 up 57.9 percent with $75 million under management. We decided not to accept additional money until we were prepared to invest it. Why? Adding too much new capital to a portfolio too quickly is a problem. It creates undue pressure to find new investments or to add to existing positions. We do not deploy new capital into existing positions unless they are either fresh ideas or positions to which we really want to add. However, while professional money managers habitually put new money into existing ideas, we don't feel comfortable doing that when an investment is already in the middle innings. If we buy something at $10 thinking it is worth $20, do we really want to add to it at $16 if we think the value hasn't changed? It is better to wait for a fresh opportunity or to close the fund to new investment. On the other hand, when the portfolio is fully invested, adding new assets helps investment performance. It allows room for new opportunities without selling existing positions prematurely. We have accepted new capital from time to time under those circumstances.

Fifty people attended the 1997 partners' dinner at the Penn Club. We expected it to be a celebration. It was not. After our presentation, we took questions. Several partners complained about how fast the assets under management had grown. They worried we would not be able to keep up the returns. I explained that we closed the fund and would not accept new money until we were fully invested and emphasized that we did not expect to make 57 percent ever again, under any circumstance. As we never expected the results to be so good, we did not believe them sustainable at any asset size. Our goal is to make 20 percent per year. This will not happen each year, but we hope to average that over time with demonstrably less risk than the market. This is a challenging goal, which we may not achieve. I believe in setting high goals rather than easily clearable low ones. However, the strong initial result was no reason to raise the bar. No matter, the dinner was a tough experience. I learned that if we were going to have question-and-answer sessions, I had to be prepared for anything.

We started 1998 well, as the fund returned 9.9 percent through April. Then, Computer Learning Centers (CLCX), our largest short position, became a problem. CLCX was a for-profit education company that took advantage of generous government student loans and ripped off both students and the government. The company charged $20,000 a year to teach computer skills to uneducated people on obsolete technology. They accepted anyone. Another short-seller sent someone to intentionally fail the admissions test at one of the schools. The admissions officer gave her the answer key and then asked her to take the test again. Because the company offered a poor product and engaged in misconduct, we took a large short position. A local TV station in Washington, D.C., ran a feature that interviewed a bunch of angry students complaining about the poor facilities and showed an admissions officer on hidden camera promising a prospective student an absurdly high expected starting salary upon graduation. The stock market reaction: yawn.

CLCX announced a strong first quarter. Reid Bechtle, the CEO, confronted the short-sellers, telling *The Washington Post*, "Every dollar the stock goes up is $4 million the shorts take out of their bank accounts." The *Post* said he told an investor, "We've already gone through Hiroshima and it's time for Nagasaki" for the shorts. Shortly thereafter, the shares began to decline when the Department of Education announced a program review to examine compliance and the Illinois attorney general filed a civil fraud complaint. The stock sank. Sensing that the end was near, we increased our short position.

A couple of months later, CLCX paid a $500,000 fine and promised better business practices to settle with the Illinois attorney general. The attorney general thought this was a big penalty, but the stock market judged it a trivial cost of putting their problems behind them. Bulls spread the word that the Department of Education completed its program reviews and would not take strong action. Three large mutual funds in Boston each added to already enormous positions. The stock doubled quickly. It looked as though CLCX might actually get away with it. I decided to swallow my medicine and covered the short in July. We lost about 2.5 percent of our capital on that position.

Covering the short was a poor decision because it turned out we were right about the company. The publicity from the regulatory action and more conservative behavior by the company caused enrollments and earnings to fall short of expectations, which killed the stock. This actually happens a lot in controversial short sales: Many times, the bulls win the battle on the core criticism (in this case, regulators didn't immediately kill the company), but the bears win the war, as business or accounting reforms cause disappointing performance. It took the Department of Education two more years to complete its work. When it did, it demanded that CLCX return all the student loans it had ever advanced to the government. This put them out of business. (For a good summary, go to http://chronicle.com/free/v47/i23/23a03501.htm.)

A key problem for investors who short a company that is subject to government oversight is that the government, even when it acts, does not move at the same speed as the stock market. Two years might make a prompt government investigation, but it is an eternity for investors such as Greenlight reporting monthly results, even in a long-term strategy. Based on my decision to cover CLCX, I developed a stronger stomach and learned to become even more patient. CLCX is one of the more expensive of many examples that have taught me this lesson.

Unfortunately, as we covered CLCX, the stock market made a near-term top. Around that time, we also covered a couple of other successful shorts. One was Sirrom Capital, named for the founder, but with his surname spelled backwards. Sirrom was in the same business as Allied Capital, with which we were unfamiliar at the time. Sirrom was a business development company (BDC) making mezzanine loans (senior to equity, but subordinate to senior debt) to private companies.

BDCs are a special creation, formed by Congress as a way for small businesses to have more access to capital and receive professional management expertise. They have existed in some form since the Investment Company Act of 1940, but their current structure was born through Congress with the Small Business Investment Incentive Act of 1980. BDCs lend small businesses money, advise them, and in return collect interest and fees. In essence, BDCs are publicly traded private-equity firms that give the public an opportunity to participate in the growth of young companies. BDCs raise capital in equity offerings and act like closed-end mutual funds. They are subject to the Sarbanes-Oxley Act of 2002 and the Securities Exchange Act of 1934. BDCs are required to maintain 200 percent asset coverage on the debt they issue. In other words, the value of the assets they invest in must be twice the amount of debt they take on, which caps their ability to leverage. They also don't pay corporate taxes, provided they pass through their taxable earnings directly to shareholders.

Sirrom funded rapid growth through a virtuous cycle where it raised equity at a sizable premium to net asset value (book value), which increased its net asset value and provided fresh, cheap capital to grow its portfolio. This cycle enabled Sirrom to grow its earnings and dividends, which caused the stock price to appreciate further, allowing Sirrom to repeat the cycle beginning with another stock offering.

As an investment company (a BDC is a type of regulated investment company), Sirrom did not report or consolidate the results of its underlying investments. Instead, Sirrom marked its portfolio to "fair-value." We took Sirrom's SEC filings and built a database that tracked the cost and fair-value of every investment in each period. By tracking the performance of loans by the year of origination, we determined that although the overall portfolio statistics appeared appealing, rapid asset growth masked poor results. We estimated that from inception to final maturity, roughly 40 percent of the loans went bad. Moreover, the data indicated management had ample advance warning of problems and was slow to recognize them in the portfolio markings.

Many mezzanine lenders receive free equity warrants known as equity "kickers" because the free warrants kick up the returns. Sirrom marked the loan and the equity kicker separately for valuation purposes. The database revealed that when trouble arose, management would mark down the equity kicker, but would leave the loan at full value. Obviously, if the equity value is reduced, then the risk in the loan has increased, making the loan less valuable as well. Management did not take that into account and kept the loans at full value until it determined that a loss on the loan was inevitable. In looking at the history of the loans, not surprisingly, writing down the equity kicker proved a reliable predictor of future loan write-downs. Further, an initial loan write-down often preceded a further write-down until eventually there was a final loss, or write-off.

This should not happen. If Sirrom's management marked the portfolio fairly, then future adjustments should be independent of prior adjustments. No pattern should exist. In trading markets, when bad news arises, the market resets the value of securities to the point where at the new price the securities are expected to generate a positive future return. If Sirrom did this, then write-downs should not beget further write-downs. The only explanation was the management was slow to fully acknowledge bad news. And there were other red flags. For example, Sirrom's auditors, Arthur Andersen, wrote in the 1996 audit opinion that "We've reviewed the procedures used by the Board of Directors in arriving at its estimate of value of such investments and have inspected underlying documentation, and in the circumstances we believe the procedures are reasonable and the documentation appropriate." In the 1997 audit letter, Arthur Andersen removed that sentence.

People began to ask questions and raise doubts. The company managed a final equity raise led by Morgan Stanley in March 1998. In July, Sirrom announced slightly disappointing quarterly results, with two bad loans losing around $10 million, or about twenty-five cents per share. The shares fell from a high of $32 in May to around $15 in July. We covered our short at $10 a share, just before the shares collapsed to under $3 in October.

We got wonderfully lucky in demutualized Summit Holdings Southeast (SHSE), a Florida workers' compensation specialist. The combination of conservative accounting as a mutual, all the IPO proceeds going to the company and a management team with a large initial stock and option grant, made this appear to be a fat pitch. We invested about 15 percent of the fund at $14 per share in May 1997.

Even better, SHSE had recently begun reducing risk by purchasing reinsurance on very favorable terms. Essentially, reinsurance companies were willing to take most of the risk and pay SHSE a huge fee. We believed that when the market realized SHSE evolved from a risk business to a high-quality, predictable-fee business, both the earnings and multiple would expand. We were actually disappointed when SHSE announced its sale to Liberty Mutual for $33 per share in cash in June 1998.

It turns out that management was savvy and we were fortunate. At the IPO road show, the CEO made the offhand comment that he wanted to sell the company "before the warranty ran out." I heard the comment, but it did not fully register until later that year when Unicover was exposed. Unicover was a reinsurance broker that induced reinsurance companies to reinsure workers' compensation on uneconomic terms. Sometimes the same risk was passed around several times. With each transfer, Unicover charged a fee. When the reinsurers saw what happened, several refused to pay claims. Almost every workers' compensation insurance stock collapsed as the scheme unwound. I suspect the favorable reinsurance Unicover offered enabled SHSE to change its business model. Unicover's exposure probably would have caused SHSE to implode along with the other workers' compensation companies. However, any problem belonged to Liberty Mutual rather than us. Sometimes it is better to be lucky than smart.

Another short that did well was Century Business Services (CBIZ), a "rollup" of accounting service firms with lousy accounting itself. In a rollup, a consolidator buys small, private companies at a lower multiple than the consolidator receives in the public markets. Every acquisition is accretive to earnings, which drives the stock price higher and enables the consolidator to use its currency to do more acquisitions of private companies in a never-ending virtuous cycle. Michael DeGroote, a famous and wealthy former partner of H. Wayne Huizenga of Blockbuster fame, led CBIZ. Like most roll-ups, CBIZ claimed to improve the operations of the acquired companies and generate 15 percent internal annual revenue growth. In fact, the sellers tended to be entrepreneurs toward the end of their careers. They sold their businesses to CBIZ and hit the golf course.

CBIZ's accounting was not compliant with generally accepted accounting principles (GAAP) in several ways. First, CBIZ recognized revenue on newly acquired firms starting on the "effective" acquisition date, which occurred before they actually closed the deals. Second, CBIZ valued the stock it issued as currency at a 40 percent discount to the market value. These tricks enabled it to recognize revenue prematurely, understate goodwill, and mislead investors about the multiples it paid for acquired companies.

For the first time in Greenlight's history, we wrote letters to the SEC. We critiqued CBIZ's accounting and asked the SEC to insist on clearer disclosures in future filings. The SEC never responded to us. However, a year later CBIZ restated its acquisition accounting to use "closing" dates rather than "effective" dates to begin recognizing revenue and to increase its goodwill. It reduced the "internal" growth rate, missed budget by a wide margin, and replaced the management team. The shares collapsed from $25 in August 1998 to less than a dollar each in October 2000.

But because we covered CLCX and Sirrom just before the market began a rapid descent into the Russia default, Long-Term Capital Management, and Asian economic crises, we had greater-than-usual net long exposure at the wrong time. As a result, we lost money for five consecutive months, from May to September 1998.

August was our worst month ever. The market had a huge sell-off at the end of the month. I was on vacation in upstate New York that week. The prices were crazy, and there was nothing to do about it. We couldn't look at the screen and say these were "fire sale" prices generated by other investors going through "forced liquidations." As detailed later, these were the type of excuses Allied would use to hold its impaired investments at inflated values. The price was the price, and we marked the portfolio to reflect that. We lost more than 8 percent that month. Ouch.

One of our largest partners was a semi-retired, well-known hedge fund manager with a fine, lengthy track record. We were proud to have him as a partner. As the story goes, he claims he called our office on that last day of August and no one returned his call. Keswin, who was not on vacation, said it was absolutely impossible that he would have ignored this partner or his call. The partner soon summoned us to his office. He said he could not believe how irresponsible he thought we had been. He asked about our portfolio. We described our largest investment in Agribrands, an animal feed manufacturer that had been spun off from Ralston Purina. With its Asian market exposure, it had fallen in the sell-off that summer. It was still a great opportunity and would be an enormous winner in 1999. Ultimately, Cargill bought the company a couple of years later for twice where it traded in late 1998. As we told the story, this semi-famous investor scoffed. "I thought you were moneymakers!" At his first opportunity, he fully redeemed his investment in Greenlight. For the next five years, every few months someone told me they'd met him and heard how lousy we were.

He was not alone. A good number of our partners reconsidered their investments after our bad five-month run. While we had worked hard to explain our program and the related risks, some of our partners probably paid more attention to the short-term track record. Our partners redeemed about half their accounts between August and January. It would have been worse except our portfolio of depressed securities recovered with the market in the fourth quarter. Some partners maintained confidence and even increased their investments, and we attracted some new partners. Overall, new investments matched redemptions. We finished the year up 10 percent and ended with $165 million under management.

Though we generated attractive risk-adjusted returns in 1998, we didn't hit our goal. Growth stocks and large-capitalization companies were the flavor of the day. Many of the huge stocks leading this advance would take years to grow into the nosebleed valuations they achieved that year. The S&P 500 shrugged off the Asian crisis to return an eye-popping 28.3 percent. Coca-Cola led the market, trading around fifty times earnings. The earnings were low quality because the company divested its bottling operations one at a time, creating gains that counted in the earnings. I did not have the guts to short Coca-Cola, but I should have. I figured with a company that large I couldn't possibly have a unique insight. Instead, I contented myself with explaining Coca-Cola's problems in investor meetings and quizzing prospective hires about their views on the subject.

CHAPTER 4

Value Investing through the Internet Bubble

From the 1998 low, the Internet bubble launched to its full glory. I believe the battle between America Online and the short-sellers catalyzed the bubble.

America Online traded at a high multiple of what many short-sellers believed to be low-quality earnings. America Online spent heavily on marketing or "customer acquisition costs" to generate monthly fee-paying subscribers. Short-sellers believed America Online inflated its income statement by capitalizing these costs and writing them off over the expected life of the subscriber relationship. America Online's accounting did not comply with GAAP, which required the costs to be expensed as incurred.

I evaluated shorting America Online and determined that even if the accounting were wrong, it was a lousy short because the true economics of the business were incredibly compelling. The stock was inexpensive considering the company's economic profits. I calculated the net present value of

33

a subscriber by comparing the up-front cash customer acquisition costs to the subscription payments over the expected life of the customer relationship. America Online was adding so many new customers that it would not take long to justify its seemingly lofty stock price. Add in the possibility of new revenue streams, including advertising, and I saw it was a really bad short idea. Perhaps this is what "value investor" Bill Miller saw that convinced him to step out of the box and take a large long position. I did not have the guts to buy America Online, but contented myself by not shorting it and arguing with those who did.

When America Online bit the bullet and took a huge write-off of its capitalized customer acquisition costs and agreed to expense them as incurred in the future, the short-sellers had nothing left to criticize. Though America Online had lower earnings under the more conservative accounting, the market understood the high return America Online generated on its investment in customer acquisition costs and looked through the lower reported earnings. As the market appreciated America Online's powerful model, after a small initial decline, the stock soared. America Online traded at a higher multiple than Coca-Cola and was still a buy! Coke lost its market leadership. Now, no multiple was too high to pay for a leading "new economy" stock. Many misunderstood the real chain of events and interpreted America Online's soaring stock as proof of the dubious theory that traditional valuation measures no longer applied.

By early 1999 the market saw that the best and the brightest of the short-sellers had been proved wrong on America Online. If they were wrong about America Online, they could be wrong about every other Internet stock. Never mind that only a handful had viable, let alone robust, business models. Bearish arguments were no longer considered. I believe the hubris from the victory over the America Online shorts was a primary cause of the Internet bubble.

For the most part, we avoided the damage in the short portfolio by refusing to sell short anything just because its valuation appeared silly. We reasoned that twice a silly valuation is not twice as silly. It is still just silly. Kind of like twice infinity is still infinity. Instead, we concentrated on selling short companies with high valuations combined with misunderstood fundamentals and deteriorating prospects. As always, frauds were preferred.

We found several good frauds in 1999. One of them, Seitel, had a multi-client library of seismic data used to find hydrocarbons. Energy companies partnered with Seitel to "shoot" (shaking the ground and measuring the reaction) data—a costly investment. The energy partner received an exclusive period to use the data. After that, Seitel could re-license it to other energy companies. Seitel capitalized the investment in shooting the data and expensed it in proportion to the *expected* licensing and re-licensing revenue. Seitel assumed that a dollar invested in data would generate $2.50 in revenue. As a result, under Seitel's accounting it was guaranteed a 60 percent margin on any license or re-license revenue.

However, Seitel did not generate anything close to $2.50 of revenue per dollar of investment. Seismic data do not have an indefinite life. If the data shows a high probability of hydrocarbons, somebody drills to find out. After that, who needs the data? Most of the license revenue came from licensing, rather than re-licensing. As a result, the 60 percent margin assumption inflated Seitel's earnings.

Worse, the initial licenses covered only a small fraction of the cost of shooting the data. Under Seitel's accounting, shooting data and the related initial licensing fee generated earnings but burned cash. Re-licensing generated cash, but re-licensing sales were harder to make. In an effort to maintain accounting profits, Seitel increased uneconomic, cash-burning investments in new data shoots.

Based on this analysis, we sold Seitel short during a strong period for energy service stocks. When that cycle ended, Seitel's shares fell sharply and the short contributed to our 1999 return. However, we did not cover because the accounting story had not played out. Seitel was heavily leveraged and we thought it would go bankrupt. Seitel shares made a strong recovery in 2000, and we stuck with it for a three-year fight until it did finally go bankrupt in the next downturn in the spring of 2002. The CEO was eventually sentenced to five years in prison.

We also found a good long idea that year. Reckson Associates, a large real estate owner, spun off a nondescript entity called Reckson Services. In early 1999, I met the CEO Scott Rechler, who was young, aggressive, and smart. I left our two-hour meeting with only a vague sense of the strategy, but a strong sense that Rechler was going to do exciting things. Reckson Services was an assortment of opportunities, including speculative real estate ventures in student housing and gaming; a shared-office space business; a concierge services provider; and OnSite, which was a money-losing start-up that wired office buildings for Internet access. I calculated there

was enough intrinsic value in the traditional businesses to justify the current
share price of about $5 without giving any value to OnSite. I wanted the
free option on OnSite and felt that Rechler would do something great, so
Greenlight invested 3 percent of the fund in Reckson Services.

As Rechler and his team huddled for a few months, the stock began to
rise as investors seeking new Internet stocks noticed OnSite, and the stock
took off when an Internet tout under the name "Tokyo Joe" highlighted
Reckson Services. Reckson Services hired a fellow from General Electric.
GE's management was so well regarded that hiring anyone who worked
at GE lent instant credibility. Reckson announced that it would lever OnSite
and the shared-office-space company to transform the company into an
incubator of Internet companies, catering to small and medium business.
An incubator is essentially a publicly traded venture-capital company. (The
leading Internet incubator CMGI had a $10 billion market capitalization
at the time.) Reckson changed its name to Frontline Capital Group. The
market loved the hire from GE, the new strategy, and the new name. The stock
soared, reaching $60 a share by the end of the year, valuing the company
at $2 billion. We sold one-third of our Frontline Capital position near what
would be the top. This was not a brilliant call on the stock: Frontline had
simply become too big a percentage of the fund given its valuation. The
market had begun to properly (in hindsight, excessively) value the option
we had acquired for nothing.

The explosive rally in Frontline Capital, the recovery of Agribrands,
the first collapse of Seitel and the early success of a spin-off investment,
Triad Hospitals, fueled a 39.7 percent return in 1999. At this point,
Greenlight hit "critical mass." Having survived the 1998 market meltdown
and capitalized on the 1999 market melt-up, our results were much better
than most value-oriented funds, many of which spent 1999 "fighting the
tape." Seemingly overnight, everyone wanted to invest. Our assets under
management hit $250 million.

But in early 2000, things became difficult for us. First, Frontline began
to fall. OnSite had trouble over a non-compete clause in its CEO's con-
tract with his former employer that delayed its planned IPO. Though the
Internet bubble still had several weeks to its final top, Frontline did not
exceed its late 1999 highs.

We also lost money shorting Chemdex, a publicly traded start-up setting
up a business-to-business (B2B) network for companies to sell chemicals to

one another. Chemdex paid for its customers to install computers and software to use its network. Chemdex induced a couple of large chemical companies to test the service at a discounted commission by giving them stock. While Chemdex hoped to earn a small commission on each transaction, it booked the entire value of the goods exchanged as revenue. Chemdex had almost no chance to generate enough commissions to cover its enormous up-front investments or its operating expenses, which were plainly not being controlled. We invested 0.5 percent of our capital to short Chemdex at $26 in September 1999, which was up substantially from its $15 IPO price in July.

In November, Chemdex announced a strategic alliance with IBM Global Services, where IBM would sell technology to Chemdex's customers. I could not figure out why that was exciting, but the shares doubled in a week. I missed the joke and doubled the position at $71 per share. In mid-December, Morgan Stanley's star Internet analyst, Mary Meeker, reiterated her "outperform" rating, writing, "We think Chemdex has got what it takes." There really was no more substance to her analysis than that. As a result, the shares soared another 50 percent that week. In late February, Chemdex changed its name to Ventro. The name change indicated Chemdex would expand its network to other industries—"verticals"—and needed a new name to express its bolder ambition.

I got a clue and gave up. We covered at $164 per share on February 22. This made Chemdex/Ventro our biggest short loser of all time, costing us 4 percent of capital. Did I feel smart when the shares hit $243 on February 25? No. That was not ten times as silly as $26. Both were stupidly silly. Of course, after the bubble popped, the shares touched $2 later that year . . . on their way lower.

■ ■ ■

At the top of the bubble, technology stocks seemed destined to consume all the world's capital. It was not enough for all the new money to go into this sector. In order to feed the monster, investors sold everything from old economy stocks to Treasuries to get fully invested in the bubble. Value investing fell into complete disrepute. Julian Robertson's Tiger Fund, which had an extraordinary multi-decade record and became the largest hedge fund in the world, performed poorly while holding a variety of old-economy stocks. Robertson liquidated.

February 2000 was our second worst month ever. We lost 6 percent, mostly in our longs, as capital fled traditional industries. We lost several percent more in early March until the Nasdaq peak on March 10. We lost a little bit of money every day for five weeks. Other than cutting our losses in Chemdex, there really was not much to do about it.

Then . . . the market reversed. Just like that. Partially informed by our Chemdex/Ventro experience, I believe the Internet bubble made its ultimate top the day the last short-seller could no longer afford to hold his position and was forced to cover. Market extremes occur when it becomes too expensive in the short-term to hold for the long-term. John Maynard Keynes once said that the market can stay irrational longer than you can stay solvent. From the peak, the market returned to rationality. The leading stocks suffered a devastating bear market and value investing made a "bottom." These enormous excesses would be completely reversed over the next few years.

This was a good environment for our strategy, and we recovered from our bad start to the year. However, the Frontline Capital stock we held fell sharply and cost us, and we lost money shorting the mail-order contact lens seller 1-800 Contacts. We believed it sold lenses without properly verifying the prescriptions, as required. The Food and Drug Administration (FDA) investigated, but decided not to act. Again, we could not stand the pain and covered the short at a large loss. Subsequently, the shares collapsed when its supplier, Johnson & Johnson—possibly fearing legal consequences of improper consumer use of its lenses—cut off 1-800 Contacts' lens supply.

We successfully shorted CompuCredit, a credit card issuer to customers with poor credit. Its rapid asset growth masked the losses in its reported results. We looked at the losses on a "lagged" basis. This allowed us to analyze the credit performance without the influence of fresh loans that had not yet had time to default. We saw that CompuCredit's losses adjusted for growth were 18 percent a year, rather than the 10 percent touted by management. The company held an analyst day in Atlanta and, aware of our bearish view, pointedly told us that we could only listen by phone. One brokerage firm analyst helpfully pointed out, "Buy the stock. They are having their first analyst day ever. If the news weren't good, they wouldn't be calling the meeting." The stock doubled in our face. This time, we stayed patient. Weeks later, the company announced disappointing results, and our losses turned to gains. As credit losses mounted, CompuCredit's next quarter's results were even worse.

Triad Hospitals (a spin-off from Columbia/HCA) and MDC were two large long positions that each doubled during the year. Most of the rest of the shorts contributed to our returns, and we recovered from our tough February to finish 2000 up 13.6 percent. Again, we did not achieve our annual target, but demonstrated a lower risk profile than the market— where the S&P lost 9 percent and the Nasdaq imploded, falling 39 percent. No one was complaining. We finished the year with $440 million under management.

We closed the fund a second time. Except for a few formal capital-raising rounds when the portfolio was fully invested and we needed capital to pursue new opportunities, we have remained closed ever since. The market continued to return to rationality in 2001. Like 1997, we went the whole year without a serious setback. The large long positions all performed, as did our biggest short position, Conseco, an insurance and annuity company.

Conseco started as a "capital structure arbitrage," an investment based on our assessment that one part of a firm's capital structure is mispriced relative to another. We do not do a lot of arbitrage, but participate in extreme opportunities. Conseco had terrible news: It lost its A-rating from the A. M. Best rating agency. This made it difficult to compete to obtain and retain customers without making dramatic price concessions that eliminate the profit opportunity. Conseco bonds traded at sixty-five cents on the dollar, while the equity market had a different view and valued the company at $10 billion. The debt yielded over 20 percent, while the equity traded as if bankruptcy were improbable. We purchased the bonds and sold short the common stock.

At first, we lost more on the short sale of the stock than we made on the bonds. Conseco brought in a new CEO, Gary Wendt, who had a great record running GE Capital. Wendt signed for $45 million cash and 3.2 million shares of stock up front. He led an analyst day and promised an immediate turnaround. He would implement fancy-sounding GE management concepts like *Six Sigma,* where its people would be trained to become *Six Sigma Black Belts* and turn Conseco from its present weak state into a strong man, which he depicted with a cartoon of a powerful weightlifter. Wendt convinced the market that the problems would soon be fixed, and Conseco refinanced some of its debt at 11 percent.

I attended a meeting Wendt held in Conseco's office in the GM build-ing. About thirty investors and analysts stood around in a warm confer-ence room until the group was fully assembled. When Wendt was ready to join us, we were asked to sit around a very large conference table. When everyone was seated, an assistant came in dragging a conspicuously fancy chair. Space was cleared at the middle of the table and when the throne was in place, Wendt joined the meeting. After a lengthy pitch, Wendt took some questions. To any question that involved the numbers, Wendt had no answer. Over and over, his response was, "Someone will get back to you." I had seen enough. We sold our bonds and added to our short.

Conseco issued a series of "turnaround memos." These self-congratulatory tomes appeared designed to provide good news to juice the stock at ran-dom times. It seemed to work, and the shares doubled. However, each time Conseco reported quarterly earnings, there were more questions without answers. For example, in one quarter, corporate overhead magically turned to a corporate profit. How do you turn overhead into a *profit*? No answer. The next quarter, the premiums and float fell in the insurance business, but capitalized customer acquisition costs and profit rose. How? No answer. Quite simply, the numbers did not add up, and Team Wendt was not inter-ested in clarifying them. The stock continued to rise. Until it didn't.

The next quarter, Conseco reported better-than-expected results. The results were, again, of low quality and raised many questions. The results were no worse than the previous batches. Nonetheless, this time the mar-ket did not buy it. The shares imploded. Eventually, Wendt resigned and the company went bankrupt. Subsequently, the company has reorgan-ized, but is now much smaller. Its name lives on most conspicuously as the Indiana Pacers' home court, the Conseco Fieldhouse. Some have observed that naming a sports arena is a good way to identify short-sale candidates.

Another troubled company with odd accounting was Orthodontic Centers of America (OCA), a rollup of orthodontist practices. The com-pany accelerated revenue recognition and recorded more than all the profit from patients in the first months of a multiyear treatment cycle. As a result, toward the end of the treatment cycle, the average patient generated a reported loss. OCA had to rapidly grow the number of new patients to outnumber the old patients. Additionally, though OCA was 40–60 part-ners with the orthodontists, OCA back-loaded expenses by recognizing the orthodontists' compensation expense on a "cash" basis rather than on an accrual basis. Based on our research, we discovered that OCA front-loaded revenues and back-loaded expenses to compound the impact of dual aggressive accounting practices on reported earnings.

For the second time, we outlined our concerns to the SEC. In March 2001, OCA announced that the SEC required it to change its revenue recognition to record patient revenues on a straight-line basis. The company delayed filing the annual report to restate results with 10 percent lower revenues and 25 percent lower profits than previously believed. Though the stock fell initially, the bulls believed OCA had put its accounting problems behind it. The restated results created easier future comparisons because OCA re-recognized the same revenues that it had improperly front-loaded and reversed in the restatement. By May, the shares recovered almost back to their previous highs. Partially changing the accounting, however, did not improve the overall bad economics of the business. By the following year, the cash flows badly lagged the earnings, and the shares collapsed. This created discontent among its orthodontists, who had bet their businesses on OCA stock. OCA eventually underwent a massive financial restatement and went bankrupt.

When the books closed in 2001, almost everything had worked. The fund returned 31.6 percent, and our assets under management reached $825 million. The bear market deepened, with the S&P 500 falling another 11 percent and the Nasdaq 20 percent.

Then, early in 2002, our two longest-standing and hardest-fought short sales finally paid off. As described above, after three years, Seitel finally imploded under the weight of its own bad business model and aggressive accounting.

Elán was a different story. Elán, an Irish specialty pharmaceutical company, had a small portfolio of branded drugs and a drug delivery technology applicable to a wide number of possible drugs. We sold Elán short in 1999. Elán entered into a series of licensing deals that appeared to be shams. Elán would invest $10 million in XYZ biotech company. XYZ, often a tiny company, would put out a press release trumpeting that Elán's investment "validated" their technology. XYZ would use most of Elán's investment to license Elán's drug delivery technology to use on drugs in XYZ's pipeline that were years away from commercialization. Elán recognized the license fee as revenue at 100 percent margins. Essentially, the money traveled a circle from Elán's pocket to XYZ as an investment and back to Elán as a license. The market paid a rich multiple for this.

We also noticed that Elán's line-by-line revenue and expense reports were usually nowhere near analyst models. And yet, the bottom line was always a penny or two ahead of estimates. A reported shortfall in one place would almost magically be made up in another. Additionally, Elán had a number of off-balance-sheet, special-purpose entities to hold various assets. These vehicles created an unexplained and growing benefit to Elán's earnings. There were many other financial statement anomalies apparent almost every quarter. Like Conseco, Elán was not interested in clarifying the issues and, for a long time, the bulls didn't care. In 2001, the SEC delayed approval of Elán's financials. We thought the truth would come out, but it didn't. The SEC completed its review, and Elán had to restate earnings—by one penny . . . one lousy penny! With the review behind them, Elán was "home free," and its shares took off to new highs.

Over the years, I debated Elán with brokerage firm analysts. After discussing the numbers and the various problems with the earnings, they would conclude by asking, "So what? Why would you short Elán? They never miss earnings. They never will miss earnings. If they don't miss, you are never going to win. How are you ever going to get paid on your short?" Elán was a rig job, but it was not up to the analysts to notice. Perhaps they noticed, but thought Elán should be rewarded for executing it so well.

In January 2002, *The Wall Street Journal* ran a lengthy story on the front page questioning many of the aspects of Elán's accounting that we had observed for years. In the post-Enron environment, the reaction was quite different, and the shares cratered. Though most of Elán's senior managers were accountants, the company began a serious accounting review. When it was over, the accounting fraud was even worse than we suspected. Elán had been selling off its drug portfolio to other manufacturers and booking the proceeds as "product revenue." This explained some of the gaps in the financial reporting that we never understood. The shares that peaked at $65 upon completion of the SEC "review" in June 2001 were in the low teens in the spring of 2002 on their way to $1 in October of that year.

Fraud can persist for a long time, and investors, analysts, and the SEC miss things. But, sooner or later, the truth wins. If you *know* you are right, all you need is patience, persistence, and discipline to stay the course.

The year 2002 started nicely. We were up 12.9 percent by the end of April. Just around that time, we completed our research on Allied Capital, an investment that would require all of my patience, persistence and discipline. And more patience.

CHAPTER 5

Dissecting Allied Capital

In early 2002, the managers of a small hedge fund that specializes in financial institutions called to discuss Allied Capital. They came over and walked through their critical analysis, pointing out anomalies with Allied's portfolio valuations. They wanted our opinion because they knew of our success shorting Sirrom Capital in 1998, a company with the identical business development company (BDC) structure and a similar strategy to Allied. The story was intriguing.

Allied Capital is the second-largest publicly traded BDC in the country (American Capital Strategies is the largest). Allied was founded in 1958 by George C. Williams as a small business investment company (SBIC) to take advantage of the Small Business Investment Act of 1958. Williams had worked for the FBI for much of the 1950s, and since the Small Business Administration (SBA) and all that new funding that was available from the SBA was also right there in Washington, Williams had the good sense to headquarter Allied in the city. The company went public in January 1960, selling 100,000 shares at $11 each. The company began making quarterly distributions to shareholders in 1963. Over the years, several affiliated companies were spun-out or created with similar mandates to make debt and equity investments in small, mostly private businesses that would provide recurring cash flows. Several of these companies would go public, but some remained private partnerships. Williams served as president, chairman, and CEO of Allied and its affiliated companies from 1964 until 1992, when he was named chairman emeritus.

Allied Capital Corporation I, Allied Capital Corporation II, and Allied Capital Lending were closed-end management companies that elected to be regulated as BDCs under the Investment Company Act of 1940. They made private-equity and mezzanine investments in small businesses. Allied Capital Lending made loans through the SBA's 7(a) loan program. Allied Capital Commercial Corporation was a real estate investment trust (REIT) devoted to investing in small business mortgages sold by the Resolution Trust Corporation and the Federal Deposit Insurance Corporation. Allied Capital Advisers managed the assets of the four other Allied Capital companies. On December 31, 1997, these five publicly traded affiliated companies merged to form Allied Capital Corporation in a tax-free stock-for-stock exchange.

At the time of the 1997 merger, Bill Walton (no relation to the former basketball star) was chairman and CEO of all the merging companies. He assumed the roles from David Gladstone, who resigned as chairman and CEO of the Allied Capital companies in February 1997. Gladstone was a long-time Allied Capital executive, having served as an executive officer of the affiliated Allied Capital companies since 1974. (Gladstone would go on to co-found American Capital Strategies before starting his own publicly traded BDC, Gladstone Capital.) Prior to assuming these positions at the Allied Capital companies, Walton had been a director of Allied Capital Advisers and president of Allied Capital Corporation II.

The rationale for the merger of the separate Allied companies was to simplify Allied's internal operations and create critical mass to raise the company's profile with Wall Street and make it attractive to institutional investors. As of December 31, 1997, Allied reported $800 million in total assets, including a $200 million private finance portfolio with investments in eighty-nine portfolio companies.

I asked one of our analysts, James Lin, to replicate our Sirrom work on Allied. He built a large database of all of Allied's loans showing the cost and value of every investment each quarter for several years. The database showed that Allied's valuation patterns repeated Sirrom's. Allied marked down the equity kickers of problem investments, while holding the related loan at cost. This was a good predictor of a future write-down of the loan. Small write-downs disproportionately preceded further write-downs. As in the Sirrom analysis, this indicated that Allied was slow to write-down troubled assets.

The pattern of loan and equity-kicker marks revealed the problem loans. Allied invested in a few public companies, where we analyzed the SEC filings and checked trading prices to see evidence of aggressive carrying values. To protect its existing investment and delay the day of reckoning, Allied often put more money into apparently troubled situations and/or restructurings without taking proportional markdowns.

According to its own customized scheme, Allied grades its investments on a five-point scale to track the progress of its portfolio:

- Grade 1 is used for those investments from which a capital gain is expected.
- Grade 2 is used for investments performing in accordance with plan.
- Grade 3 is used for investments that require closer monitoring; however, no loss of investment return or principal is expected.
- Grade 4 is used for investments that are in workout and for which some loss of current investment return is expected, but no loss of principal is expected.
- Grade 5 is used for investments that are in workout and for which some loss of principal is expected.

From James's database and Allied's SEC filings, we assembled a list of questions to ask the company. We arranged a call with Suzanne Sparrow and Allison Beane of Allied's Investor Relations department on April 25, 2002. This would be my first contact with Allied, and in many ways would reflect Allied's general investor relations practice: Officials answer the easy questions and avoid the hard ones. During this call, and in a follow-up call the next week with Penni Roll, Allied's CFO, we raised all of our issues and concerns and listened to the company's responses. The first call, which we recorded in accordance with our standard practice, lasted about two hours.

Early in the conversation, I asked the key question of how Allied determines the value of its investments. "How do you . . . decide what to value the equity for? What do you need, like another financing round to come in that validates the value of the equity or do you do an appraisal? How do you do it?" I asked.

Sparrow described what she called Allied's *Mosaic Theory* of valuation, "It is not quantitative definitively. Certainly, there are quantitative factors, but there are also qualitative factors," she said. "And that's where some of the BDCs, I think, diverge on methodology with respect to valuation. You see some others who treat it truly as a quantitative exercise."

"That's the beautiful thing about a BDC as a vehicle," she said a moment later. "You don't have, you know, the bank regulators leaning on you to say you must write-off this asset."

I asked whether Allied began writing loans down when the risk increased so it would require a higher yield or whether it waited until it realized the investment was a certain loser. She responded that write-downs started "when we believed that we had permanent impairment of the asset."

This was wrong. As a BDC, Allied has to use "fair-value" accounting, which requires them to value securities based on what they are worth today. An arm's-length buyer would take into account higher risk and would demand a higher return on a loan that deteriorated. A higher return requirement translates to a lower value. It was aggressive and, in my opinion, improper to wait for an investment to be permanently impaired before writing down the value. My job during these calls was not to argue, but to hear their side of the story. I responded only, "I see."

Sparrow continued to defend carrying loans that deteriorated at cost. "Grade 3 tends to be carried at cost because nothing has been lost yet; we don't believe there is permanent impairment there yet," she said. "So, it's only when we believe that truly it's gone and once there is a write-down we take the position that it is permanent. We're not taking it down because we think it's going to come back. I mean, obviously we're going to work real hard to make it come back if we possibly can, but we don't want to tell our shareholders, 'Oh, it's down today, but it's back tomorrow.' You know, if we write it down, we think it is gone and so it's permanent."

It was plain she was openly admitting improper accounting. "Right, I understand," I said. I wondered whether Allied realized that what it was doing was wrong or whether the company was simply unsophisticated.

Then I asked her about writing down the loans when the equity kicker has been written down. Allied doesn't need to, she said, because it believed at that point it was not losing principal or interest on the loan.

The market values debt based on Treasury bonds, which are presumed to have no risk, and then adds a spread representing the credit risk of the particular debt instrument. So, I asked whether Allied valued its loans based on spreads to Treasuries.

"No," she said, "long term it's tended to show fair-value over what a willing buyer and willing seller over a reasonable period of time would be willing to exchange assets. So it's not supposed to be a fire-sale or a liquidation kind of valuation."

This seemed like a non sequitur. I hadn't referred to a fire-sale or liquidation values. I knew her answer was wrong, and thought she was plainly avoiding my question. "Sure, I understand," I said.

We discussed several winning investments in the portfolio. She volunteered Business Loan Express (BLX), Hillman, and the Color Factory. We discussed Allied's rapid growth in fee income. This came from Allied's strategy to have more "controlled" companies, meaning Allied owns the majority of the equity. By controlling companies, Allied can charge various fees for services. Allied was principally a mezzanine lender until around 2000, when it shifted strategy to add controlled companies to the portfolio. According to Sparrow, almost everyone working at Allied helped provide services to controlled companies. Allied even billed Sparrow's time. We reviewed the real estate portfolio and then asked to discuss the specific private finance loans. Sparrow suggested a follow-up call with Allied's CFO, Penni Roll, to cover those.

So we reassembled on May 1 for a lengthy call with Roll. I wanted to create the same kind of static pool data we created with Sirrom. A static pool analysis looks at loans in groups based on when they were originated. This analysis is particularly helpful in analyzing growing portfolios, where new loan growth can sometimes mask the developing losses in earlier loans. We hadn't been able to do this for Allied because it did not disclose the loan maturity dates, even though this is required by SEC Regulation S-X. (Allied began disclosing individual loan maturity dates in its 2004 annual report.) We had trouble tracking loans by year of origination because Allied's corporate restructuring in 1997 made data older than that difficult to compile.

Lacking the data, I asked Roll about the historical credit loss rate. She indicated it was less than 1 percent of principal per year. (Later, Allied showed this figure in its SEC filings, but stopped after we questioned its accuracy.) That figure seemed absurd to me. In a low-interest-rate environment, Allied charged interest rates in the teens for mezzanine loans to middle-market companies. No one achieves a credit loss under 1 percent a year over time on these types of risky loans. An excellent average annual loss rate would be 3 percent to 4 percent. Allied's loans had to be riskier than high-yield loans, and much riskier than bank loans, which recently experienced loss rates much higher than Allied claimed for its portfolio of mezzanine loans. Loss rates on risky corporate debt instruments spiked in the bear market. Apparently, none of this hit Allied's books. Was it truly better investing or simply an accounting regime that delayed losses until they were deemed *permanent*?

I asked her whether Allied's loans were more or less risky than an index of publicly traded high-yield bonds. Roll said, "We think what we do from a structural perspective of the instrument itself is less risky. If you look at a high-yield bond portfolio, a high-yield issuance typically has very little teeth in the financial instrument itself. And very little covenants, and payment default is always the biggest thing that can put you in default versus a lot of financial ratios.

"So Bill Walton, our chairman, kind of equates it to, if you're going to a basketball game, if you're the owner of a high-yield instrument, you have a ticket to watch the game. If you have a subordinated debt instrument like ours, you're on the court playing the game. So, you don't have a lot of rights as a high-yield bondholder. As the holder of a highly structured privately placed subordinated debt instrument like we would have, you have a lot of teeth in your document. You have tight financial covenants, you have covenants with respect to what they can and can't do with the company, assets they can or can't sell, people that have remained in the company to ensure its success. You have rights to review any acquisitions, rights to look at corporate structure, change in corporate structure, and a lot of teeth in your document."

This was not true. While investment-grade bonds often have skimpy covenant packages, it is standard for high-yield bonds to have exactly these types of covenants and restrictions—that's teeth. People with hands-on experience in bankruptcies and financial restructurings know the absurdity of Walton's in-the-game-vs.-watching-the-game analogy and Roll's clueless parroting of it.

Rather than argue, I moved to a more dramatic example. I asked her to compare the risk in Allied's portfolio to non-investment-grade commercial bank loans, which would have better asset protection, seniority, and even tighter covenants than the loans Allied made. Though these loans were plainly safer than Allied's subordinated loans, industry figures indicated they recently suffered much greater losses than 1 percent per year.

Roll replied that banks aren't structured to work out problem credits. Their regulators pressure them to dispose of non-performing assets, so they can't be as patient. As a result, they would have to "take haircuts on getting out of an investment that we wouldn't be willing to take because we have staying power," Roll concluded.

It was now clear to me what was going on. The company had a qualitative method of valuation, where write-downs occurred only when they determined money would be permanently lost. They could hold the investments as long as they wanted to, for years perhaps, hoping that they would eventually get their money back and avoid a loss. As a result, they reported a loss rate superior not just to high-yield bonds, but also to much safer senior bank loans. This made no sense.

I pictured Allied management sitting in a room saying, "Do you think we'll eventually get our money back?"

"I think so. This business could turn up."

"All right, then we don't need to take a write-down."

I knew this had nothing to do with fair-value accounting.

We continued the conversation, covering specific problem investments. One of them, Cooper Natural Resources, had performed "sideways," a euphemism for performing badly, but not yet bankrupt. The senior lenders asked Allied to convert its debt instrument into equity. Allied did that, but did not reduce the value. Roll admitted that Cooper performed below plan and the balance sheet needed to be restructured to appease the senior lender.

"Why wouldn't that lead to some, even modest, mark-down in value?" I asked.

"Because sometimes in these cases, you haven't really moved any further down the balance sheet," she said. "You just recharacterize it in a different security—and if you look at the long-term projections of the company, then we were still in the money . . . so, when you look at the value of the company, you have to look at where they are today. But you also have to look in the future, and we didn't see that we had any permanent impairment from this transaction."

Time would reveal the suspect nature of this treatment. Eventually, in September 2003, Allied *began* to write-down the equity piece of Cooper Natural Resources. Allied valued the equity piece at zero in March 2004 and recognized a realized loss in 2006 (see Table 5.1).

Table 5.1 Allied's Investment in Cooper Natural Resources

Date	Debt Investments		Equity Investments		Comment
	Cost	Value	Cost	Value	
June 30, 2001	3,724	3,724			
September 30, 2001	1,686	1,686	2,259	2,259	Recapitalization; no write-down
December 31, 2001	1,750	1,750	2,259	2,259	Increased investment may be PIK
March 31, 2002	1,782	1,782	2,259	2,259	Increased investment may be PIK
June 30, 2002	2,114	2,114	2,259	2,259	Added money
September 30, 2002	2,148	2,148	2,259	2,259	Increased investment may be PIK
December 31, 2002	2,183	2,183	2,259	2,259	Increased investment may be PIK
March 31, 2003	2,218	2,218	2,259	2,259	Increased investment may be PIK
June 30, 2003	2,254	2,254	2,259	2,259	Increased investment may be PIK
September 30, 2003	2,292	2,292	2,259	1,822	First write-down
December 30, 2003	2,300	2,300	2,259	984	Gradual write-down
March 31, 2004	2,120	2,120	2,259	–	Gradual write-down
September 30, 2006	–	–	–	–	$2.2 MM realized loss

Note: Dollars in thousands

We asked about several additional investments that we suspected were troubled, including Galaxy American Communications, a rural cable provider, and three publicly traded bankrupt companies: Startec Global Communications Corporation, NETtel Communications, and the Loewen Group. We were following the Loewen Group bankruptcy because we had shorted its stock. It appeared that Allied carried its bond investment above the trading price. We asked Roll how they marked the bonds.

"What we were doing is, because there were really no trades going on in this bond once the bankruptcy hit, any trade that was made was a privately negotiated sale," she said. "And given the status of the company, you were, if you wanted to sell versus hanging in in bankruptcy, we would just have to take probably more of a haircut than you otherwise would have. So what we were doing is, we were looking at trades, and you couldn't really say they were market trades, as one data point. But we were on the secured [sic] creditors' committee for a long time, so we were actually using the data we were getting from the secured [sic] creditors' committee to value the company, on the underlying assets in the company and where they thought they would be in the emergence from bankruptcy."

Roll's story that the bonds did not trade was—not to put too fine a point on it—a lie. These were registered, publicly traded bonds. We received pricing sheets from dealers daily, quoting Loewen bonds at relatively narrow bid-ask spreads. There was an active market for Loewen debt, and the quotes were reliable. Greenlight itself had reviewed the possibility of buying Loewen debt several times during the bankruptcy. Her comment that a sale would cause more of a haircut was simply an admission that Allied carried the investment above market. Allied determined the value itself, based on its view that there was no objective market measuring the value. In fact, there was a market. Allied just didn't like the price.

The conversation then turned to the limited facts disclosed about Allied's controlled companies: BLX and Hillman. Finally, I observed that at the end of 2001, Allied's auditor, Arthur Andersen, removed a sentence from Allied's opinion letter that appeared in previous years. The auditors no longer opined, "We have reviewed the procedures used by the Board of Directors in arriving at its estimated value of such investments and have inspected the underlying documentation, and in the circumstances we believe the procedures are reasonable and the documentation appropriate." Andersen had removed the same confirmation with Sirrom years before.

I questioned whether this removal indicated that the auditors conducted a lesser level of review or inspection, or perhaps didn't agree with the values or procedures. Roll explained that the Audit Guide changed in 2001, which caused Andersen to change the standard language in its opinion. I called Greenlight's auditor to check whether this was true. The partner on the audit researched the subject and concluded that the relevant sections were identical between 2000 and 2001. We also checked the bond prices on some of the other troubled Allied investments like Velocita and Startec and determined that Allied valued its holdings well above the quoted market prices.

Based on our independent research and what I learned on these lengthy calls with management, Greenlight put 7.5 percent of the fund into the Allied short sale at an average price of $26.25 a share.

Having been invited to speak at the Tomorrows Children's Fund charity conference on May 15, 2002, and asked to present my most compelling investment idea, now I knew I had one. Nervously, I stepped up and made the speech. (If you have not done so already, you can see it for yourself at www.foolingsomepeople.com. It makes the story much easier to follow.) And yet, at that moment, I had no idea the story was really just beginning.

PART TWO

Spinning So Fast Leaves Most People Dizzy

CHAPTER 6

Allied Talks Back

After my speech, the reaction was immediate. When I showed up for work the next morning, a junior analyst from a mutual fund company that held a large long position in Allied was waiting outside our locked door. He heard that I said something important about Allied and came over to get a first-hand account. I brought him into a conference room and summarized what I had said. When I started discussing BLX, he said he hadn't even heard of it.

When I finally got to my desk, my e-mail inbox was full of complimentary messages from people who had attended the speech, and I took a number of kind phone calls. When the stock market opened a few minutes later, there were so many sell orders for Allied that it took the specialist about thirty minutes to find a balanced price to open the stock. When it did open on May 16, 2002, the price was $21, almost a 20 percent drop. I was surprised the stock fell so far so quickly. Even so, I did not for even a minute consider covering any of our short.

I heard that Merrill Lynch told people that someone made a speech characterizing Allied Capital as another Enron. They didn't know exactly what had been said in the speech, but they were confident that whatever was said was wrong. Obviously, one way to find out what I had said would be to contact us or ask for a copy of my speech. Though there were about a dozen analysts at brokerage firms covering Allied, not one reached out to us on that day to find out for themselves. In fact, to the date this book went to press, no brokerage firm analyst has ever done so. Whatever contact I have had with them has been at my initiation.

Allied announced it would hold a conference call later that morning to respond. When we dialed into the conference call number, we were unable to connect because the call was so well attended that Allied had not reserved enough phone lines. We called another fund that we knew was participating and listened through its connection partway through the call. Though no one from Allied contacted us to find out about my speech, nonetheless, Bill Walton, the chairman and CEO, began the call, saying, "We've been gathering information on this speech throughout the morning, and I think some people have actually gotten to the person who gave the speech, and so we've got some items here that we think we ought to discuss, but because of the fact that *we're not really fully apprised of what we know were said last night, all of which we feel are misguided* and talk you through those and then we plan to open it up for Q&A."

Walton began what would become a pattern of making general comments and taking personal shots, while Joan Sweeney, the chief operating officer, spun the substantive issues. Allied said it charged BLX and Hillman comparable interest rates to the rates Allied charged for mezzanine investments. Management claimed the rates were not as high as they seemed because Allied did not earn a current return on the equity investments they made to those companies. Allied encouraged investors to concentrate on the "blended" return on their combined debt and equity investment, which Allied said was not excessive. Besides, according to Allied, the controlled companies could afford to pay.

Despite management's claim, the rates charged to the controlled companies were not customary, as no other companies paid Allied 25 percent interest. At the time, Allied charged most companies about 15 percent interest. Guiding investors to focus on a blended return that included the return on the related equity investment was a red herring, because from a legal and accounting perspective Allied treated the debt instruments as discrete from the equity instruments. In fact, Allied did earn a return on the equity investments through realized and unrealized increases in the fair-value of the investments and from dividends.

The high interest rates padded Allied's earnings, even if BLX and Hillman could afford to pay them. Future disclosures ultimately showed that BLX didn't have the ability to pay anyway, as it did not then, nor does it now, generate any cash. Instead, Allied periodically injected money into BLX to enable BLX to pay the 25 percent interest rate and other fees back to Allied. Sometimes, rather than have Allied infuse more money, BLX borrowed on its bank line. Since Allied guaranteed the banks against the first 50 percent of any loss on the bank line (and charged BLX a hefty fee for the guarantee), bank borrowings weren't substantively different from Allied, simply adding to its investment in BLX directly.

Next, on the issue of Andersen omitting its confirmation language from its audit opinion, Sweeney repeated Roll's line about the Andersen audit language being removed, "The Audit Guide simply changed."

On the issue of the funding gap created by reported earnings, which included non-cash (payment-in-kind [PIK]) income, and its required shareholder distributions, Sweeney responded, "I think what people miss in that analysis is in the case of a mezzanine loan, you're taking cash interest for a very, very high coupon. You're taking PIK interest for a smaller proportion, so let's say you take 14 percent cash interest and 2 percent PIK, as long as your cash interest is above your cost of capital, the PIK is a very good thing because the PIK is added to the note and it compounds, and that note is subject to cash interest as well as PIK interest. So in a sense, PIK actually becomes accretive for shareholders, not dilutive, and really isn't a cash drain."

Got that? Me neither. PIK interest means that the lender accepts additional securities, growing the balance of the loan, rather than cash, as interest. It may or may not be a good thing, but Allied gave no response to my point that it has to pass the non-cash PIK income on to shareholders even though Allied has not received cash from its underlying investments to distribute.

Walton explained that cash flow, including principal repayments but before new investments, easily covered the distribution. Allied, however, did not generate cash earnings to satisfy its distribution requirements. Using principal repayments to fund the distribution without making new investments would shrink the portfolio, lowering future earnings. Essentially, this would be analogous to burning the furniture to heat one's home.

Walton further explained that Allied's purchases of senior debt at a discount without writing down the existing subordinated debt investment reflected fire-sales of assets that did not reflect the credit quality of what Allied bought. He added, "In fact, it was a huge opportunity for us and very good for the shareholders. Now in cases where we're buying down senior debt of companies where we have a subordinated debt investment, we recapitalize the business and write down the subordinated debt appropriately to reflect the overall value of the business. So it's not a question of us buying down senior debt at a discount and leaving the sub-debt in place at its previous structure and value. That simply does not happen."

Though Walton recognized this as inexcusable, all of our research strongly suggests that this *simply did happen* at three Allied portfolio companies prior to Walton's remark: ACME Paging, American Physician Services and Cosmetic Manufacturing Resources. Allied eventually had large write-downs on all three. The recapitalizations delayed the write-downs, giving Allied time to outgrow the problems by repeatedly issuing new shares.

Regarding fair-value accounting, Sweeney explained, "I think what people miss when they try to understand fair-value accounting is fair-value accounting takes into consideration the fact that a BDC is holding private illiquid securities held for the long term. It is not meant to take into effect the liquidation or fire-sale accounting."

There is no such thing as "fire-sale accounting." A fire-sale means a sale of assets at reduced prices to raise cash quickly. Sweeney invoked the colloquial term "fire-sale" because an SEC administrative law judge used the term in an opinion and indicated that investment companies should not value investments at "fire-sale" prices. I hadn't said anything about fire-sale accounting.

For BDCs, the SEC requires fair-value accounting, the price at which an informed, arm's-length buyer and seller would transact. For the next several weeks, Allied repeatedly and disingenuously claimed that we insisted on "fire-sale accounting." In an effort to discredit our analysis, Sweeney redefined what I said to make it refutable. She knew most listeners hadn't heard my speech and must have believed they wouldn't know the difference.

Furthermore, Sweeney's answer made no sense. The anticipated holding period is not relevant to fair-value accounting. By referring to the long holding period, she may have been referencing "hold-to-maturity" accounting, which permits loans to be held at amortized cost as long as all the holder expects are the payments to be made when due; fair-value accounting does not permit this method. Further, illiquidity is a reason to discount the value.

Walton discussed the troubled investments that had not been written down to fair-value. He started with NETtel, a bankrupt telecommunications company "that's been written down to basically the realized value of some asset sales, which are imminent." The truth was that at the time of this statement, NETtel had been in Chapter 7 liquidation for over a year, and its assets had already been sold. Two quarters later, Allied hid NETtel from further disclosure by quietly moving it from "investments" to "other assets" on its balance sheet. The September 30, 2002, SEC Form 10-Q showed that $8.9 million of receivables related to portfolio companies in liquidation were included in "other assets." Though they did not disclose which investments these were, we were able to reconcile the disclosure to indicate that they included NETtel and two other investments. Five years later, Allied still has not recognized a realized loss on NETtel.

Walton described Velocita as a partnership between AT&T and Cisco Systems. "We're in the senior debt," he said. "We took down [the value] aggressively in the first quarter of this year to about $4 million, which is roughly where we think the company is fairly valued. We do understand that Cisco has written down its investment. But Cisco is in the equity, which, of course, is the first thing to go in a troubled telecom situation. We're in with a fairly sophisticated group of bondholders here, and we think there are some very interesting recovery possibilities."

Allied wasn't in the senior debt but the subordinated debt. Cisco held the equity *and* the senior debt. Cisco wrote both to zero two quarters earlier. As for the interesting recovery possibilities, weeks later on its June 30 balance sheet, Allied recognized its Velocita bonds to be worthless.

"In the case of Startec," Walton continued, "if you look at the statement of loans and investments, we have a $24 million debtor-in-possession (DIP) facility, which is the first money out, and this is a company with roughly $130 to $140 million of revenue and operating above . . . breakeven . . . so there's value here and certainly there is value in our DIP instrument. We've also got a $10 million secured piece of paper in there, which we also feel, based on our views about how the company will come out of bankruptcy, will be money good."

Startec's bankruptcy records indicated monthly revenues had fallen to $5 million. Eventually, we learned that Walton's quoted revenue figure included revenue from discontinued business lines. Startec, a communications company, was losing money and burning cash. Again, weeks later, on the June 30 balance sheet, Allied wrote the "money good" portion to zero.

Dan Loeb, who manages Third Point Partners and is never afraid of asking tough questions, asked the first question on the call. "On your fair market valuation, you seem to draw a distinction about where things trade versus where you mark them."

"Let me be clear, they don't trade," Walton interjected.

"Okay, but let me give you an example," Loeb said. "Velocita debt does trade. It trades at about two cents on the dollar. My understanding is that you are carrying Velocita at a price of forty. And these aren't just distress fire-sale, you know, sales. This is a real market level."

Sweeney argued, "Yeah, but I think you also have to look and say, 'Is that a market?' I mean, in the case of Velocita, if it trades at all, it's by appointment."

"Well, I can make an appointment to buy those bonds at two," Loeb responded. "Yet, you're still carrying yours at forty."

"Yeah, but the question is, who are you buying them from because . . . "

"It doesn't matter," Loeb said. "I mean, there is a level. Put it this way, you're so far off the market. Put it this way, are you buying more bonds, then, at these levels? Are you buying them at twenty, twenty-five, and thirty?"

"No, because that's not our business to do that," she said.

"Look at it this way," Walton said a moment later. "We had a total investment in this that's roughly $15 million. It's down to $4 [million] and we feel that's a very aggressive write-down. We're evaluating the situation as we go forward. We're working with—talking with management, etc., etc. If we feel like it's going to be less than that based on our continuing to work with it, we'll take it down the rest of the way."

"I know you have a big portfolio with a lot of things in there. That one slipped through the crack," Loeb quipped.

Sweeney defended the valuations by arguing that when Allied exits investments, it achieves the most recent carrying value. According to Sweeney, this proves that the investments couldn't be mismarked and shows that "we are pretty good when it comes to fair-value accounting."

Her reasoning suffers two basic flaws:

- First, there is selection bias: Allied chooses which investments it exits. Suppose Allied has two investments carried at $10 million. If Allied tries to sell them and receives a bid of $10 million for one and $5 million for the other, Allied can decide to sell the first one and keep the second at an inflated value. Allied can hope that the overvalued investment will eventually grow into Allied's carrying value. As Allied sells additional shares and grows its equity base, the overvaluation becomes a smaller proportion of Allied's equity, which makes the overvalued investment less material over time. The technical term for this might be *pyramid-scheme* accounting.
- Second, because the investments are typically not registered securities, it usually takes Allied more than a quarter to negotiate, structure, and close sales. This gives Allied time to *revalue* investments tantalizingly close to the actual sale price just prior to exiting them. Comparing exit prices versus the previous quarter's carrying value after Allied had an opportunity to revalue the investment to reflect the pending sale price is a meaningless exercise. When you have perfect knowledge, it's really easy to get the valuation exactly right. Certainly, it does not validate Allied's general valuation practices.

Loeb wasn't done. He asked if Allied's business resembled a closed-end fund. Walton responded that Allied is actually an operating company, providing significant managerial assistance to its portfolio companies. The transactions are privately negotiated, and Allied has board observation rights or serves on the board in every deal. Allied provides significant assistance in financing, mergers and acquisitions (M&A), employee benefits, marketing and all sorts of areas to help grow the business. "So our business is not a passive buy-and-hold and trade business," Walton said. "It's an actively managed portfolio . . . deeply involved with each management team to grow the business. And it's a very hands-on process. We have thirty-five investment officers handling 130 companies."

The next private-equity investor I meet who says he just puts money in and sits on his hands will be the first. They all say they provide services and add more than money to their investments. Still, they realize the funds they manage are investment vehicles, and few, if any, would consider themselves to be "operating companies."

The time-consuming nature of negotiating and structuring the entry and exit of each investment and looking for new opportunities suggests that the thirty-five investment officers didn't have a lot of time left to make large contributions to marketing and human resources at 130 companies. In 2001, fees totaled $46 million, or $1.3 million for each of the thirty-five investment officers providing part-time assistance. At those implied rates, it was no wonder most of the fees came from controlled companies that were not deciding for themselves whether to engage Allied for auxiliary services.

"That wasn't really my question," Loeb said. "The observation was that—what compelling argument would you make to invest in your company?"

"Dividends," Walton said.

Now we're at the heart of the matter. Allied has paid a steady or rising dividend for over forty years. It has paid the dividend whether it had profits to cover it or not. Allied's dividend is a holy covenant between itself and its shareholders. Its payment proves to them that all is well. After all, you never have to restate a dividend.

Just as the Elán bulls had argued that Elán was a lousy short, because it would *never* miss its earnings forecast, the Allied bulls argue that Allied's dividend is unlikely to be cut regardless of whether it deserves to be cut. They raise the same question: "How are you ever going to get paid on your short if Allied *never* cuts the dividend?" Of course, when Elán was ultimately revealed to be a fraud, it did miss the earnings forecast, and the short worked out well.

As bizarre as this sounds, *Allied's "dividend" is not really a dividend.* Traditionally, a dividend represents excess profit that a company pays to shareholders because it does not need to retain the capital in its business. Though Allied's "dividend" of about 8 percent is about three times the average yield in the S&P 500, it isn't a "dividend" in the traditional sense. Traditional companies that pay large dividends do not generally issue fresh equity because the dividends reflect an unneeded surplus of capital. However, Allied does not have excess capital. So, its "dividend" is not paid from surplus it doesn't need to retain in order to maintain or grow its business. In fact, Allied routinely sells freshly issued stock to satisfy its ongoing need for additional equity.

Technically, Allied's "dividend" is a tax distribution. As an investment company, as long as it distributes its taxable earnings to its shareholders, Allied does not pay corporate taxes. This is the same tax regime practiced by mutual funds and every other type of U.S. investment company. When mutual funds pay large annual tax distributions, its investors are unhappy. In fact, a good mutual fund seeks to minimize its tax distribution by keeping its winners and selling its losers. No mutual fund strives to smooth and grow its tax distribution. No one would value a mutual fund based on the yield implied by its tax distribution.

As a stroke of investor-relations genius, Allied breaks its tax distribution into four quarterly pieces and calls them "dividends." Wherever I refer to Allied's "dividend," "tax distribution," or just "distribution," I am referring to the tax distribution Allied calls its "dividend." Unlike almost every other investment company, Allied principally judges itself by how well it maximizes its taxable income rather than by its investment results. As a result, it sells its winners and keeps (and often supports) its losers. In the money management industry, this is known as "picking your flowers and watering your weeds," and it's a recipe for disaster. The *maximize taxes* strategy, of course, increases Uncle Sam's take. Allied has taught its shareholders to pay taxes and like it!

Later, Walton said: "We're a dividend company that wants to grow the dividend 10 percent a year." Then Walton addressed me. "I'd like to just point out to Mr. Einhorn that he's so generous by giving up half his profits," he said. "We've got 85,000 retail shareholders that depend on the dividend. We really operate the business for dividends. I think that's a pretty good social purpose, too. . . . We find it unusual that somebody gets up and gives a speech about a company who never bothers to talk to management. I think most informed investors would appreciate some time spent with us so they can talk these things through unless you're simply trying to develop the short thesis to scare people and make a quick buck and move on. I don't find that a very high social purpose. Maybe other people do."

Walton and others at Allied *knew* we had talked to management and gone through the issues with them at length. Their responses on the conference call weren't different from what Sparrow and Roll told us. They knew there wasn't any misunderstanding, and they had no interest in calling us to work through the issues to try to show us we were wrong. Instead, they desperately needed people to question our motives and to think we didn't do our homework.

Walton responded to a question about how much of the distribution is covered by ordinary income. "For the last four years, our exclusive strategy is to build the interest and fee income from the portfolio to provide more ordinary income to cover the dividends." He continued, "Last year, our ordinary taxable income was about 90 percent of income, which we think provides a lot of stability for the dividends. We think capital gains are great, but they're less predictable, and so, therefore, we try not to build that into the dividend growth model."

Beginning with that quarter, Allied has been unable to sustain the 10 percent distribution growth it projected, and ordinary income never again came close to covering the distributions. Instead, Allied shifted to a capital gains strategy. All it had to do was make shareholders forget Walton's words and convince them that capital gains are actually predictable.

Then Walton finished with an Orwellian wrap-up. "We're delighted to talk about our business and we're committed to transparency and full disclosure," he said.

Allied's entire strategy is extensive disclosure on some things, but little disclosure on what a skeptical investor might really wish to know. For example, Allied provides terrific detail of its industry and geographic investment diversification, but barely a word about the business results, prospects or valuations of its individual investments.

It occurred to me that people who are willing to lie about *small* things have no problem lying about *big* things.

CHAPTER 7

Wall Street Analysts

C oming out of the conference call, I felt great. Allied management did not make any points that seriously challenged our analysis and continued to repeat what they had told us previously. Their comments were convoluted, their tactics desperate. When a reporter for *Dow Jones Newswire* called, I told her, "They talked around all my issues without really addressing any of them." I decided to sell more shares short.

Starting that day, a number of law firms began filing class-action suits, repeating the criticisms I had made in the speech. Though Allied and its supporters claimed Greenlight was behind the lawsuits, we had nothing to do with any of these lawsuits, and we were surprised by them. The lawyers were simply reacting to the news of the day and rushing to court hoping to earn fees. It seemed Allied wanted people to sympathize with them as victims of an intricate, though, in fact, imaginary conspiracy.

Later that day, Allied's investment banker, Merrill Lynch—which earned millions in fees underwriting Allied's recent equity deals—published a report titled "The Song Remains the Same." Though our view was outside Wall Street's thinking about Allied, the company and its supporters pretended that Greenlight offered nothing new, so no one needed to pay heed. Of the conference call, Merrill opined, "The company provided meritorious defenses to all the criticisms leveled."

"As a business development company, the company is required to mark its investments to long-term value, and disclose these investments to investors quarterly in their SEC filings," the Merrill report declared. "From time to time, the company has had investments in publicly traded companies (equity and debt) where the mark to market on the investment differs from where the investment trades in the market (or where a deal has been announced). There have been both undermarket gains (such as WyoTech currently) and debt and equity that has traded below where Allied has carried it (such as Velocita debt currently)." Then, Michael Hughes, the Merrill analyst, underlined his next sentence for emphasis. "The nuance here is that Allied is required to mark to long-term value, not mark to market." That would have to be some nuance, because it was clearly wrong. As I said in my speech, the Merrill Lynches of the world would defend the stock to the death.

Indeed, the next morning Wachovia resumed coverage of Allied with a "Strong Buy" rating and a $29 price target. Joel Houck, its analyst, published a report that might as well have been written before my speech. It talked about the business model, Allied's long history, and how cheap the stock was. The report discussed how the business model evolved after 1997 when Walton became CEO and Allied's predecessors merged. Allied made larger deals, raised capital, and took more control positions, such as BLX, Hillman, and Wyoming Technical Institute (Wyotech). When Houck presented his recommendation to the Wachovia sales force, he also said that I "didn't raise anything new."

At my request, a few hours later we had a call with Houck. Houck told us that he had drilled down on our issues for twelve to eighteen months, and while Allied's transparency isn't where it needs to be, the weaknesses in tech-oriented names are where their long-term approach to valuations doesn't really hold up well. Because the transparency isn't good, he can judge only the portfolio-wide results, and, as Sweeney said, since exit events occur at valuations consistent with Allied's most recent marks, there is no reason to question the portfolio valuation as a whole.

While he acknowledged that Velocita, Loewen Group, and NETtel valuations are "almost indefensible," he thought there was offsetting upside in the valuations of Hillman, WyoTech, and BLX. I pressed him on his admission of "indefensible" valuations. He tried to clarify, "What I meant was, absent the proprietary information Allied is sitting on, the valuations are indefensible." I pointed out Velocita is a public company with SEC-filed financials. What proprietary information could they have to justify carrying it at cost at the end of last year?

He asked if I had seen the internal documents Allied used to value its portfolio. I told him that I hadn't, but if he could show us a document to justify the year-end valuation of Velocita, we would publicly recant our entire analysis. He said he would pass that along. He also said that the investment company valuations allow the company a hold-to-maturity approach to valuation. I called him on that by pointing out that the Investment Company Act of 1940 doesn't permit that. Suddenly, he didn't seem to know everything. "What does it say?" he asked.

I said the Act says you have to use fair-value. He quibbled over the difference between "fair-value" and "market value," so I asked him to explain the distinction.

He responded, "Value is a tricky concept, David."

Then, I pressed him on his claim that I had not said anything new. I pointed out that he didn't hear my speech and he hadn't called to find out what I said. He said that the audit letter was a new issue, but it was "easily dismissible" because the Audit Guide had changed. I challenged that, and he said he would look into it further. Then, he asked me what I thought was new. I questioned how the portfolio survived a recession without significant credit losses. I compared Allied to a high-yield bond portfolio and pointed out that Allied's loans were generally riskier because the companies are smaller than high-yield issuers and had less access to capital. According to Allied, it had performed even better than Finova, a senior lender.

He said, "Finova was fraud." In fact, Finova was not a fraud, just a company that mismanaged its credit and liquidity risks.

"How do we know this isn't fraud?" I asked him.

"David . . ., nobody knows. Nobody can say definitively whether it is fraud or it isn't fraud," Houck acknowledged.

"How do you know Finova was fraud?" I asked him.

"Well, you know it was fraud after the fact," he replied.

Then, he told me we had spoken to the "wrong people" at Allied. This continued the story that *we hadn't done our homework*. I told him that we went over our issues through normal investor-relations channels. He said that we needed to talk to Sweeney, not Roll. "Joan Sweeney is the chief operating officer, has her finger on the pulse of all these companies," Houck said. "Do you know where she was before Allied?"

"Where was she before?" I asked. "I don't know her history."

"She came from the SEC Division of Enforcement," Houck said. "I mean, look, anything is possible: SEC investigation; I hear what you're saying, not a good event. But I'll take my chances that Joan Sweeney knows the. . . rules and regs and is going to come out on the right side of the issue given her background."

This wasn't just Joel Houck speaking. This was Allied's story. Repeatedly, I heard from shareholders and short-sellers Allied's whispers that Sweeney's experience at the SEC Division of Enforcement made it implausible that she would break rules, or, more cynically, if she did, that the SEC would give her a pass.

■ ■ ■

Even though my wife wrote for *Barron's*, I didn't have a lot of contact with journalists at other publications. Obviously, because of my wife, I could not bring the story to *Barron's*; the editors and I had a policy that I would not discuss investments with anyone on the staff. I had recently met Jesse Eisinger, who wrote the excellent story about the fraud at Elan for *The Wall Street Journal*. Though the *Journal* is owned by Dow Jones, which also owns *Barron's*, the publications are run separately. Eisinger told me to call if I ever had a story. I called and arranged a meeting, in which James Lin and I spent a couple of hours describing Allied. Eisinger expressed interest and asked for an exclusive until his upcoming vacation, which was to start in a few weeks. We agreed.

■ ■ ■

The next week, Hughes, the Merrill Lynch analyst, wrote another supportive report titled "Allied Capital Auditor's Opinion—Much Ado about Nothing."

> Allied Capital's stock price has been on a roller coaster for the last few days as the market sorts through a series of allegations including

improper investment valuation procedures. During this period we have written that we believe these allegations are unfounded and uninformed and have attempted to produce as much factual rebuttal as possible. As outlined below, we believe we can now factually dismiss the allegation of a less thorough audit.

The report continued:

The AICPA (American Institute of Certified Public Accountants) audit guide was revised in May 2001. A key revision of the guide: auditors are no longer instructed to specifically comment on the reasonableness of a company's investment valuation procedures if they find them acceptable. And the only audit opinion provided for use if the fair values are reasonable is exactly the audit opinion used in Allied's report.

We knew this was wrong. James Lin got the pages from the Audit Guide that supported Merrill's research. Merrill gave James pages with a fax header from BLX. The pages with the old language came from the 1993 Audit Guide. From this, Merrill had no way to determine that the change occurred in May 2001. I re-examined the Merrill report closer and saw that Merrill had footnoted the 1993 Audit Guide in an eye-doctorish microscopic font. The footnote indicated that Merrill must have noticed what BLX sent them and wrote the report anyway—proving that Merrill willingly participated in the spin job.

Greenlight's auditors determined that the actual Audit Guide change occurred in 1997, not 2001. I complained to Hughes's boss at Merrill about his apparent bias. His boss told Hughes to call me. Rather than acknowledge that Allied's management misled him and reassess Allied's credibility, Hughes dug in his heels. He asked, what if they argued that Andersen missed the change in the 1997 Audit Guide and only put in the new policy in 2001? I had the impression that Hughes wanted to create a story we could not refute. It seemed to me that it didn't matter to him whether it was true or not; he had no interest in determining and analyzing the facts. I told him I knew this was wrong. Arthur Andersen had also been Sirrom's accountant and made the same change to the audit language at Sirrom in 1997.

Then I turned to the point from his first report where he emphasized that Allied is supposed to mark its portfolio to "long-term value."

"You're going to have me on this one, because I know the technical language is fair-value," he said.

We then debated whether it was permissible to carry Velocita bonds above the publicly traded market price. I told him, "You do not have an ability under Allied's own policies as explained in the 10-K when there are quoted market prices to carry it at a premium."

He replied, "It's never been my reading of the 'K,' but I'll have to get a lawyer to look at it."

"I can read it to you verbatim if you like," I offered. "Do you want to know what it is?"

"Actually, I've read it many a time," he said. "I just didn't have the same interpretation."

"Here, let's read it and let's see how you might interpret it differently," I said. "What it says is: 'The value of investments of public securities is determined using quoted market prices discounted for illiquidity or restrictions on resale.'"

"Is there a sentence after that?" he asked.

"No."

"Well, I'll tell you what. I'm going to go back and read the whole thing."

"I think, if you're mistaken, I think you should publicly correct it," I said.

"I think if I'm mistaken, I should publicly correct it."

A week later, after I followed up with Hughes's boss, Merrill published a follow-up acknowledging, "We were mistaken. The audit guide changed in May 1997." But they did not admit or correct their error that Allied isn't supposed to mark its portfolio to "long-term value" or that it can't carry publicly traded securities above their quoted prices.

■ ■ ■

During the weeks following the speech, I received phone calls and e-mails from long and short investors who were trying to understand both sides. Many contacted Allied, as well. Even when the e-mails had an edgy tone, I tried to respond matter-of-factly. Through these dialogues, we kept up with Allied's latest spin, and I believe they kept up with our views. Through these intermediaries, we debated without direct contact.

Table 7.1   Velocita and Startec Bonds

Date	Velocita Price (%)		Startec Price (%)	
	Quoted	Allied	Quoted	Allied
June 2000			80	100
September 2000	77	100	80	100
December 2000	97	100	60	100
March 2001	60	100	45	100
June 2001	60	100	3	100
September 2001	60	100	4	100
December 2001	10	100	2	–
March 2002	1	37	2	–

At Greenlight, we continued our research. We gathered the historical bond prices from Chase Securities for Velocita and Startec and compared them to Allied's historical carrying values. As Table 7.1 shows, Allied did not take timely markdowns.

Allied structured its loan to Startec to be *pari passu* with Startec's bonds. That means that even though they owned a separate piece of paper, it had the same status as the bonds. As a result, the bond price was a good indication of value. If anything, under SEC rules, Allied should have carried its investment at a discount to reflect the relative illiquidity of its private investment.

■ ■ ■

One fund manager sent us a copy of a recent BLX securitization prospectus. It showed that 14.5 percent of BLX's loans were delinquent as of December 31, 2001. We called the credit rating agencies to learn more about BLX's securitizations. The agencies told us that they got the data used to rate the securitizations from BancLab, which tracked Small Business Administration loans. We licensed BancLab's analysis of BLX's portfolio. It would take them about a month to prepare a report.

CHAPTER 8

The You-Have-Got-to-Be-Kidding-Me Method of Accounting

Just two weeks after the speech, Allied held a second conference call on May 29, 2002. Walton came out firing. "We understand [our business] better than any external individual, and we are going to continue to communicate our understanding to you," he said. "But let's be clear: We are not having an academic, intellectual debate. The shorts are people with an agenda and a lot of money and reputation riding on trying to get investors to deconstruct our company and to view the Allied Capital glass as half empty."

Allied first tackled the Audit Guide problem. The company conceded that its argument about the Audit Guide changes was false and acknowledged that the Audit Guide, in fact, changed in 1997. Now, Sweeney asserted on her honor that Arthur Andersen had not identified any problems with

the audit. Andersen had shut down due to Enron-related liability, and
Allied had just hired a new auditor. Though we will never get to the bottom
of why Andersen changed the language, we know Allied's first explanation
was a lie. In any case, whoever opined that Velocita debt was worth par at
the end of 2001 didn't do much of an audit.

Walton continued the call with a valuation discussion. "The other issue
is that shorts seem to think that we should write loans down to zero at the
slightest sign of trouble, regardless of whether there has been money lost,"
he said. Obviously, we don't believe that loans should be written to zero at
the slightest trouble. Walton is smarter than that. Finally, he repeated what
Roll told us, "We write loans down to the amount that we believe we will
collect."

Larry Robbins of Glenview Capital pressed the company about the
carrying values of troubled credits. Roll explained, "Sure, Grade 3 assets,
really we don't see any real risk of principal or interest loss in what we call
[loans] in 'monitoring.' In other words, we're working with the company,
and it can be a Grade 3 for a variety of reasons. They can be a Grade 3
because they're working on something with their senior lenders, they can
be a Grade 3 because we've had companies go into Grade 3 because we're
working with them and they're up for sale and, as a result, [they're not
paying us] for whatever reason until they sell. But they can be a Grade 3
for a variety of different reasons.

"Grade 4 is where we get a lot more concerned, because Grade 4
we think we've lost contractual interest due to us. In other words, the
deal we went into with respect to what they were supposed to pay us in
interest, we don't think we're going to get that contractual interest. Now, we
don't think principal's impaired, but we do think we have contractual interest loss. Grade 5 is where we think we've not only lost contractual interest,
but we've actually lost principal. And this is principal, so it's cost basis. In
other words, it's money that went to them that we don't think we're going
to collect back. So if an asset is in that situation, [it] is a Grade 5."

Robbins persisted. "But your carrying values of Grade 4, for example,
there is a likelihood that you would not receive guaranteed interest, but
you would still receive contractual principal. Where are you carrying those
Class 4 loans?"

"It depends on the asset, but most of those would be carried at original cost and . . ." Roll said.

"So, it's only a Class 5 loan that would get written down below cost?" Robbins asked.

"Right," she said.

Here we are back to day one of freshman investing class, where beginning students learn that when an investment reaches a stage where the investor would not repeat the investment, it is no longer worth the original cost. As a result, loans to companies performing below plan, violating covenants, or even not making interest payments—including to the point that Allied realized it would never collect the interest—are not worth cost. Nonetheless, if Allied believed it would eventually recover its principal (Grade 4), it valued the investment at cost. This might be called the "*you-have-got-to-be-kidding-me*" method of accounting. Walton wanted people to believe that we thought loans needed to be written down to zero at the first sign of trouble. What we believed was that these loans might be worth more than zero, but they certainly were not worth 100 cents on the dollar, as Allied's financial statement indicated.

Sweeney then introduced a white paper (essentially a research paper) that she and Roll authored describing Allied's valuation strategy. "We have a consistent process we've used to determine fair-value, and that process is clearly outlined in our disclosure document," Sweeney said. "In addition, if you visit our Web site, you will see that we have written a white paper on fair-value accounting and our interpretation of its application. We wrote this paper for a conference on BDCs in February. We encourage you to read the white paper to obtain a better understanding of fair-value."

Investors didn't need to read Allied's white paper to learn about fair value. It's not up to Allied; it's up to the SEC. In 1969 and 1970, the agency issued accounting series releases (ASRs) describing how investment companies need to value investments. ASR 118 says, "As a general principle, the current 'fair-value' of an issue of securities being valued by the Board of Directors, would appear to be the amount which the owner would reasonably expect to receive for them upon their current-sale." Then, it elaborates on how to value both marketable and unmarketable securities. ASR 113 indicates it is improper to continue to carry securities at cost if cost no longer represents fair-value as a result of the operations of the issuer, changes in general market conditions, or otherwise. Furthermore, investment companies have to take into account restrictions on selling when determining fair-value.

Shortly after the conference call, I did as Sweeney asked. I downloaded the white paper, *Valuation of Illiquid Securities Held by Business Development Companies*. It comes right out and challenges the SEC-issued ASRs. It argues, "The concept of 'current sale' in ASR 118 is particularly troubling if applied to a BDC's illiquid portfolio, because if such a portfolio were subject to a current sale test, the portfolio would need to carry a significant discount from the face value of its underlying securities." The white paper continues, "The concept of current sale for the purposes of determining fair value in ASR 118 is difficult, if not impossible, to apply in the case of a BDC's portfolio."

The paper boldly asserts, "The current SEC regulations and interpretive advice for valuing a security at fair value applicable to investment companies [is] . . . not specifically applicable to BDC's." Further, according to the paper, the SEC-mandated rules "are not easily applied to the unique characteristics of a BDC portfolio, primarily because the securities in which a BDC invests cannot be put to the test of current sale for purposes of valuation."

So, according to Allied, the SEC rules don't apply to the company. Indeed, if it had to follow the SEC rules, which require the current-sale test, the company's portfolio would have to be carried at a significant discount. In fact, Allied conveniently said that a current-sale test is too difficult to employ because the securities are illiquid.

The white paper brazenly flaunts Allied's use of non-SEC-sanctioned accounting. Instead, it calls for more lenient SBA accounting. Under SBA methods, assets are written down only when they are deemed to be permanently impaired. "SBA policy is far more applicable to the portfolio of a BDC than the valuation guidance set forth by the SEC in the ASR's," the white paper explains in alphabet-soup fashion.

The conclusion of the paper could not have been clearer. "SBA policy, with minor modifications, appears to provide the best overall guidance for valuation of fair value for the portfolio of a BDC . . . BDCs, therefore, should adopt investment policies that encompass the guidance provided by the SBA, taking into account that all private illiquid securities may have unique characteristics that impact value." I have never before or since seen a company publicly indicate that it ignores SEC rules. *Somehow, Allied did this without fear of repercussions.*

After producing the white paper, Sweeney said on the conference call that Allied isn't a normal investment company and investment company accounting should not really apply to it. She indicated the public markets don't value BDCs at net asset value, but rather based on dividend yield. While they are subject to the Investment Company Act of 1940, they are different from mutual funds because they are "internally managed operating companies" and don't report results like mutual funds, but, instead, file 10-Qs and 10-Ks like operating companies.

Sweeney continued to explain why Allied shouldn't be viewed as an investment company:

"What we do think is important to our valuation as a public company is our net income, which communicates our earnings power to shareholders. The idea that we should be marking long-term, illiquid investments to some artificial or theoretical market instead of telling shareholders what we really think we have made in gains or lost in principal seems theoretical at best and at least confusing. We don't hide what we've lost by claiming a temporary decline in market. When you read our income statement and look at net income, you know where we think we actually are and don't think it serves any purpose to cloud our results with a lot of temporary unsustainable ups and downs.

She continued, "Net income is the predictor of future dividends for shareholders. [Investment losses] will decrease dividends; real investment gains will increase dividends. Mutual funds trade in the public markets at net asset value, and they mark their portfolios daily because they are simply pools of securities that have a value that is shared by the fund's shareholders. Mutual funds are typically externally managed. Mutual funds must stay very liquid and be very precise on their net asset value calculation, because they are subject to daily redemptions should their investors take money out of the fund by selling their shares. Net asset value is the primary method by which mutual funds trade. In contrast, Allied Capital, like most BDCs, invests in long-term illiquid securities. Any increases in value are realized over a long period of time. BDCs typically do not trade their securities; they invest until maturity or until ultimate sale of the company that has issued the securities. BDC shares are not subject to redemption."

Allied's 2001 annual report issued in early 2002 echoed Sweeney's conference call statement, Roll's private description, and the white paper's thesis. For example, Allied's official policy stated, "The company's valuation policy considers the fact that privately negotiated securities increase in value over a long period of time, that the Company does not intend to trade the securities, and that no ready market exists. . . . The Company will record unrealized depreciation on investments when it believes that an asset has been impaired and full collection for the loan or realization of an equity security is doubtful."

This, cleverly enough, is the SBA standard for valuation. But as a regulated investment company, Allied is subject to the tougher SEC standard that requires write-downs as soon as a willing buyer would no longer pay cost.

The 2001 annual report continued to echo Sweeney's conference-call statement: "Under its valuation policy, the Company does not consider temporary changes in the capital markets, such as interest rate movements or changes in the public equity markets, in order to determine whether an investment in a private company has been impaired or whether such an investment has increased in value."

Oddly, though, the previous year's annual report lacked most of this language. Clearly, it was brand new in the 2001 report. Obviously, this could not be part of Allied's forty-year-old "consistent" accounting practices. The new language plainly reflected new practices, with new prose now justified by the white paper. Had Allied modified its accounting policy to avoid taking write-downs in the mini-recession of 2001–2002?

Later, we learned that the white paper wasn't Sweeney's first attempt to obtain lenient SBA-styled accounting treatment for BDCs. In 1997, Sweeney represented Allied in the SEC's annual Government-Business Forum on Small Business Capital Formation that recommended, "[a] safe harbor . . . be established in the '40 Act for the 'mark-to-market' evaluation of investment companies' portfolio of illiquid investments in small businesses to protect directors of such companies from possible liability."

The panel elaborated: "The Investment Company Act requirement of [sic] that fund boards determine the 'fair value' of portfolio securities for which market quotations are not readily available discriminates against the illiquid securities typically issued by smaller companies. Using an established valuation guideline such as the one developed by the SBA should provide sufficient information and consequently some protection for the investment company's directors from liability under federal securities laws."

The SEC never granted the requested safe harbor.

In summary, Sweeney went to the SEC and asked permission to use the SBA standard. When the SEC didn't agree, *Allied did it anyway*. Then, Sweeney and Roll wrote a white paper to justify it. In 2004, when we learned of Sweeney's 1997 failed attempt with the SEC, I realized Allied's improper use of SBA accounting was no accident. Rather than an unsophisticated lack of understanding, it was a willful, intentional act—a sham that had been in the works for years.

■ ■ ■

We called Doug Scheidt, the associate director of the SEC's Division of Investment Management, who had written open letters to the Investment Company Institute clarifying the SEC's views on fair-value accounting that appeared to conflict with Allied's analysis. We asked him for the SEC's view of Allied's argument. We began the conversation in generic terms without bringing up Allied by name. I asked Scheidt whether the SEC's 1940 Act current-sale test valuation standard is primarily for mutual funds, rather than for BDCs, which instead could use an SBA impairment test standard for valuation because they hold illiquid securities for years.

"Disagree," Scheidt said. "The guidance that we were providing applied to all investment companies, open-end and closed-end. . . . Closed-end funds or BDCs, though, publish their NAVs (net asset values) if they're trading on an exchange . . . and all of these NAV calculations that they are required to make or that they do make are subject to the 1940 Act and regardless of whether they redeem or repurchase or sell their shares. So it is, and for example, their publication of their NAV may have an effect on market prices.

"I know that closed-end funds have tried to argue that they shouldn't be subject to the same standards because of the differences between closed-end funds and open-end funds," he said. "But the Act and the law doesn't differentiate between the two. It says for all investment companies, they are required to use market quotes and do fair-value. And we have had closed-end funds make the same argument that since they don't have to do redemptions, that if they invest in a bank loan participation fund, they typically hold until maturity or they should be able to value it at what they can get for it at maturity unless there is some sort of impairment in the credit or the collateral that's underlying the bank loan. So, and we said no, and . . . it's inappropriate for a fund to value it at what the fund would expect to get for it at some point in the future because the appropriate standard is: What can you get for it today?"

Again, without mentioning the company by name, I asked Scheidt about Allied's argument that since it custom-tailors the loans, which are illiquid, they know the borrowers better than any potential buyer and plan to hold the loans for five to ten years, any sale would have to be a "fire-sale."

"I would say we're not forcing you to sell," Scheidt said. "The way that I've told people when they raise the argument about how do you value illiquid securities, how do you apply the standard that says you use the value that you would get today from a willing buyer when it would take me months or weeks to sell this thing. I say assume that weeks or months ago you started beating the bushes for a buyer. And it took however long it took, and now today you have a willing buyer who is willing to buy from you, what would they [pay]? So it's not a fire-sale like 'Oh my God, I've got to get rid of this, will somebody take this off my hands?'"

I pointed out that they might argue that these types of loans are rarely sold, and the only time anybody ever sells them is when either the loan is distressed or the owner of the loan is distressed. As a result, potential buyers would perceive any sale as a fire sale.

Scheidt shot back, "I would say that would be all the more reason to hold it at a lower value because that's what it's worth."

We were quite pleased to hear the SEC so decisively support our view.

Though we conducted the majority of our call without mentioning the company in question, at the end we told Scheidt that Allied Capital had made these and other claims. We asked if it made sense to outline our concerns to the SEC and, if so, to whom should we address them? Scheidt said that we should, and that he was the guy. This was good.

We sent a letter and an eighteen-page summary of our analysis, describing our concerns that Allied was not complying with SEC valuation requirements and abusing intercompany accounting available for controlled companies. We detailed Allied's responses and the various events that I have discussed here. As a betting person, I felt that Scheidt's disagreement with Allied's story made it only a matter of time before the SEC would resolve the dispute—and not in the way Allied's shareholders hoped.

CHAPTER 9

Fact—or Maybe Not

O*ff Wall Street* is an independent researcher started in 1990 by Mark Roberts that publishes buy and short-sale recommendations. We have been customers for years. It is an expensive, high-quality publication, sold to hedge funds and traditional long-only institutional investors. Unlike most of its peers, *Off Wall Street* continues to follow up on its ideas and provides substantive updates until it closes out a recommendation. Whether long or short, *Off Wall Street* is deeply concerned about its track record and treats its recommendations similarly to how serious fund managers treat their portfolios.

On June 12, 2002, *Off Wall Street* published a twenty-one-page "Sell" recommendation on Allied that highlighted its own conversation with the SEC, an analysis of ASR 113 and ASR 118, and Allied's white paper. It reviewed a number of Allied's portfolio companies highlighted in my speech, and wrote its own analysis. Though Allied's stock had recovered to over $25 per share—or almost all the way back to where it traded before my speech—the shares fell sharply, again, upon the release of the *Off Wall Street* recommendation.

Part of what was so compelling about *Off Wall Street's* analysis was its research into Allied's largest subsidiary, Business Loan Express (BLX). Allied Capital formed BLX when it bought BLC Financial Services Inc., and merged it with its own SBA lending subsidiary, Allied Capital Express (also know as Allied Capital SBLC). *Off Wall Street* reviewed BLC Financial's SEC filings before Allied purchased it and determined that BLC Financial generated 63 percent of its revenue as a public company through gain-on-sale accounting. Gain-on-sale accounting, which allows the recognition of the value of assets when originated, is fundamentally more aggressive than traditional portfolio accounting, which requires recognition of earnings over the life of the assets.

We believed Allied refused to disclose financial information about BLX to conceal its use of gain-on-sale accounting. That accounting, which front-loaded revenue and assumed good loan performance, combined with BLX's high delinquencies, were a potentially lethal combination. BLX's earnings were of unusually low quality, and it was probably not generating much cash. This cast further doubts on the appropriateness of the 25 percent interest rate Allied charged BLX. Clearly, Allied used these related-party fees to prop up its income statement.

Off Wall Street also questioned Allied's $39 million carrying value of its loan to Galaxy American Communications Inc. (GAC). It pointed out that GAC was an affiliate of Galaxy Telecom LP, which went bankrupt and shared the same business address. While there were no public filings on GAC, *Off Wall Street's* review of Galaxy Telecom's SEC filings, which included information about GAC, confirmed that GAC had minimal revenues, lost money, and had more liabilities than assets.

A few days later, *Off Wall Street* followed up:

> We think that the company's approach now seems to be that it will attack the short thesis with a combination of *ad hominem* attacks, obfuscation, and specious syllogistic reasoning. A great deal of this approach has to do with the integrity or lack of integrity in using language, and with the use of language to distort and confuse, in our opinion. In the past, we have seen this approach used to good effect in the political arena . . . the integrity of language used might have some relationship to the integrity of the speaker.

Off Wall Street concluded by asking:

> By the way, who is writing this convoluted stuff for Allied? And, further, if its accounting is so obviously correct, why did Allied even think it had the need to issue the white paper in the first place, and why does it continue with these new tortured explanations to justify its methods?

■ ■ ■

We decided to put our analysis on Greenlight's Web site. We wanted to share it with the public because we wanted everyone to be able to better understand it and to see for themselves how Allied mischaracterized it. I was tired of Allied's putting words in my mouth, suggesting that my speech had been part of a secretive "whisper campaign," claiming that we hadn't done our homework and didn't know what we were talking about.

As we put the finishing touches on the analysis, Allied announced it would hold yet another investor conference call on Monday, June 17, 2002. I had never before seen a company assemble everyone three times in a month. The Friday before the call I gave a nearly complete draft of our lengthy analysis to journalists who covered or expressed interest in Allied. I thought they would benefit by reading it in advance so that they could have time to prepare informed articles. In fact, none of the journalists wrote about our analysis. Worse, at least one of them passed our draft analysis to Allied.

On the morning of this third conference call, we posted the twenty-seven page report, *An Analysis of Allied Capital: Questions of Valuation Technique*, and issued a press release containing a summary and offering the public an opportunity to view the full report on our Web site. The analysis included our concerns over the accounting, valuation, Allied's white paper, controlled company transactions, specific valuations, our conversation with the SEC, the payment-in-kind income, and the strange history of the Arthur Andersen audit letter.

The afternoon conference call had a different tone than the earlier ones, where management had spoken almost off-the-cuff. This call was organized, scripted and apparently well rehearsed. I believe having an advance copy of my analysis aided management. They had a clear message, and management's confident, forceful presentation compensated for its lack of veracity. The phone call was quite a significant event, because the company recanted virtually all of its previous claims about how appropriate its accounting was. It capitulated by agreeing with the SEC, and with us, that it should use fair-value accounting. It removed its previously trumpeted white paper from its Web site.

Allied hired a world-class spin expert, Lanny Davis, to guide management's presentation of the change. Management was effective at completely changing its story, while claiming it was "consistent." Many listeners apparently fell for it and accepted Allied's assertion that it had been the victim of a manipulative "Big Lie." The hiring of Davis, known for spinning the Monica Lewinsky affair as White House counsel for President Bill Clinton, seemed to me like an admission of wrongdoing. "When you parachute him in, you know you've got a serious problem," Ed Mathias of the Carlyle Group told *The Hill*, the newspaper that covers Congress, about hiring Lanny Davis generally. Davis's clients have included Seitel, the seismic data shooting fraud discussed earlier; Lernout & Hauspie, a European speech recognition technology company that perpetuated a multibillion-dollar fraud; and HealthSouth, a significant accounting fraud. It was clear that Allied's problems required a political-style spin job, and Davis was a perfect choice.

In the conference call, Walton recalled Allied's forty-year history and described the issue as a battle between a great company and a group of stock manipulators. Walton's description of the situation was, to my mind, blatantly misleading and scurrilously dishonest. Yet, his introduction to the subject represented a brilliant distortion of the facts:

> The purpose of today's call is to set the record straight in response to a systematic campaign by certain individuals who have been circulating statements about Allied Capital in recent weeks that are either misleading or downright false. Many of these individuals appear to be motivated by personal profit because they have taken substantial short positions in Allied Capital stock and, thus, stand to benefit by driving our stock price down.
>
> Their core charge is that Allied Capital has deliberately and thus fraudulently inflated values of companies in our investment portfolio in order to inflate the value of our stock. That is a lie and the facts will prove it is a lie. Indeed, this is a classic example of the Big Lie,

which repeated so many times and in so many different versions to so many different constituencies, usually behind closed doors, using whispers and rumors that the victims have had little chance to catch up and defend themselves with the truth.

Many public companies have been faced with systematic attacks by short-sellers. Sometimes those attacks have performed a public service when, for example as in recent months, they have helped to uncover an actual fraudulent financial reporting of wrongdoing. This has led to an unfortunate but understandable skepticism by many investors to the integrity of financial reporting by many public companies. But those engaging in the current misinformation campaign against Allied Capital are cynically trying to take advantage of the current post-Enron environment by tarring a great and honest company like Allied Capital with the broad brush of a Big Lie.

[Some] . . . companies under such attack choose to ignore such cynical short attacks out of a concern for dignifying them or publicizing them. Well, we at Allied Capital have made a fundamental decision. We are not going to let them get away with it. We owe it to our shareholders, we owe it to ourselves and we owe it to our famil[ies]. We are going to confront our accusers in the daylight with the facts and the truth until the truth prevails. Transparency goes both ways. It is time for our accusers to be held accountable in the light of day for the misinformation they are circulating. We would certainly welcome a full inquiry by the SEC and the New York Stock Exchange concerning the use of such misinformation to manipulate the market.

Walton continued his defense that Allied used fair-valuation methods and didn't inflate the value of its investments. He repeatedly criticized the motivations of short-sellers. Here is Walton's description of what he claimed to be a coordinated, greedy, and "tortious interference" attack against Allied by the short-sellers, lawyers, and the media:

I think it's . . . [created a] whole industry of hedge funds who . . . [, now that the] stock market's not going up, they're trying to find things to go down. And they're trying to find things that they can help go down and there seems to be a pattern. You develop a position; you then have some sort of an event; in our case it was a speech. One is closely linked with law firms who then very quickly file suits, everybody says the company's been sued, so therefore, something must be wrong. . . .

There's been a lot of rumors out there about articles that are going to get published, or this is going to happen or that's going to happen. We've had hedge funds call the SBA to find out, to tell them we're in trouble. We're seeing a lot of things that I'd characterize as tortious interference of our business model and that sort of thing should be outlawed. And we're going to do the best we can to be part of that process, and I think the fact that we're speaking out the way we are I hope sheds some light on that, and maybe other people will maybe join us in fighting this stuff.

Walton wanted everyone to focus on our "motivation." For Greenlight, Allied is one of many ways for us to make money. It is a part of a large portfolio. However, Allied's management was quite "motivated" to say whatever they could to get themselves out of this pickle. Certainly, Walton and Sweeney had much more at stake personally than anyone else. *For management, Allied is the whole ball of wax.* If Allied is shown to be fraudulent, the consequences would be more dire than losing a few dollars. Top management players could lose their jobs and possibly go to jail.

Next, Allied recanted the white paper—acknowledging that SEC accounting rules applied to them after all—and came up with a fresh description of its accounting. Sweeney spoke about the valuation issue and described the white paper (incorrectly) as if she believed most people wouldn't know what it said:

Now, let's look at the valuation methodology we use. It is simply beyond dispute that it is both appropriate and consistently applied. Allied Capital developed a white paper, which is posted on our website to describe this valuation methodology. To summarize: Allied Capital's Board of Directors makes a judgment in good faith to appropriately value the portfolio on a quarterly basis using a valuation policy that has *been consistently applied based on the estimated price that a portfolio company could be sold for if a willing buyer and willing seller were to negotiate at arm's-length*. That judgment includes factors recommended by the SEC in accounting series releases that go back thirty years. It includes such factors as the company's current and projected financial condition, cash flow and profitability, net liquidation value of tangible business assets, yield to maturity with respect to debt issues, debt to equity ratios and so forth.

While this comment is interesting, it is not accurate. In fact, the Allied white paper stated the *opposite*. As discussed in Chapter 8, the whole point of the paper was to rationalize *not using* the SEC accounting series releases. Clearly, Allied had received some advice (the advice probably came from the SEC, though it is possible Allied hadn't yet heard from the SEC and simply realized its own mistake) that its white paper, with its brazen view that SEC valuation guidance did not apply to them, was wrong. Allied now ran away from its white paper as fast as it could. Allied changed its tune and would no longer claim that SEC policies don't apply or that measuring the value between a willing buyer and seller at arm's length was difficult or impossible to apply to its investments.

Sweeney continued her script with what she called "FACTS" or, better yet, "INDISPUTABLE FACTS." This type of wordplay was typical of Allied's approach. Apparently, Sweeney felt that if she said the word FACT loudly enough, with enough emphasis, many people would accept what she said as true.

She then tried to defend Allied's accounting policies. "Regarding the question of propriety of our methodology," she said, "here are a few indisputable facts. FACT: The valuation methodology outlined in our white paper is nearer in our form and to [the] shelf registration statement, which is filed every quarter with the SEC, and the SEC has consistently found these filings satisfactory." Of course, Allied had only introduced this language in its SEC filings earlier that year, giving the SEC little time to opine on it.

Further, Sweeney said that Allied's statement of accounting policies matched the white paper and was Allied's actual practice. Allied's current annual report echoed the white paper, stating, "The Company will record unrealized depreciation on investments when it believes that an asset has been impaired and full collection for the loan or realization of an equity security is doubtful."

However, starting with this conference call, Allied switched its descriptive language from an impairment test to current-sale valuation based on where willing buyers and sellers would transact. Without fanfare, in its next SEC filing, Allied eliminated the offending language that had described its valuation methodology in terminology consistent with its discredited and withdrawn white paper. Eventually, Allied would say the white paper was a "discussion piece for an industry conference" and claim that it never actually used that type of accounting.

Sweeney continued, "FACT: Mark-to-market and fair-value are not the same thing. It has been falsely stated that the appropriate valuation method to be used is a rigid mark to market or fire-sale." Presumably, she meant it was falsely stated by short-sellers, though I don't know who.

Of course, this was more wordplay. We argued that fair-value accounting required a mark-to-market approach. She simply added the part about fire-sale. This was a convenient invention because the SEC said fair-value accounting should not require a fire-sale valuation. Having now falsely tarred us as claiming that Allied needed to use fire-sale values, she had no trouble explaining that we were wrong. She continued, "The experts do not agree, and for good reason. Fair-value is a regulatory concept that includes the concept of current sale, which is not the same thing as fire sale. The term is defined by the AICPA guide as a current sale means 'an orderly disposition over a reasonable period of time between willing parties other than a forced or liquidation sale.'"

A few minutes later in the call, in response to a question about whether Allied complied with the Investment Act of 1940, Sweeney again rejected the white paper and adapted the current-sale test: "We apply a current-sale standard, and how we do that is every quarter we actually determine the value of the portfolio company if it were to be sold today in a current-sale. In other words, what in an arm's-length transaction would a willing buyer pay for a company? . . . If the enterprise value of the company is in excess of our last dollar of capital, we have no need to depreciate a debt security and, in fact, we may have evidence of appreciation for an equity security."

This was a changed description of Allied's accounting. Gone was the analysis that it marks investments to what it believes it will *eventually* collect. Gone was the discussion that the current-sale test was difficult or impossible to apply to a BDC. Gone was the notion that it should ignore temporary changes in value and use SBA-styled accounting treatment, where assets are written-down only when they are deemed to be permanently impaired. In fact, Allied retracted almost every description it had used for its accounting that it had made over the past several weeks. Now, suddenly, the current-sale test, which always applied to everyone else, also applied to Allied. Not only that, but according to management, this had always been the case because its accounting was "consistent."

Sweeney was getting closer to the correct SEC interpretation of the meaning of current-sale, but she wasn't quite there. The required definition of current-sale refers to the price that an arm's-length buyer would pay for the *specific security* Allied held and not for the *entire company*, if it were sold. This was confirmed by the SEC's Doug Scheidt, who had written to the Investment Company Institute and cited an SEC case captioned *In Re Parnassus Investments*, where the SEC found "that a board's valuation of a portfolio security based upon what the security would be worth upon the sale of the entire company as a going concern, when no such offers were forthcoming, was not determined in good faith." Certainly, Allied's management was aware of the distinction of the value of the entire company versus the value of a specific security in that company. Allied cited this case in its white paper. It is the same decision that says investment companies should not value investments at "fire-sale" prices.

While a total enterprise value calculation makes sense for valuing equity securities—you determine the value of the firm and subtract the net debt to calculate the equity value—it does not make sense for valuing debt instruments because debt instruments have limited upside. The most a debt holder can expect to receive is the principal and the interest due. Because of this, debt securities are valued based on the risk of default. For example, if there are two debt securities yielding the same interest rate, the debt security with the lower risk of default is worth more than a debt security with the higher risk of default. If the enterprise value of a firm falls, then the risk of default increases and the value of the debt instrument declines, even when the enterprise value is still greater than the amount of debt outstanding.

Allied's argument that debt securities are worth par whenever the enterprise value exceeds the debt outstanding is fundamentally flawed and ignores the impact of increased risk of default when the enterprise value falls. It is market practice to reduce the value of debt instruments when the equity cushion shrinks. In Allied's view, as long as there is *any* cushion, the debt is worth cost. Allied's comparison of enterprise value to the last dollar of debt in this manner is simply another description of an improper "impairment" test rather than a current-sale test.

When a questioner pressed Allied on its practice of valuing nonperforming loans at cost, Walton backed off and tried to soften Allied's previous position stating, "We say freely a Grade 4 loan is at par because we think that's the amount we're going to get in the value chain and that we're getting a par return on it. Now, investors when they look at our portfolio can say, 'Well, gee, they've got this amount in Grade 4 that aren't earning any interest, I think those things are worth a little less.' They're free to do that. That's part—that used to be called security analysis. And then they can say, 'Okay, I think it should be a little less.' But that's not because we're trying to hide losses. There's nothing there we're hiding. We're saying this is the way we do it."

Thus, Walton admitted the obvious: The Grade 4 loans, where Allied believed it eventually would recover the principal but not the interest, were not really worth cost even as Allied valued them at cost on its books. Nonetheless, it is Allied's job to determine how much less they are worth and reflect that on its financial statements. Allied can't delegate this responsibility to investors as "security analysis." It is absurd to expect investors to understand by how much Allied overstates its loan values, particularly since Allied does not disclose the performance of the underlying companies, most of which are private.

Next, Sweeney addressed BLX. "The criticism from the shorts seems to be centered on two allegations. First, they say that Allied is taking excessive money from BLX in interest payments and fees. Second, they claim that we have chosen not to consolidate BLX's financial statements, with the innuendo that BLX is really nothing more than a sham company reminiscent of Enron's off-balance-sheet special-purpose entity. These allegations are totally baseless. Let's look at the facts. "

She said BLX had met its business plan goals, was current on its bank debt, had average delinquencies on its SBA portfolio, and received the highest SBA rating for a preferred lender. She said that Allied performed substantial consulting services for BLX, including loan systems integration, marketing, human resources, Web site development, and board recruitment, which more than justified the management fees. (Eventually, we would learn that BLX's board consisted entirely of BLX and Allied insiders, including Walton and Sweeney. How much did they charge for that board recruitment exercise?) She repeated that 25 percent wasn't an excessive interest rate to charge BLX because Allied earned nothing more on its equity investment in BLX. This was consistent with Allied's past comments on BLX.

She continued, "FACT: The consolidation issue is *absolutely* black and white. Since Allied Capital is a BDC, the rules for accounting for investment companies is quite clear. No investment companies may consolidate the financial results of its portfolio companies into its own. Nevertheless, if Allied Capital could consolidate BLX's results, our reported earnings would have been higher, not lower."

In fact, Sweeney's statement must have been knowingly false. In consolidation, Allied would eliminate the unrealized appreciation, fees, interest, and dividends it recognized from BLX and replace them with BLX's actual earnings. Allied carried BLX at a premium to Allied's cost, which was itself a large premium to BLX's book value. Consolidation would have lowered Allied's earnings and book value by eliminating the premiums.

Certainly, Allied's management knew that the consolidation of BLX was far from black and white. Indeed, years earlier, Allied consolidated the financial results of BLX's predecessor, Allied Capital Express, in its financial results. Why couldn't it consolidate Allied Capital Express's successor as well? Robert D. Long, a managing director of Allied, spoke to me at Allied's investor day a couple of weeks later and contradicted Sweeney. He told me that BLX *should* be consolidated. He said that there is a way that they could do that *if they wanted to*.

Our subsequent review of the technical accounting literature indicated that investment companies are precluded from consolidating entities *other than another investment company*. BLX is a lender and could be structured as an investment company. Quite likely, Allied took pains to structure BLX so it wouldn't have to consolidate it. In fact, part of the motivation to acquire BLC Financial and merge it with Allied Capital Express may have been to deconsolidate Allied Capital Express. Considering that Allied owned substantially all of BLX, guaranteed most of its financing, consolidated a predecessor entity, and considered and often referred to BLX as its small business lending "subsidiary," consolidation was far from "absolutely black and white." Further, since investments were being transferred back and forth between Allied and BLX, there are serious doubts as to whether BLX is even operated as a separate company.

During the Q&A, Todd Pitsinger, an analyst from Friedman, Billings & Ramsey, asked how much of BLX's revenue came from gain-on-sale accounting—a low-quality revenue stream that investors often discount. Sweeney avoided the question and instead gave a lengthy response, which concluded with the erroneous statement that SBA loans last an average of about eleven years. A later questioner pointed out that she hadn't answered the question and asked for an answer. Management ducked the question a second time.

Sweeney repeated the eleven-year loan life number at an investment conference sponsored by Bank of America on September 22, 2002. In 2003, Wachovia Securities published a report estimating BLX average loan life to be less than four years. Since one of the key assumptions in calculating the gain-on-sale is to estimate the life of the loans, if BLX assumed eleven years, then it dramatically overstated its revenues because the longer the term, the more interest payments are assumed to be paid. (If BLX used an assumption that was closer to four years, then Sweeney was misleading the market.) Its gain-on-sale assumptions remain top secret to this day. Incidentally, if Allied consolidated BLX, it would have to disclose the assumptions.

During the call, Allied said that Hillman had made a typographical mistake in the 10-K and Hillman's senior debt was worth face value. The point refuted our analysis that Allied's subordinated investment in Hillman was not worth par, because Hillman's 10-K conceded that the fair-value of Hillman's senior debt was only 75 percent of face value. We believed that if the senior debt wasn't worth face, the subordinated investment wasn't worth face, either.

We, of course, had assumed Hillman had filed an accurate report with the SEC. Indeed, in my next letter to the SEC, I wrote, "In our earlier analysis, we had relied on that disclosure in asserting that Allied's investment in Hillman was impaired. Assuming that it was in fact a typo, we would withdraw the criticism based on their erroneous SEC disclosure. We would, however, continue to assert that the 18 percent rate of interest Allied charges Hillman is not arm's-length or market and should not be permitted."

Before Allied bought Hillman, it advanced an unsecured subordinated loan at 13.9 percent interest, while Hillman's publicly traded preferred stock yielded 19 percent. By the time Allied obtained control, Hillman's credit improved so that the preferred yielded only 12 percent. Nonetheless, Allied reset the rate it charged Hillman to 18 percent, increasing Allied's reported interest income. A fair rate on a subordinated loan should be lower than the prevailing yield on the preferred equity. However, as Allied controlled Hillman, it set the rate as it saw fit. Though Allied eventually sold its equity investment in Hillman for a large gain and claimed vindication, Allied gave Hillman a new subordinated loan at a market rate of 10 percent, further confirming our view that the earlier 18 percent rate was not arm's length.

More inaccuracies followed. Sweeney spoke about Galaxy American Communications (GAC) and explained that GAC, in which Allied held an investment valued at $39 million compared to the original cost of $49 million, was a different company from its affiliate company, Galaxy Telecom, which had gone bankrupt. She said the criticism of GAC was, "bogus . . . almost comically bogus."

"It appears that our critics not only don't do simple math, but they don't do their simple homework," she said, castigating us. "Is it possible that our critics, so quick to accuse and so oblivious to our facts, had confused these two companies? Or without evidence, are suggesting that the adverse results of Galaxy Telecom has [sic] any impact on the financial results of Galaxy Communications? Apparently so, which tells us all about their credibility."

We hadn't said anything about GAC. The only applicable comments we knew about came from *Off Wall Street*, which was certainly not confused. It clearly distinguished between GAC and Galaxy Telecom in its report. Since the vast majority of listeners did not have access to *Off Wall Street*, they would be unable to see that Sweeney was just making this up, with a fabricated attack on our "math," "homework," and "credibility."

After several questions by brokerage firm analysts and sympathizers, one caller asked, "I'm just wondering whether you're going to take some calls from the so-called shorts you're complaining about." To which, Sweeney's reply was basically, "the line is open." Once again: untrue. On this and the previous conference call, I tried to get into the queue to ask questions. Though the calls went for a long time, Allied did not take a question from me. The service that operates the conference calls provides the company with a real-time list of who is on the call and who is interested in asking questions. The company determines whose questions will be accepted, and no one gets through without its consent.

Sweeney added another untruth for good measure: "We've never had a call or visit from the two organizations who have written papers about us." I couldn't believe that Sweeney still claimed we had never called Allied. According to a *Dow Jones Newswire* story, "Allied Capital: Short-Recommendation Reasons 'Unfounded'" (May 16, 2002), "The Company confirmed that investor relations director Sparrow and Chief Financial

Officer Penni Roll both had spoken to the hedge fund manager [me] within the last month." Despite this, Sweeney *again* insisted we never called. I continued to hear this lie repeated for years.

The next question related to my conversation with Doug Scheidt, the SEC official, which we detailed in the analysis on Greenlight's Web site. Sweeney answered, "If you look at the question and answer between Doug Scheidt and I guess it was Mr. Einhorn, Doug answered the questions that were asked. They weren't the right questions. The way Mr. Einhorn characterized what we do is not, in fact, what we do. So, if he wants to put a hypothetical in front of Doug Scheidt and get an answer, that's one thing. But it's not specifically Allied Capital."

There was no dispute: I conducted my conversation without identifying Allied. However, we discussed what Allied said and wrote, and Scheidt responded that it was "inappropriate." Sweeney knew this and, in my opinion, was kicking dust in the air.

■ ■ ■

A couple of days later, on June 19, Allied issued a press release announcing that Sweeney had met with Scheidt, who confirmed the conversation had been generic. Sweeney never revealed what else she and Scheidt discussed during their meeting. Did Allied ask Scheidt to comment on the white paper and accounting policies, and what did he say? Did the conversation with Scheidt cause Allied to change its description of its accounting methods, which it did in its next SEC filing? Had the answers to these questions been exculpatory to Allied, I believe Allied undoubtedly would have shared more details of Sweeney's conversation with Scheidt in the press release.

At the end of the June 17, 2002, conference call, Walton promised to disclose more information about its control companies, including BLX's gain-on-sale accounting assumptions. He said, "It's the right thing to do." And, of course he was correct that it was the right thing to do. Subsequent events, once again, revealed his unwillingness to do the right thing. Though Allied began providing summary information on BLX in the next 10-Q, it never revealed the promised detail on gain-on-sale, and Allied never provided more information about its entire portfolio of controlled companies, as Walton pledged.

Allied's stock, which began to fall again after the *Off Wall Street* report, fell further, reaching $20 per share following the conference call. A few days later, Sweeney decided to turn up the volume on her personal attacks and said in a *Bloomberg* article that our plan was a strategy of "let's scare the little old ladies."

I told *The Washington Post* at the time, "We're not critical of this company because we are short; we are short because we are critical of this company." Ladies, be they little, be they old, or be they both, had nothing to do with it.

CHAPTER 10

Business Loan Express

I n early June 2002, I heard from Jim Carruthers, a partner then at Eastbourne Capital Management in San Rafael, California. I had met him nine years earlier while working on my first short sale of a fraudulent company, Home Care Management, while at Siegler, Collery. Carruthers was a *digger*, an analyst who developed alternative sources and searched public records to gather valuable information not generally contained in press releases.

During our conversation, Carruthers told me he had discovered fraud at Business Loan Express, Allied's largest investment. At March 31, 2002, Allied carried BLX at $229.7 million, or 17 percent of Allied's net asset value. Furthermore, Allied had additional exposure through its guarantee of BLX's bank debt. Again, Allied formed BLX by purchasing BLC Financial Services Inc., a publicly traded company, and combining it with its own SBA lending business, Allied Capital Express. (As I describe the various troubling and sometimes fraudulent BLX loans throughout this book, I am referring to BLX or either of its two predecessors.)

Carruthers identified BLX's SBA loans that were the subject of court proceedings by searching through PACER, a legal database. He obtained the related filings and spoke to a number of the participants. One case related to loans extended to a woman named Holly Hawley for car washes in Michigan that, according to Carruthers' interviews, "violated every convention and lending practice."

Carruthers found that Hawley had previously been criminally charged and convicted of a federal crime involving the illegal conversion of Federal Housing Administration property in an embezzlement case. Carruthers found a transcript of Hawley's sworn testimony that detailed her experience with BLX. To summarize: Prior to obtaining the loan from Allied, four banks cited her lack of operating experience—a requirement to obtain an SBA loan—in denying her application for construction loans to build car washes. Hawley's loan broker introduced her to Allied (prior to the formation of BLX), which issued her an SBA loan. Hawley wanted to obtain more financing to build additional car washes, but was ineligible to borrow from the SBA, which permitted only one loan per person. Because she was "loaned up" at the SBA, Allied suggested that she form a new corporation and use her brother to sign the loan documents.

Hawley's fraudulent loans were made and supervised by Allied executive vice president Patrick Harrington and vice president William Leahy. Harrington headed the Detroit office of BLX in Troy, Michigan. After Hawley's two SBA loans defaulted, Harrington and Leahy tried to cover up the loss by granting her additional loans. She formed yet another entity to take another loan and used the proceeds to pay $150,000 of past-due interest owed on the existing SBA loans and pay off liens filed by contractors.

Allied instructed her to put the loan into her twenty-year-old daughter's name, and Hawley even bought an airline ticket for her daughter to attend the closing. However, an employee at Allied's Washington, D.C., office rejected the loan due to her daughter's inexperience and status as a full-time student. Allied suggested that Hawley issue the loan to yet another brother, who lived in California. She signed her brother's name at Allied's office in Leahy's presence, at his direction.

Carruthers found another dubious loan to Jefferson Fuel Mart, a gas station in Detroit. According to his interview with one of the attorneys involved in the case, BLX entered into a loan that was "wholly inappropriate given the asset and cash flows associated with the property," on which BLX appeared to "conduct zero due diligence." The appraisal was so inflated, at about three times the actual value of the property, as to suggest fraud. The borrowers who were given the loan had no business experience. Apparently, they bought the gas station from one of the bor-rowers' brother, who had run into trouble with loan sharks. The borrow-ers never made a single payment on the loan, but BLX waited a year and a half before attempting to collect on the default.

In the related litigation, it was alleged that, "Allied Capital Corp. delayed for a year and several months in collecting or bringing any action on the defaulted 'loan' for the reason that they did not want their stock-holders and investors to discover the nature of this bad loan and the inad-equate collateral underlying the loan."

Prior to forming BLX, Allied made a loan to Victor Lutz, who planned to expand his hotel in Michigan with a "funland" and a bakery restau-rant. According to Carruthers' interview with Lutz, Lutz informed the loan officer before the closing, "We're having a real rough time right now" because the road leading to the hotel had closed. Lutz asked whether the loan would "stay with him, because we may miss a few payments because of these issues." According to Lutz, the Allied loan officer said not to worry, they would understand if he fell behind. Lutz defaulted.

In addition to these anomalies, Carruthers also found a firm called Credit America, a third-party business loan broker operated by Kevin J. Friedrich out of his home, that was doing business with BLX. Carruthers discovered that Friedrich had been investigated and sanctioned by the Pennsylvania Securities Commission and the National Association of Securities Dealers for various securities laws violations. According to Carruthers' source, Credit America generated $40 million of loans per year for BLX.

Carruthers also found several other loans that appeared to have sig-nificant problems. My immediate reaction was, "So what?"

BLX was just one piece of Allied Capital, and these loans represented only a small piece of BLX. I didn't see how a handful of bad SBA loans could make a difference in view of what we perceived to be the much larger and broader problems at Allied itself.

Yet, a few days after we published our research on Allied, we received the BancLab report. It showed that BLX's portfolio performed far worse than we imagined. BLX's loans defaulted about three times more often than the average SBA loan. Even after adjusting the loans for age, size, geography, industry, and other factors, BLX's loans defaulted more than twice as often (see Table 10.1). I hypothesized that the excess defaults at BLX reflect its aggressive or even fraudulent underwriting practices.

Table 10.1 Average Annual Default Rates from BancLab Report

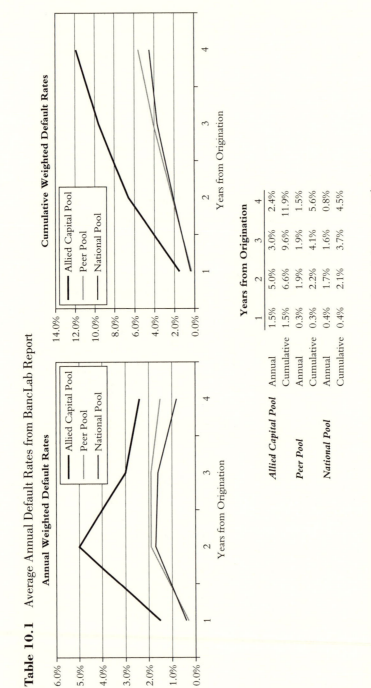

Annual Weighted Default Rates

Cumulative Weighted Default Rates

Years from Origination

		1	2	3	4
Allied Capital Pool	Annual	1.5%	5.0%	3.0%	2.4%
	Cumulative	1.5%	6.6%	9.6%	11.9%
Peer Pool	Annual	0.3%	1.9%	1.9%	1.5%
	Cumulative	0.3%	2.2%	4.1%	5.6%
National Pool	Annual	0.4%	1.7%	1.6%	0.8%
	Cumulative	0.4%	2.1%	3.7%	4.5%

Loan defaults are tracked on a static pool basis from the time of origination. For example, a loan defaulting in the 18th month after the initial loan disbursement will be reported as a default occurring in the second year.

Carruthers told us that he shared his findings with the SBA's Office of Inspector General (OIG), which is responsible for internal audit and investigations for the agency. He asked if we would speak with the OIG and I agreed. A few days later, Keith Hohimer called from the SBA's OIG and said he was looking into BLX. I didn't have anything to tell him separate from what Carruthers found. I sent him the BancLab report at his request.

■ ■ ■

On June 26, 2002, a former employee of BLX, who read our analysis of Allied on Greenlight's Web site, e-mailed me. He identified himself as a former senior vice president of BLX who had previously been at Allied Capital. He wrote that he "left in October 2001 because I was basically forced to resign by BLX's new management team due to the fact that our secondary market loan sale premiums declined so significantly."

> The reason for the decline was principally due to the poor performance of the loan portfolio, as you noted. As a result, BLX was forced to establish its own securitization facility to sell the unguaranteed portion of their SBA and 504/piggyback loans. This eliminated my position with the company. *The CEO wanted me to leave because I often pointed out the massive underwriting deficiencies to Allied's executive management.*
>
> In my three years at Allied I was promoted annually by Joan Sweeney and I was given the highest possible rating an employee could achieve in my annual review the last two years. My raises and bonuses exceeded 20%. In other words I was an outstanding employee and thus a very credible person to speak with concerning Allied.
>
> Although I have not covered any new information in this e-mail, I would be willing to meet with you in order to give you some critical additional insight that would be valuable information regarding BLX . . . that you may not be aware of. If you are interested, please let me know the next time you are in the D.C. area.

I never met him, but we spoke on the phone and he had more damning things to say. He said BLX focused on issuing as many loans as it could, as fast as it could, so that it took severe shortcuts in underwriting loans. According to him, BLX management consciously de-emphasized underwriting by installing underwriters with "no lending experience." BLX did not properly check a borrower's creditworthiness or collateral. Most notably, BLX did not verify that each borrower had invested equity in the business (called an "equity injection"), which is a basic SBA lending requirement to ensure that the borrower had "skin in the game." As a result of all this, BLX experienced increased loan defaults.

The former employee said BLX developed the reputation for selling shoddy loans that went into early default. He said BLX used accounting assumptions on these loans "that were crazy" because they relied on outdated historical information on the average life of its loans that failed to account for the more sophisticated nature of today's borrowers, who are more likely to refinance with cheaper capital when it becomes available. As a result, he said the company's average-life assumptions were way too long. No wonder Allied took great pains to keep the gain-on-sale assumptions from public review. Even when Allied provided voluntary supplemental disclosure about BLX, it never revealed the gain-on-sale assumptions.

The former employee told us to look into the questionable background of Matthew McGee, the head of BLX's top-producing office in Richmond, Virginia. In short order, we found that McGee was convicted of felony securities fraud in 1996 and spent a few months in prison. Apparently, as an employee of Signet Bank, he siphoned money from institutional customers into his family's account. The SEC banned him from ever again working in, or affiliating with, an investment company.

His father, Robert, had been a vice president of Allied Capital in 1992 and later became a senior executive of BLC Financial. BLC Financial hired Mathew McGee after he got out of prison, while he was still serving two years of supervised release. According to the former employee, Matthew McGee sat on BLX's credit committee. This would have violated the terms of the SBA's waiver to BLC Financial to permit McGee's employment after his release from prison. Moreover, the former employee told us BLX honored Matthew McGee at a recent corporate summit and held him up as an example to its other loan officers, asking, "Why can't everybody be as productive as McGee?"

When Jesse Eisinger from *The Wall Street Journal* confronted Allied about McGee's role, it denied McGee was on the committee. However, additional former BLX employees have also told us that McGee was, in fact, a voting member of the credit committee.

BLX had a lot to gain from pushing these substandard loans. Gain-on-sale accounting enabled the company to recognize its income at the time the loans were originated. The more loans BLX made, the more earnings it reported. Churning out loans was good for its bottom line and good for its executives' bonuses. Not only that, but taxpayers bore most of the risk because the federal government guaranteed three-quarters of each loan against loss. This sort of arrangement can promote reckless behavior by unscrupulous operators like BLX.

BLX split the SBA loans into a government-backed guaranteed piece and an unguaranteed piece, which retains credit risk. Historically, BLX sold the guaranteed piece to banks at a 10 percent premium and retained an annual servicing fee of about 1 percent for collecting payments and working out problems. The premium reflected the value of the spread between the interest rate on the loan, generally the prime rate plus 2.75 percent—the maximum rate allowed in the program—less the servicing fee and the risk-free rate. BLX pooled the unguaranteed pieces and securitized them. This front-loaded income and meant that BLX only had exposure to the junior residual, which it retained.

Sweeney would explain how it worked in the next quarterly conference call: "If you originate a million dollars [sic] SBA 7(a) loan, you immediately sell $750,000 of that loan into the secondary market. Those are paying cash premiums today of ten percent. You get $75,000 of cash right on that sale. You then only have [$250,000] left in the loan . . . and you sell that via securitization, . . . but you sell off of that $250,000, $245,000 and you get cash back through a securitization. So, out of that million-dollar loan, you only end up with [$5,000] of equity capital required to capitalize it. So, [$5,000] in and your first year cash proceeds are the $75,000 gain on sale. You get $7,500 on your servicing fees that you get on that loan that you sold. And, you get $9,800 in interest on the [$245,000] piece sold for a first year . . . revenue of $92,000. So on a $5,000 investment, you get $92,000 of cash in the first year."

Banks that purchased the guaranteed pieces of these loans were taking a hit on the 10 percent premiums they paid BLX. When a loan defaults, the government guarantee reimburses the owner the face amount of the guaranteed piece. However, the owner loses any premium it paid for the loan. As a result, though the SBA (which doesn't track defaults efficiently) didn't notice the rising default rate, the banks did, and became hesitant to pay a 10 percent premium. As a result, BLX had to accept a lower premium to sell the loans.

In response, BLX restructured its sales so BLX retained the early default risk by selling the guaranteed piece without any premium and keeping a larger servicing spread. This change reduced BLX's cash flow because it no longer received cash premiums up front. Instead, BLX booked more non-cash revenue through gain-on-sale accounting, recognizing its estimate of the future value of the larger servicing spread it retained.

The former employee also gave us the names of representatives at financial institutions that purchased loans from BLX. We contacted several of them and asked about their dealings with BLX. We inquired about adjustments to the debt-service ratios—calculations designed to make sure that the borrower would have sufficient profits to make interest and principal payments on the loans, the adequacy of appraisals and the level of due diligence, verification of the sources of equity injections, history of first-payment defaults, and other related topics.

While a couple of the sources declined to speak with us and one had favorable things to say about BLX, the majority confirmed a negative view. A representative of Zion's Bank told us that BLX works with riskier clients with less price sensitivity. The official from GE Capital looked at many BLX deals, but passed on most of them for a variety of reasons, including being outbid by other banks and not being comfortable with the credit risks. He said BLX is recognized as having customers with credit problems that keep them from going to other SBA lenders. Bank of the West told us they recently reviewed thirty BLX loans and funded just one due to credit quality concerns. The underwriting was "not what I'm used to," the bank official said, and referred to BLX as a "production office. Get it in, get it out and get it funded. That's how it felt . . . [in] dealing with them."

As we synthesized our understanding of Carruthers' work, the BancLab report, the views of the former employee, our field calls, and both Allied's disclosures and refusals to disclose, it became clear that Allied's exposure to BLX was a problem much bigger than excessive management fees and an inflated 25 percent interest rate on the subordinated note.

Allied formed BLX to get itself out of a mess. Instead, BLX was an even bigger mess, and Allied knew it.

CHAPTER 11

Disengaging and Re-engaging

At the end of June 2002, WorldCom, a large telecommunications company led by Bernie Ebbers, acknowledged it had issued fraudulent financial statements. It filed for bankruptcy in July. Greenlight held a large position in WorldCom's debt, which fell overnight from about forty cents on the dollar to twelve cents. It was the biggest single day's loss in our history. As the rest of the market reacted negatively to the fraud, we suffered additional losses in other positions. Between June and July we lost more than 7 percent, the second worst decline in the history of our fund.

At the same time, I was getting tired of the Allied fight. I like stocks. I enjoy finding provocative opportunities on the long side. I am an optimist and want to participate in the market's long-term positive trend. We always have more exposure to longs than shorts. The press began referring to me as a "noted short-seller," a label I didn't care for. Allied had been calling me names that were far worse than "short-seller."

Allied was just one position in our portfolio, so I decided I would be better off paying attention to other things. Obviously, this book proves this was a resolution not kept, but it was my intention. I reasoned that the Allied controversy would work its way out on its own. The SEC would surely investigate what I sent to them, and, perhaps *The Wall Street Journal* could tell the rest of the story. I decided I did not need to be the public spokesman for this any longer. Originally, I had asked James Lin to prepare a Greenlight response to Allied's June 19, 2002 press release. Now, I asked him to stop.

On July 2, 2002, I was on the train on my way to work and opened *The Wall Street Journal* editorial page, where Holman W. Jenkins Jr. wrote about Allied's dispute with us. The column headlined "One CEO's War for 'Investor Confidence'" with an enlarged "pull quote" that read, "Differences of opinion are increasingly phrased as accusations of fraud." Clearly, Jenkins sided with Allied.

Jenkins did not contact us in preparing the article. Generally, people named in a story get an opportunity to comment. One would think that Jenkins would want to at least hear the other side of the story before publishing. Later, I learned that Jenkins was a columnist, and the rules for columnists are different than the rules for reporters. They can write their opinion and do not have an obligation to offer the opposing party a chance to respond.

As for the column itself, I had been careful not to accuse Allied of "fraud." Actually, I did the opposite of what Jenkins was complaining about. I criticized Allied with toned-down language, using terms such as *improper* and *non–arm's length*. I consciously did not used the "F" word—fraud—because at that point I was not certain whether Allied's actions were intentional or merely unsophisticated.

Jenkins's column said that auditors had not found any problems with Allied's accounting and that Merrill Lynch had written that Allied had put up "meritorious defenses against the criticisms leveled." Then Jenkins said my speech "smacks of a mugging" and linked it to the class-action lawsuits that followed, before finally concluding, "Somehow we prefer the example of Mr. Walton, a CEO who seems to be taking every chance he can find to answer any criticism thrown at him."

When I read the article, I knew I was going to have to continue the fight. I believe that Allied planted the article. Another hedge fund manager called to tell me that Lanny Davis once boasted that he "owns *The Wall*

Street Journal editorial page." I e-mailed Jenkins and asked him to call me to discuss the article. When he called a little while later, I told him that he had his facts wrong. I had not, for example, been in contact with class-action lawyers. He seemed mildly amused at my call and suggested that he would like to learn more about the short-selling business and we could chat in late August after his coming vacation. But his curiosity stayed on vacation: He never followed up.

I took the issue to his editor. After several e-mails and phone calls, the editor suggested I write a letter to the editor, which I did. They printed a portion of it a couple of weeks later under the headline "Our Short Position in Allied Capital." I wrote:

> We are writing in response to Holman Jenkins's . . . [July 2 Business World column] regarding our short position in Allied Capital . . . We are not critical of Allied because we are short and have an agenda; we are short because there is a lot to criticize at Allied.
>
> For example, Allied does not carry its assets at fair-value as defined by the SEC's interpretation of the Investment Company Act of 1940. We identified approximately 35% of Allied's port-folio that appears to be carried above fair-value, because Allied uses the Small Business Administration's (SBA) more liberal valu-ation policy, rather than the SEC's. Allied generates low quality earnings through non-arm's-length dealings with unconsolidated subsidiaries such as Business Loan Express, even as Business Loan Express's portfolio has deteriorated. Allied has responded that the SEC rules are "difficult, if not impossible to apply" and "do not contemplate Business Development Companies (BDCs) and their unique portfolios," and, therefore, are "not specifically applicable to BDCs." Allied believes that "SBA guidance is far more appli-cable to the portfolio of a BDC than the valuation guidance set forth by the SEC." We have spoken with the SEC and confirmed BDCs should use SEC rather than SBA guidance.
>
> We were surprised that Mr. Jenkins gave voice to a conspiracy theory without contacting us to comment or at least to check his facts: Greenlight has had no contact with any of the law firms that are suing Allied. Linking us to them based on the motivated comments of a defensive CEO without corroboration is irresponsible, in our view.

■ ■ ■

The next day, I wrote Walton and Sweeney. In the letter, I pointed out that I had refrained from personal attacks and said they were not practicing similar professional courtesy:

> We understand that you may not appreciate us in our role as whistle blower. We do not understand why rather than addressing our issues in a professional manner, you have engaged in a pattern of false personal attacks for which you have no basis. According to press accounts you have engaged professional assistance in public relations in an effort to better attack us. Be advised that no matter how far into the mud you roll, we have no intention of joining you there.

At the end of the letter, I pointed out:

> We have published our analysis and do not believe it contains any misinformation. We have listened to three conference calls and read several press releases from you designed to refute our criticisms and have yet to hear any factual errors in our research. Generally, your responses have been non-responsive, out of context or refutations of your mischaracterizations of our actual criticisms. However, if we have made any factual errors, we invite you to point out specifically where in our analysis we are factually mistaken. In the event any such errors exist, we will publicly correct the record.

Allied's name-calling was part of its playbook to distract people from the real problems, and I did not expect it to retract or apologize. However, we had put out a lengthy analysis on our Web site, and I sincerely wanted to be sure we hadn't made any errors. Sweeney responded about a week later in a brief letter that said we were wrong, as they showed in the conference calls. She wrote about my "false statements" and innuendos without identifying them. "Your attack on Allied Capital is inaccurate and irresponsible; you are no 'whistle blower,'" Sweeney wrote.

When she declined to identify any actual errors, I took that as yet further confirmation of the soundness of our analysis. I would just have to put up with their attacking our criticisms as a "campaign of misinformation for personal profit," which sounded like a cheesy slogan in a dirty Senate race. A few weeks later, *Forbes* published an article outlining some of our criticisms, and Allied's response was to continue the personal attacks by denouncing me as a "predator" and declaring, "We're not going to let [the] shorts get away with this."

CHAPTER 12

Me or Your Lyin' Eyes?

A few days later, on July 23, 2002, Allied announced its second-quarter earnings. We've seen a lot of examples in short sales where the company maintains that the short-sellers are wrong, but at the same time the company has to change either its accounting or business practices so that the results fail to live up to previous standards. This process began for Allied with this quarterly announcement.

Allied announced only forty-one cents per share of net investment income (this term excludes write-ups and write-downs of investments and is used interchangeably with operating earnings) compared to fifty-three cents per share the prior quarter and forty-six cents in the year-ago quarter. Analysts expected fifty-seven cents per share. Weeks before, Walton highlighted the importance of these "recurring earnings" from interest, fee, and dividend streams that excluded volatile gains and losses in the portfolio. Interest income was less than expected, because non-accrual loans more than doubled from $40 million in the March quarter to $89 million in the June quarter. PIK (payment-in-kind) income fell from $13 million in the first quarter to $8 million in the second quarter, and fee income fell from $16 million to $11 million.

Clearly, Allied adopted a more conservative revenue recognition policy. Because Allied recognized PIK income in a wide number of loans, there was no other explanation for the 40 percent sequential decline. Allied probably took a new, more conservative view of non-accruals, interest income and fees that caused the sudden shortfall. Allied also changed how it wrote-up and wrote-down investments. In previous periods, Allied made few adjustments to the investment values, but now adjusted a large number of investments. Allied wrote-down the "money good" investment in Startec's operating company from $10.2 million to zero and did the same to the remaining $4.3 million investment in Velocita.

Allied took $67 million in other write-downs. According to Sweeney, Allied wrote-down five companies by $20.6 million due to softening in the manufacturing sector, five other companies affected by declines in technology spending by $14.7 million, two media companies by $7.7 million due to declining values in the sector, and, finally, two others suffering "difficulties, as a result of the attacks on September 11," by $11.3 million. Allied didn't explain why it took over nine months to recognize September 11 impacts. It was plain that all these bad things did not happen in a single quarter, but reflected Allied's response to scrutiny.

Allied also found a large number of offsetting write-ups. In fact, the headline earnings were 71 cents per share, which exceeded analysts' forecasts. The commercial mortgage backed securities (CMBS) portfolio, which Allied historically valued at amortized cost, was now worth $20.7 million more because, Sweeney said, "in accordance with ASR 118, we determined the fair-value of the portfolio on an effective yield-to-maturity basis." Tellingly, Allied still contended the mezzanine loan portfolio shouldn't be valued on a yield-to-maturity basis, as per ASR 118.

During the earnings conference call Q&A, Don Destino, a bullish analyst from Bank of America, observed that this was the first time Allied meaningfully changed the valuation on the CMBS portfolio and asked whether it planned on doing the same exercise from now on. "Yeah, well, Don, actually, we do this every quarter," Sweeney replied. Sure.

Even more problematic, Allied increased the value of Business Loan Express by $19.9 million and provided one of the most convoluted explanations I've ever heard. When Benjamin Disraeli said, "There are three kinds of lies: lies, damned lies, and statistics," he could have used this as a case study. Penni Roll, Allied's CFO, said that in 2002 BLX had $85 million of revenue, $43 million of earnings before interest, taxes, and management fees (EBITM), $4 million of pretax profits, $286 million of total assets, and total debt of $183 million. Roll said financial service companies are valued using net income.

The problem was, with all the fees and interest Allied charged BLX, it had minimal net income. "So to value BLX," Roll explained, "we determined what this company's net income would be with a capital structure that would likely be imposed upon this company by a buyer if it were sold today." Allied already owned BLX and could impose any capital structure it liked on BLX. Why would a different owner use a better capital structure, if there were such a thing?

"As you know, we have capitalized BLX with $87 million in subordinated debt in addition to our preferred and common equity investments," she continued. "For purposes of valuation, we assumed that our subordinated debt would be treated as equity and that BLX would be able to increase the size of its senior debt facility."

How could this be? BLX, with Allied owning it, had a much smaller senior lending facility. That facility could only be obtained with Allied guaranteeing the first 50 percent of any loss the lender would have. Why would a different owner be able to obtain a larger senior facility on better terms?

The analysis continued. "We believe that BLX could have by the end of 2002 borrowed senior debt of approximately $155 million secured by assets on their balance sheet[, since]. . . at any point in time roughly 30 to 40 percent of their assets are in cash or government-guaranteed interests."

How did they come up with $155 million? Thirty-five percent of $277 million in assets was about $95 million, roughly what BLX had drawn on its line. What was the rest of the collateral? (Incidentally, though Roll said BLX had $286 million in assets a few moments earlier on the conference call, Allied's 10-Q indicated BLX had only $277 million in assets at the time.)

Roll continued, "We included an annual interest cost of $5 million and subtracted that from their approximate $43 million of EBITM to arrive at a pro forma profit before tax of about $38 million." This implied a 3.25 percent interest rate on $155 million of debt. This is approximately the rate Allied charged just to *guarantee* BLX's existing bank debt, which

BLX paid in addition to what they paid the senior lender. How could the hypothetical larger bank facility also come at a reduced rate? Allied, a much better credit, paid about 7 percent on its own debt. If BLX could really borrow $155 million at 3.25 percent, it should have done that.

"We exclude management fees paid to Allied Capital in the pro forma calculation because the majority of our integration services have been completed and a new buyer for BLX would not need to incur these expenses going forward," Roll said. How could they exclude the management fees? Weeks earlier, Allied explained it provided essential, value-added, and easily justifiable services to BLX for the fees. It was suspicious that now that Allied was under scrutiny, suddenly BLX wouldn't need to purchase as many services from Allied.

Next, Allied explained that it took the $38 million of pro forma pretax profit, taxed it and applied a price-to-earnings (P/E) multiple. It calculated the multiple through several methods, including looking at the trading multiples of comparable companies. Allied selected CIT, Financial Federal and DVI as comparables. However, CIT and DVI traded around book value. When the market values companies based on book value rather than earnings, the earnings multiples lose relevance. Further, CIT and Financial Federal employed portfolio-lending accounting, where income is recognized over the life of the loan, instead of gain-on-sale accounting, where income is recognized up-front at origination. The market generally rewards more conservative accounting with a higher multiple. Here, Allied imputed the relatively higher multiples of the portfolio lenders to BLX's lower-quality gain-on-sale-driven results.

Allied completed the valuation of BLX by adding back the $155 million of hypothetical senior debt and adding $15 million of future cash flow to calculate BLX's enterprise value to be $390 million. When all was said and done, Allied applied a 17 percent discount to account for sale costs in the current environment and determined that the value of BLX, miraculously increased by $20 million.

The implication of this tortured exercise was that Allied determined BLX was worth nine times EBITM, *sixty-five times net income* and about *five times book value*. Sixty-five times net income and five times book value do not pass the laugh test: No one would value a gain-on-sale securitizer that richly. Market values for gain-on-sale securitizers fell so low that once DVI went bankrupt a few months later, we could no longer identify a

Table 12.1 Allied's June 2002 Valuation of BLX

EBITM	43	a	Reported:		
Pro Forma Interest	5	b = h * 3.25%	EBITM		43.0
Pro Forma Pretax Income	38	c = a − b	Net Income		2.3
Pro Forma Taxes	15	d = 40% * c	Shareholder Equity		59.0
Pro Forma Net Income	23	e = c − d	Senior Pfd Stock		25.0
			Goodwill		6.0
P/E	9.6	f	Tangible Book Value		28.0
Equity Value	220	g = e * f			
Pro Forma Debt	155	h			
Future Cash Flow	15	i			
Enterprise Value	390	j = g + h + i	Multiples:		
BLX Debt	183	k	Enterprise		
Senior Pfd Stock	25	l	Value/EBITM	9.1	x
Equity Value Before	182	m = j − k − l	Price/Earnings		
Discount			Rato	65.7	x
17% Illiquidity Discount	31	n = 17% * m	Equity Value/		
			Tang. Book Value	5.4	x
BLX Equity Value	151	o = m − n			
Allied Ownership	93%	p			
Allied Equity Value	140	q = o * p			

Note: Dollars in millions

publicly traded company that generated a large portion of its income through gain-on-sale securitizations.

Later in the call, Darius Brawn of Endicott Partners again raised the issue of how much of BLX's $85 million in revenue came from gain-on-sale. Sweeney indicated that she didn't know off the top of her head, but after Brawn pressed her, Sweeney said that the cash portion of BLX's revenues was around 50 percent to 70 percent. This meant that the 30 percent to 50 percent of $85 million in revenues, or $25 million to $42 million, was non-cash. Since gain-on-sale revenue generally flows through the income statement without marginal expense, this meant the majority of the $43 million of EBITM was non-cash.

For the first time, Allied provided some summary financial information for BLX in its 10-Q filed weeks later. Since the last available disclosure about

BLX at its formation in December 2000, BLX's debt increased $65 million to $183 million and an intangible asset created by gain-on-sale accounting called "residual interests" roughly doubled to $106 million. As the residual interests were almost four times the tangible equity, you could call the valuation whimsical, or imaginative, or fanciful—but not supportable.

Putting it all together, BLX was a problem in three ways. First, BLX made loans improperly. Second, BLX used aggressive accounting techniques to inflate its results. Finally, Allied's valuation of BLX had no reasonable basis, even if BLX's business and accounting results had been genuine. Frankly, as we were learning more about BLX, we were coming to believe Allied's investment could really be worthless.

■ ■ ■

Allied sought to convince investors it wasn't a fraud by giving evidence that it didn't behave like other frauds. Allied paid distributions, proving the cash wasn't missing. Insiders purchased shares, signaling the market that nothing was amiss. It had consistent accounting, validating its four decades of success.

It was like the old Richard Pryor joke: "What do you do if your wife walks into your bedroom and finds you in bed with another woman? Deny! Deny! Deny! Who are you going to believe? Me or your lyin' eyes?" So, too, with Allied.

Despite the large changes in Allied's accounting practices, to maintain the confidence of inattentive or unsophisticated investors, management repeatedly advanced the illusion that Allied's accounting was consistent. During the second quarter of 2002 earnings conference call, Walton led off his discussion of valuation, "as a result of our *consistent* process of determining the fair-value of our portfolio in good faith . . ." Moments later, Sweeney echoed, "As we stated in our public filings, we used a *consistent* methodology to value our portfolio companies in keeping with the guidance provided by the SEC and industry practices." Before turning to the Q&A, Walton reiterated, "Let me emphatically state that we will continue to apply a *consistent* and prudent valuation methodology that is in accordance with all regulatory guidelines as we have always done."

The evidence that Allied changed its accounting is overwhelming. There were remarkable sudden changes to non-performing assets, PIK and fee income, and write-downs and write-ups. A few weeks later, Allied dramatically changed the narrative description of its accounting in its new 10-Q.

Allied eliminated the questionable language that echoed the white paper that first appeared in the 2001 annual report. The company replaced it with new prose describing its use and interpretation of the current-sale test based on enterprise value. The June 2002 10-Q declared for the first time, "The fair-value of our investment is based upon the enterprise value at which the portfolio company could be sold in an orderly disposition over a reasonable period of time between willing parties other than in a forced or liquidation sale. The liquidity event whereby we exit a private finance investment is generally the sale, the recapitalization or, in some cases, the initial public offering of the portfolio company."

Over time, the effects of the new accounting persisted. Fees, interest, and PIK income stayed lower. The number of write-ups and write-downs recognized each quarter remained more pronounced. Earnings that had been growing steadily and predictably became volatile and unpredictable. Net investment income per share, which grew in a straight line for several years through the first quarter where they reached fifty-three cents per share, reversed their steady upward trend and became more volatile and stopped growing. They have yet to return to anywhere near that first quarter of 2002 level (see Figure 12.1).

Allied not only changed how it evaluated its portfolio, but also changed how it wanted investors to evaluate the company. In the past, Walton directed investors to focus on recurring net investment income (also called operating income) and observed that capital gains were nice but unpredictable. With the new accounting, Allied's net investment income no longer approached the quarterly distribution. Instead, Allied refocused investors on taxable income, which consists of net investment income plus realized capital gains. To that end, Walton announced that the company would no longer give earnings guidance and from then on would only provide "dividend" guidance for its tax distribution.

"The dividend, as you know, is based on taxable earnings," he said. "We find that the timing differences between tax and GAAP earnings result in our GAAP earnings being less meaningful to shareholders. . . . The reality for Allied Capital and its shareholders is taxable income supports the dividend, and although GAAP earnings are useful as a predictor of future taxable income, our primary focus is on cash distribution to shareholders, which are paid from taxable income."

Distributions are much more predictable and manageable than earnings. Distributions are declared at the discretion of the board and limited only

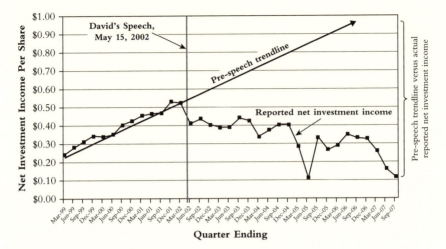

Figure 12.1 Quarterly Net Investment Income

by the company's ability to fund them. Taxable income is managed and maximized by selling winners and keeping losers and Allied has significant control over which investments it exits.

In May, Sweeney had said, "What we do think is important to our valuation as a public company is our net income, which communicates our earnings power to shareholders." Now, just two months later, Allied wanted everyone to ignore that and concentrate solely on easily manipulated "taxable earnings" and its distributions.

Allied let me through to ask a question on the second-quarter earnings conference call. Perhaps my complaints that I had been screened got back to them. I questioned Allied's new enterprise value valuation technique, and referenced *In Re Parnassus,* a case where the SEC ruled that investment companies should value the actual securities they own, as opposed to the value that could be achieved in the sale of the entire company when there were no bids pending. Sweeney gave a lengthy speech, indicating that the value of a company is linked to the value of its securities and how Allied interacts with other co-investors. She did not answer my question. Walton chimed in, pointing out that liquidity events happen when the company is sold, and that they had no plans to sell the securities.

I pointed out that the SEC current-sale test is based on the securities they actually own as opposed to the whole enterprise. I described how debt securities fall in value if the equity cushion erodes. I observed that under their standard, they would carry the debt at the same value regardless of whether it was supported by a fat equity cushion or an extremely thin one. Sweeney replied, "I think that you end up with the identical result," and proceeded to talk about how equity values rise and fall in the same way that enterprise values rise and fall. I pressed that I was talking about debt instruments, not equity instruments. Sweeney responded by stating the obvious, saying that this is why there is equity beneath the debt, so it is the equity that suffers first.

Finally, Walton effectively ended the discussion, "David, we really have written and talked about this extensively. I would love if you wanted to give us a call to chat about it. We would be delighted to talk with you about it, but I think right now people want to learn a little bit more about our company."

CHAPTER 13

Debates and Manipulations

Following the disappointing second-quarter earnings, Allied's stock fell to $16.90 a share on July 24, 2002. The stock has never traded below that since. I sent a second, fifteen-page update to the SEC on July 31, 2002. I discussed Allied's aggressive comments in its white paper and compared it to the annual report, demonstrating that Allied incorrectly followed SBA, rather than SEC accounting. I described Allied's accounting transition to the enterprise valuation method and explained why it still was not SEC compliant. I dissected Allied's unreasonable write-up of BLX and discussed the inflated interest rates Allied charged BLX and Hillman. I noted Allied's false statements that its accounting was "consistent" when it was not.

To the extent the revaluations reflected changes in value that should have been made earlier, I asked the SEC to force Allied to restate results to reflect when gains and losses actually occurred and explain publicly how it changed its accounting.

I questioned whether Allied matched gains with losses to hold income steady. For example, write-downs increased from $15 million in the first quarter of 2002 to $80 million in the second quarter. Write-ups increased from $14 million to $99 million at the same time. Was this a coincidence—or had Allied either created write-ups to match the write-downs or limited the amount of write-downs to the amount of write-ups it could find? Finally, I enclosed a copy of the BancLab analysis and discussed what the former BLX employee told me without identifying him.

I figured when the SEC followed up on my letter, it would call to get his contact information. Yet, no one from the agency contacted us. I was disappointed by the lack of interest and diligence.

■ ■ ■

Allied announced it would have an investor day in early August. The event would last for several hours and give us a chance to ask questions in person. James Lin and I flew to Washington to participate. It was a noncombative meeting that covered little new ground. Allied paraded on stage a large number of senior officers demonstrating a deep, experienced team. The group appeared quite presentable.

Many people think you can spot crooks by their appearance. The stereotypical crook looks like a mobster, flaunts gaudy jewelry, or sports an all-season tan. The Allied team had none of this. They were well dressed and well spoken, sounded earnest, and seemed like nice people. In fact, they were quite charismatic.

Some of my favorite movies, including *The Sting* and *Dirty Rotten Scoundrels*, feature well-spoken, attractive, confidence men and women. Perhaps the same can be said for some of the CEOs behind real-life scandals I had experienced, including Gary Wendt (Conseco), Al Dunlap (Sunbeam), and Donal Geaney (Elan), not to mention Bernie Ebbers (WorldCom) and Ken Lay (Enron).

Instead of arguing with its critics, the company played to its core audience. It was as if Allied modified P. T. Barnum, as illustrated in Mike Shapiro's cartoon (see Figure 13.1), "You can fool some of the people all of the time, so let's concentrate on those folks." Allied was much more positive, even friendly. There was hardly any mention of the issues that concerned us.

However, Allied was plainly scared of uncontrolled questions and answers. Most investor days allow a lot of time for Q&A. Here, Allied

"Remember, you can fool some of the people all of the time.
Those are the people we need to concentrate on."

Figure 13.1   Cartoon

budgeted only a half hour and pointedly required questions to be
submitted on 3" × 5" index cards. Suzanne Sparrow, the head of Investor
Relations, collected the card pile and selected softball questions to para-
phrase to Walton. I filled out about four cards and signed them. Sparrow
didn't pick any of my questions.

Sparrow asked Walton whether he would sign the financials under the
newly enacted Sarbanes-Oxley laws. He indicated that he would have no
trouble doing so. *In for a penny, in for a pound.*

In this Q&A format, Allied had nothing to worry about. Walton had
such a good time pounding the fat pitches out of the park that when time
expired, he looked over to Sparrow and said, "I'd be willing to take a few
more." There was a grumble from the room; people were plainly ready for
lunch.

Lunch was more interesting. Robert D. Long, a managing director of
Allied and one of the speakers at the event, came up to me as we were
breaking to eat. He told me that we have a mutual friend, Chris Fox, over
at Cramer Rosenthal McGlynn. I have known Fox since 1994. Long sat
down and joined us for lunch.

In addition to Long, our table included a young, aggressive analyst
from a mutual fund that held Allied shares. He was not shy in telling me
that we were wrong about the company. He said that Allied was soon
going to announce big news that would bury the shorts and implied that
his close ties to management gave him an informational edge. Long sat

next to me and also tried to convince me that our take on the company was wrong. At least he was a real gentleman about it. He conceded we made many good points in our analysis.

I asked about the sudden large number of mark-ups and mark-downs in the portfolio. He told me that Allied applied a sharper pencil. He went on to say that Allied was under a lot of heat from its regulators. Allied had told everyone that the SEC approved everything it did and our complaints were completely off base. Now I knew from the inside that Allied had not applied the valuation method consistently. And better yet, the SEC was doing something!

I pressed him on the related-party fees, interest from BLX and pointed out how circular this was. As I wrote in Chapter 11, he told me that BLX *should* be consolidated. There is a way that Allied could do that if it wanted to. His admissions were the highlights of my day. I left the meeting optimistic the system was working and Allied would get its just desserts.

Shortly after the investor day, I received a call from another professional investor. He had read our research and had wondered about Allied for years. He knew about Allied's investment in ACME Paging.

According to Allied's SEC filings, its original investment in ACME was in place by the end of 1997. At that point, Allied thought that the equity portion of its investment called "Limited Partnership Interests" had a gain. Allied reversed the gain in the March 2000 quarter and wrote the Limited Partnership Interests to zero in the September 2000 quarter. Meanwhile, it held its debt investment at cost. Allied invested additional equity in the December 2001 quarter and increased its debt and/or equity investment each quarter through September 2002.

The investor told us what had happened. He said ACME was a troubled Brazilian paging operation. Competition from cell phones and the devaluation of the Brazilian currency hurt the company. Brazil had also experienced severe economic turmoil. ACME Paging had been shopped for sale in 2001, but there were no buyers, so the company was recapitalized.

The equity holders essentially walked away and handed Allied the keys, and, as noted, Allied increased its investment. According to its SEC filings, Allied continued to value ACME at cost. The fellow's view that Allied deferred recognizing a loss in this investment proved out, as Allied gradually wrote-down the investment beginning in the December 2002 quarter, with further write-downs each quarter through March 2005, at which point, Allied carried ACME at zero value (see Table 13.1).

Table 13.1 Acme Paging

Date	Debt Investments		Equity Investments		Comment
	Cost	Value	Cost	Value	
December 31, 1999	6,618	6,618	1,456	2,100	An unrealized gain
March 31, 2000	6,714	6,714	1,456	1,456	Reversed the gain
June 30, 2000	6,811	6,811	1,456	806	
September 30, 2000	6,961	6,961	1,456	–	Wrote down equity to zero
September 30, 2001	6,989	6,989	1,456		
December 31, 2001	6,992	6,992	3,640	2,184	
March 31, 2002	7,743	7,743	3,640	2,184	
June 30, 2002	10,205	10,205	3,717	2,261	Loan before recapitalization; no write-down
September 30, 2002	3,525	3,525	13,301	11,846	Recapitalization; no write-down
December 31, 2002	3,750	3,750	13,301	9,250	Gradual write-down
March 31, 2003	4,042	4,042	13,301	7,750	Gradual write-down
June 30, 2003	4,265	4,265	13,301	6,525	Gradual write-down
September 30, 2003	4,395	4,395	13,301	6,087	Gradual write-down
December 30, 2003	4,496	4,496	13,301	2,586	Gradual write-down
March 31, 2004	4,578	4,578	13,301	2,427	Gradual write-down
June 30, 2004	4,631	3,634	13,301	1,819	First write-down of debt
September 30, 2004	4,631	2,398	13,301	1,742	Gradual write-down
December 30, 2004	4,631	–	13,301	1,230	Gradual write-down
March 31, 2005	4,631	–	13,301	–	Total investment valued at zero
June 30, 2005	4,631	–	13,301	–	
September 30, 2005	4,631	–	13,301	–	
December 31, 2005	4,631	–	27	–	$13.8 MM realized loss
December 31, 2006	4,631	–		–	$4.7 MM realized loss

Note: Dollars in thousands

CHAPTER 14

Rewarding Shareholders

In an impersonal and anonymous market, we like to know what people on the other side of our investments are thinking. To succeed, we like to feel that we have an edge through deeper analysis or better information than those who disagree with our views. We knew most of Allied's investors are individual investors. Some have held the shares and collected the tax distributions for years. They had probably not engaged in the analysis we had done and would probably hold the shares, at least until the company admitted a problem.

Allied often pointed to its institutional shareholder base as proof that sophisticated professionals held the stock. Shortly after the investor day, Ed Painter, our institutional salesman from UBS, arranged a meeting with another of his clients, Wasatch Advisors. Wasatch is a mutual fund and was the second largest Allied shareholder with five million shares. Wasatch had a great track record and an excellent reputation. Painter thought that the fund manager in charge of its Allied position and I would both benefit by hearing each other out. The fund manager turned out to be Dr. Sam Stewart, the founder of Wasatch.

Wasatch's office was just down the street, so James Lin and I walked over with a briefcase full of our research. We met with Painter and Stewart in the conference room. Stewart brought nothing but a legal pad and pen. "Okay," he said, "go ahead."

I thought this was supposed to be a two-way dialogue. "First, what did you think of our analysis?" I asked him. "Do you see anything wrong with it?" He said he hadn't read it.

While I could believe that Allied's shareholders might generally be too busy to have read the lengthy analysis we put on our Web site, it was hard to imagine a professional, who was the second-largest Allied holder, would come to a meeting with us and acknowledge such lack of preparation.

So I asked him why he held the stock. Stewart said that in the tough market he felt it was a good time to own a lot of high-yielding stocks and his Allied holding was really part of a "basket approach." He hadn't done the research we had, but he had spoken to Allied management. "They seem honest," he said. "Have you found a history of fraud or other criminal behavior in their backgrounds?"

"No, not at Allied," I replied. "But we have at BLX."

I decided that if he came to the meeting with so little to say, there really wasn't much sense in going into detail. I briefly described the work we had done and raised a couple of points. Stewart didn't have much of a reaction.

So I wrapped up by telling him that if he read Greenlight's report and wanted to discuss it, I would be happy to talk further. At his request, we followed up by sending him our Excel spreadsheet of Allied's historical valuations so he wouldn't have to recreate the work and could see Allied's patterns of write-ups and write-downs for himself.

I left with a new understanding of what we were up against. It wasn't an issue of investors understanding our views and disagreeing. In addition to the small investors, Allied's other investors were big funds managing lots of other people's money—too busy or too lazy to worry about the details, other than the tax distribution. I never heard from Stewart again, but a few quarters later I noticed that his fund had completely sold its Allied position.

■ ■ ■

Over the years, I've heard many rumors that companies can do things with their stock that create havoc in the stock-lending market. A sudden shortage of borrowable shares can force short-sellers to cover whether they want to or not. The resulting price spike is known as a short squeeze. About a month after my speech, Walton posted a letter on the Allied Web site telling shareholders, "Finally, you can help us protect your investment in Allied Capital. If you hold any of your shares in a brokerage account, please ask your broker to move your Allied Capital shares out of a "margin" account and into a "cash" account. By doing this, you prevent the brokerage firm from lending your shares to short-sellers. I have done this with my own shares. Any shares you own directly are not accessible to brokerage firms and cannot be borrowed."

How does this protect an investment in Allied Capital? In a traditional sense, it doesn't, because the value of an investment in Allied depends on how its portfolio performs and shouldn't have anything to do with whether shareholders lend shares to short-sellers. What Walton wanted was a short squeeze, where owners recall stock lent to short-sellers. If the short-sellers are unable to find another stock lender, they have to purchase the shares at whatever the market price is in order to return the borrowed shares. I think efforts to coordinate this sort of action between shareholders are overt attempts to manipulate the market. To date, however, the SEC has never prosecuted these efforts. As a general matter, companies that engage in this sort of effort have large problems.

Some people believe that stock splits, stock dividends, and rights offerings can precipitate short squeezes. Actually, it does not work this way because the share-clearing system is able to adjust. In August 2002, Allied made another attempt to manipulate the clearing system by filing preliminary documents with the SEC to do a rights offering. The stated purpose was to "reward the long-term shareholder."

The proposed method of this offering was something I had seen neither before, nor since. According to the proposal, Allied would issue "nontransferable" rights that allowed the holder to subscribe for more shares at a price to be determined, only after the holder irrevocably exercised the rights. By having the rights non-transferable, it appeared that Allied was trying to complicate the clearing and settlement process, which they hoped would force short-sellers to cover. Goldman Sachs, our clearing broker, suggested to us that market participants believed that Allied created the non-transferable rights to generate a short squeeze. If the rights could not be transferred, Allied hoped the short-sellers would not be able to create rights to return to the stock lenders. Allied was wrong; the clearing system was able to adjust for this.

According to the proposal, holders who wished to exercise their rights would be required to certify that they held the stock continuously from the record date to the exercise date. Generally, the purpose of having a "record date" for corporate actions is to enable anyone who held the stock on the record date to participate. Here, Allied proposed the unheard-of condition that if you sold your stock after the record date, you would forfeit the rights.

The exercise price would be determined during the period when the shareholders needed to certify that they held the stock continuously. Allied wanted to create a complete absence of sellers (if you sold, you would forfeit the rights), which, obviously, would make the stock rise. Then, Allied would price the rights offering at a modest discount to the artificially inflated price. This would have the dual effect of hurting the short-sellers on a mark-to-market basis and induce the existing holders to subscribe to the rights at a small discount to the inflated price. Since the investors would not know the purchase price until after they irrevocably committed to exercise the rights, there would be nothing they could do if the price turned out to be higher than they thought. Allied would pocket the inflated proceeds.

In case the scheme didn't work, the company left itself an out: If the share price fell, it would have the option to cancel the offering and simply refund the investors' money without interest. Of course, the board could not recommend to shareholders whether or not they should exercise their rights in these circumstances.

I wrote another letter to the SEC on September 3, 2002, where I pointed out the manipulative aspects of the rights offering. I don't know if my letter had any effect. However, Allied amended the deal to eliminate the requirement for shareholders to hold the shares continuously between the record date and the exercise date. Allied set the pricing at a 7 percent discount to the market price on the date the rights expired. Investors did not have to hold the shares for an extended period to maintain the rights and would not be subject to the uncertainty of exercising the rights at an unknown value. Allied gave shareholders the right to purchase one additional share for every twenty shares they held. Allied also gave shareholders "oversubscription" rights, or the opportunity to subscribe for additional shares in the rights offering for any shares that other rights holders did not purchase.

The final prospectus no longer said that the purpose was to "reward the long-term shareholder." Instead, it said, "Our board of directors has determined that this rights offering is in our best interest and in the best interests of our shareholders. The offering seeks to reward the long-term shareholder by giving existing shareholders the right to purchase additional shares at a price below market without incurring any commission or charge. . . . Our board of directors makes no recommendation to you about whether you should exercise any rights." *Buyer beware*.

If the purpose were to reward long-term shareholders, it was a reward that the management and directors, for the most part, decided to forgo. According to the proxy, nineteen insiders were granted rights to purchase 123,000 shares, in addition to oversubscription rights. As a group, they exercised about one-third of their rights. Collectively, this was less than they receive in a single quarterly tax distribution check.

Speaking of insider purchases, Allied management made several small insider purchases between my speech on May 15, 2002, and the end of the year. As one Allied shareholder asked me, "Allied insiders have been buying shares and not selling. In fact, I think the last insider sell was more than a year ago. This does not seem like the behavior of management that is hiding something. If, as you suggest, they are privy to negative information that likely would be detrimental to the stock price, it's inexplicable to me why they would put more of their own money at risk."

This, of course, is a straightforward and logical analysis. I agree that insider purchases are *generally* bullish. However, in this case, the insider purchases were so small relative to the financial wherewithal of the participants and to their existing stakes in the company that they appeared to be simply an effort to "signal the market" with news of insider purchases, thus reassuring retail investors like this fellow. In context, this was not a serious effort to increase their stakes by taking advantage of discounted prices.

Walton earned $2.4 million in cash compensation for running Allied in 2001 and held about $10 million in stock, with options to purchase many more shares. For him to invest about $46,000 to purchase an additional 2,000 shares is hardly an increased commitment. (Walton did this shortly after my speech. In the rights offering he exercised rights to purchase approximately 11,000 shares, effectively reinvesting a single quarterly distribution back into the stock.) Considering his vested interest in the outcome, $46,000 is an awfully cheap form of "advertising" his "confidence."

If insider purchases are indiscriminately believed to be a bullish indicator, bad actors can use them as false indicators at desperate times. Dennis Kozlowski and Mark Swartz of Tyco each spent about $15 million to signal the market with insider purchases in January 2002. In June 2005, Kozlowski and Swartz were found guilty on twenty-two of twenty-three counts of grand larceny and conspiracy, falsifying business records and violating business law. They were ordered to pay fines and restitution of over $200 million and given lengthy prison sentences.

■ ■ ■

In August 2002, Professor André Perold, who teaches an investment course at Harvard Business School, called to ask if I would meet with his class. He had heard about Greenlight's work on Allied and wanted to teach the story. I checked into Perold's reputation. It was excellent, so I agreed.

I met with his class in October, and Perold discussed Greenlight's Allied analysis with his students. I took fifteen minutes of questions at the end. Perold's lecture seemed supportive of our thinking. The student reaction was mixed. The class materials included the analysis we posted on our Web site, which had a discussion analogizing Allied's relationship with BLX to Enron's relationship with its Raptor partnership. One student thought the comparison was unfair. Others nodded in agreement.

I explained that we said that the relationships were analogous in that both were controlled, unconsolidated entities that contributed to the parents' earnings without any transparency in the underlying results. In both cases, the parent company guaranteed the financing. In Raptor's case this came from a pledge of Enron stock, and in BLX's case from equity investments and debt guarantees. No one in the class seemed inclined to argue. Perold said he wanted to write a case study and would invite Allied to tell its side.

While I was in Boston, I learned that Deutsche Bank initiated research coverage of Allied with a "Sell" rating. This was surprising. Analysts rarely urge investors to sell. If they don't like a stock, they usually mute their language, telling investors not to buy more and rate the stock "Hold." A "Sell" rating often angers the company, its institutional investors and creates problems for the analyst.

In an extraordinary move, the New York Stock Exchange, normally a slow-moving organization, decided to immediately investigate the "Sell" recommendation and hauled in Mark Alpert, the analyst who issued the recommendation, and the Deutsche Bank institutional salesman who covered Greenlight. The salesman had sat with me at the Allied investor day, and Allied, always looking for a good conspiracy, cried foul. The Exchange questioned the salesman and the analyst about whether Greenlight had influenced the report.

We had no role in the recommendation. I only had a single, brief conversation with Alpert several months earlier. I had no idea whether he agreed with us or not and had no indication he would begin to cover Allied. The Exchange's investigation ended without action.

As Alpert put it, "It's ironic, especially in today's world of research, that the NYSE would investigate a sell recommendation. What better way to intimidate independent thought? It was clear from the beginning that I had been accused of accepting compensation from short seller(s). I assume Allied was behind the allegation."

According to Greenlight's Deutsche Bank salesman, Allied was quite upset and wanted the "Sell" recommendation removed. At the end of the year, Allied got its wish when Alpert left and the bank ceased to cover Allied. A few months later, Allied let Deutsche Bank—which, at that point, no longer even had an analyst covering the stock and had never underwritten an offering for Allied—underwrite the first of at least five stock offerings, for which the bank made millions of dollars in fees.

CHAPTER 15

BLX Is Worth
What, Exactly?

The equity and high-yield bond markets plummeted in the third quarter of 2002, following the WorldCom fraud. Allied announced its quarterly results, which were only a few cents below analysts' estimates. Operating income actually improved, led by a pick-up in PIK income. Allied again had a large number of write-ups and write-downs during the quarter—ending in a wash. Most notably, Allied held its investment in BLX constant. It was hard to imagine how Allied justified this, since the stock prices of BLX's three publicly traded comparable companies Allied used for valuation purposes fell an average of 32 percent during the quarter.

During the earnings conference call on October 22, 2002, Allied discussed accruing income from controlled companies. According to Sweeney, "What we don't want to do is accrue interest income if we're continuing to fund them on a routine basis because we look at that as if we are

accelerating interest income that we are funding. So we don't do that."
On that basis, how could they recognize income from BLX? Allied's SEC
filings revealed BLX burned cash and needed ongoing capital for its operations. Allied routinely contributed that capital, either directly through fresh
investment or indirectly by guaranteeing bank loans.

At the end of the conference call, Walton gave tax distribution guidance. The company estimated distributions of $2.20 a share in 2002, fol-
lowed by 5 percent growth in 2003. The company's previous target had
been a 10 percent annual increase. Management explained on the conference call that 10 percent had been more of a long-term goal. The company
further said net investment income would be 80 percent of the 2002 distribution and 85 percent of the 2003 distribution. This implied net investment income in 2003 of $1.95 a share. When the dust settled on 2003, net
investment income was only $1.65. Allied filled in the gap with additional
capital gains. By then, Allied managed to convince its shareholders money
was money and the distribution was the distribution no matter how it was
funded. In fact, Allied came to argue that net capital gains are actually better than net investment income because they are taxed to the investor at a
lower rate. In May, Walton had pushed the opposite (more conventional)
view: Net investment income is superior to capital gains because it is more
predictable.

Allied defended its treatment of BLX with additional misleading comments. When questioned about the $100 million of residuals on BLX's
balance sheet at the Bank of America investor conference in September
2002, Sweeney told the audience, "I'd buy a $400 million stream of cash
flows for $100 million." This answer created the misimpression that BLX's
residuals had hidden value. However, embedded in the $400 million figure
was the absurd assumption that no loan ever defaulted or prepaid. Allied
had no interest in allowing investors to judge the value for themselves by
sharing the actual prepayment and default assumptions or history. Further,
Sweeney told investors at a Piper Jaffray conference in November 2002
that BLX's SBA loans "perform in line with the national average."

■ ■ ■

I provided reporters from both *The New York Times* and *The Wall Street
Journal* with the BancLab analysis, access to the former BLX executive

who had contacted us, and described Allied's inflated valuation of BLX. I knew Jesse Eisinger from the *Journal* had visited Allied. As time passed without an article—his initial period for an exclusive had long since passed—I came to believe there wouldn't be one, so I decided to write the story myself. Several months earlier, TheStreet.com, a financial news Web site, invited me to become a contributor. I took them up on the offer and wrote a two-part article titled, "The Joker in Allied Capital's House of Cards," which the site published on December 10 and 11, 2002. The story highlighted the problems with gain-on-sale accounting, BLX's loan performance, questioned the nonconsolidation of BLX and recounted the absurdity of Allied's BLX valuation. At the same time, we added the BancLab analysis to our Web site.

There was no measurable reaction to the story anywhere. None of the brokerage firm analysts commented on any aspect of the issue. When the stock, which traded at about $22 per share at the time, did not react, Allied's management probably thought no immediate response was necessary. On the conference call discussing fourth-quarter results held two months later, Roll responded, "We are aware of what we believe to be an inaccurate report in the market regarding BLX and its 7(a) loan portfolio quality." Again, she didn't specify any inaccuracies, but said that according to BLX's own data, the losses on the unguaranteed pieces over the last five years averaged less than 1 percent and the performance was better than the national average.

Roughly two years later, I learned the difference between the BancLab data, which showed defaults, and Allied's description of "losses." When loans become 60 days late, the SBA considers it a default. BLX notifies the SBA and requests the SBA to satisfy the guarantee, which the SBA pays. BLX continues to try to collect and/or resolve the default for as long as it can, which can be years. Neither BLX nor the SBA count the loan as a "loss" until the loan resolution is complete. So BLX's "losses" are "small" mostly because it doesn't resolve defaulted loans in a timely fashion.

However, a benefit of publicly discussing Allied was hearing from others. Jim Brickman, a retired real estate developer from Dallas, introduced himself by e-mail. Someone had pointed him to Greenlight's analysis because of his background in SBA lending. Brickman served on a creditor's committee responsible for liquidating and evaluating the value of the SBA platform of Amresco, a Dallas-based lender that went bankrupt in 2001.

With the assistance of Houlihan Lokey, a boutique investment banker, he sought to find a buyer. There was none at even a fraction of book value. So Brickman approached the BLX discussion with a clear understanding that SBA lending platforms are not worth sixty-five times earnings or five times book value, especially when the balance sheet has multiples of its book value in residual assets.

Recall that residuals are the estimated present value of future cash flows. The estimate depends on various assumptions. Historically, many companies have used assumptions that proved too optimistic, leading to future write-downs. As a result, investors take a skeptical view of residual asset values. Allied's staunch refusal to provide the assumptions BLX used to estimate its residuals raised further doubts.

Brickman's e-mail began a long dialogue. While I've spent more time on Allied than I can quantify, Brickman has spent much more; he is retired and his kids have grown. As he sees it, "These people believe they are above the law." He has become an expert at searching public records, analyzing information, and has been a major collaborator in identifying problems at Allied and BLX. He is one of the best forensic detectives I have ever met. He finds the Allied story—how it has developed and persisted—as amazing, surprising and disheartening as I do.

His first big find involved two of Allied's investments, GAC and Fairchild Industries, each of which filed for bankruptcy in early 2003. The bankruptcy documents indicated that Fairchild defaulted on $6 million of senior debt to Provident Bank in 2001 and stopped paying interest on Allied's junior debt investment in January 2002. Despite this, Allied valued its debt investment in Fairchild at cost throughout 2002 and even carried its warrants at an unrealized gain. In December 2002, Allied wrote its warrants to zero. Even after Fairchild went bankrupt, Allied carried its loan at cost in March 2003. Finally, Allied began to write-down the loan in June 2003 (see Table 15.1). Ultimately, after Allied doubled its investment, Fairchilds results improved and Allied exited with a gain in 2005.

Brickman's work on GAC showed that it was another case of Allied ignoring reality. Remember that Sweeney taunted the short sellers about not doing their basic homework on GAC. Though it was Allied's third largest investment at cost, Allied didn't feel a need to disclose its bankruptcy via press release, in its earnings announcement or even in its 10-Q. Allied appeared to announce only good news. For example, around the time

Table 15.1 Fairchild Industries

Date	Debt Investments		Equity Investments		Comment
	Cost	Value	Cost	Value	
December 31, 2001	5,872	5,872	280	2,378	Unrealized gain
March 31, 2002	5,889	5,889	280	2,378	Stops paying interest; no reversal of gain
June 30, 2002	5,906	5,906	280	1,100	
September 30, 2002	5,924	5,924	280	1,100	
December 31, 2002	5,942	5,942	280	–	Warrants written down to zero
March 31, 2003	5,954	5,954	280	–	Filed bankruptcy; no debt write-down
June 30, 2003	5,954	5,426	280	–	First debt write-down
September 30, 2003	5,954	3,534	280	–	
December 31, 2003	13,120	10,700	280	–	Recapitalized; doubles the investment
March 31, 2004	13,120	10,108	280	–	
June 30, 2004	13,099	10,089	280	–	
September 30, 2004	11,347	11,347	2,841	72	Business turns around
December 31, 2004	10,871	10,871	2,841	2,123	
September 30, 2005					$16.2 MM realized gain

Note: Dollars in thousands

of GAC's bankruptcy, Allied issued separate press releases announcing a $7 million gain on the disposition of CyberRep and an $8.4 million gain from selling Morton Grove Pharmaceuticals.

Bankruptcy documents showed that GAC had only $6 million of revenues and negative cash flow. Given what *Off Wall Street* reported about GAC, it is doubtful the business was ever profitable. Even as Sweeney had said the critics didn't know what they were talking about, Allied wrote GAC down $5 million in June, $9 million in September, and $5 million in December 2002, leaving the value at $20 million. This was a good example of Allied taking gradual write-downs to smooth its results. Walton was asked about GAC on the first-quarter conference call. Without even acknowledging the bankruptcy, he indicated there had been management changes and he thought there was "an interesting business plan going forward." We never learned just how interesting that business plan must have been.

The bankruptcy forecast indicated that GAC expected further declines in performance. Over time, the actual results came in worse than the forecast. By June 2005, Allied showed an unrealized loss of $50 million on its original $50 million investment. It had invested an additional $8 million during the bankruptcy, which it carried at $8 million. As part of its strategy of selling the winners and keeping the losers, Allied elected not to take a $50 million realized loss, which would have provided a valuable tax shield for shareholders—but would have reduced Allied's taxable income, which supports the distribution. Instead, Allied changed the name of the company to Triview Investments Inc. and infused another $78 million to make acquisitions in an unrelated field, taking an additional $15 million write-down. This was an example of Allied's sacrificing economics for improved optics (see Table 15.2).

Allied also had an investment in, and had a representative on the board of, Redox Brands, a consumer cleaning-products company. Todd Wichmann, a former CEO of Redox, called in early 2003 to tell us Redox violated its bank covenants and obtained a waiver and an additional investment from Allied in the second quarter of 2002. Though Allied added $7 million to protect a $10 million investment under duress, it did not write-down the initial investment. The very next quarter, Redox appeared likely to violate the revised covenants. Wichmann told us that *Allied put pressure on management to falsify the financial statements to hide the default from the bank.* Wichmann said management refused to go along, but carefully documented Allied's inappropriate request.

Table 15.2 Galaxy American Communications

Date	Debt Investment		Equity Investment		Comment
	Cost	Value	Cost	Value	
December 31, 1998	30,703	30,703			Initial investment
September 30, 2001	44,967	45,717			Added money and took small write-up over time
December 31, 2001	48,869	39,217			First of many gradual write-downs
March 31, 2002	48,863	39,221			
June 30, 2002	48,433	34,010			Sweeney attacks critics in June
September 30, 2002	48,989	25,000			Gradual write-down
December 31, 2002	48,989	20,000			Gradual write-down
March 31, 2003	49,704	20,000			Files bankruptcy
June 30, 2003	49,704	12,712			Gradual write-down
September 30, 2003	50,204	12,712			
December 30, 2003	50,698	12,712			
March 31, 2004	50,697	10,680	350	—	Gradual write-down
June 30, 2004	50,697	7,789	1,350	—	Gradual write-down
September 30, 2004	11,000	7,527	43,350	—	Equitizes most of the debt
December 30, 2004	11,000	7,517	43,350	—	
March 31, 2005			57,350	7,049	Equitizes remaining debt
June 30, 2005			57,356	7,661	Avoids taking realized loss
September 31, 2005	50,365	50,365	86,693	22,023	Becomes "Triview"; added money for acquisitions
September 30, 2007	44,423	44,557	119,836	82,777	Added money over time; still on books

Note: Dollars in thousands

He told us on the phone, "Things were requested of me as CEO that I resisted vehemently and I documented this to protect myself . . . I was asked to do things that violated GAAP. . . . I can't give specifics, but it was nothing that could be debated. . . . Our CFO sent a sternly worded memo [to Allied] that said it was a black-and-white issue."

Wichmann indicated that Allied wanted to sell Redox. He suggested that we pose as a buyer of the company and discover evidence of Allied's malfeasance during our due diligence. I had no appetite for that. Instead, I informed the SEC of Wichmann's story and hoped it would discover what Allied had tried to do. I have no idea if the agency ever followed up. Rather than having a conversation with the authorities, more and more it felt as if we were "having" a monologue. I worried that the audience had dozed off.

PART THREE

Would Somebody, Anybody, Wake Up?

CHAPTER 16

The Government Investigates

Late in 2002, I received a cold call from Kroll, the private investigation firm, which recently started a group to provide field research for money managers and wanted to pitch its services. Kroll impressed me and sparked the idea that a good public-data search and some active feet on the ground could aid our research on Allied. We hired Kroll to look into two of the Allied investments that were troubling us: BLX and American Physicians Services (APS). I wanted an independent third party to look into what was happening at BLX.

Allied's pattern of investment and valuation made its APS investment suspicious. The investment started in 1999 as a $16 million investment in debt securities, preferred stock and warrants. In December 2000, Allied wrote-down the preferred stock and warrants to zero, signaling a problem. In the second quarter of 2001, Allied increased the investment to $40 million and reclassified the prior equity components of preferred stock, convertible preferred and warrants into common stock. Though this suggested that APS had been recapitalized, Allied continued to value its debt investment at cost. The history looked suspect, so I asked Kroll to see what it could find out.

Just as Kroll began its work in December, *The Wall Street Journal* reported that Eliot Spitzer, the New York attorney general, would investigate Gotham Partners, a hedge fund run by David Berkowitz and Bill Ackman. Specifically, Spitzer wanted to see whether Gotham intentionally manipulated stock prices by publishing research discussing its investment opinions. Prior to Spitzer's investigation, Gotham announced it was closing, having suffered a mildly disappointing performance while concentrating its portfolio in illiquid positions. Gotham had a thin investor base, and when a few key investors lost patience, Gotham had to either sell all of its liquid securities to meet the redemption requests or shut the fund to achieve an orderly wind-down of the entire portfolio.

Because selling the liquid part of the portfolio would unfairly prejudice the remaining investors by leaving them with disproportionate stakes in the illiquid holdings, Gotham did the right thing by shutting down. I spoke with Gotham often because I thought highly of its principals. Though our styles were different, we had some overlapping positions, including short sales of MBIA and Farmer Mac, about which Gotham had published compelling analyses. My immediate reaction was that this type of investigation would have a chilling effect on the sharing of ideas among investors.

In an e-mail to another manager, I wrote, "It seems that at the end of the bear market, people would love to blame short-sellers for the misery. The establishment is very anxious to blame the corporate malfeasance on the ones that have already blown up (Tyco, WorldCom, Adelphia, and Enron) and hope that by everyone swearing that the financials are accurate and putting the known bad guys in jail, that it will all go away. After all the talk, the SEC doesn't have funding. The Bush Administration doesn't want the SEC acting as a tough cop. Try to get *The Wall Street Journal* to write a scandal story where there isn't already blood in the water. They won't do it. Even 'Heard on the Street' goes nowhere that could expand the scandal culture."

Many investors share analysis and opinions on both longs and shorts. This discussion and debate helps make the markets efficient. I never considered that publicly sharing Greenlight's research, particularly because it clearly disclosed our short position, was likely to provoke regulatory interest. Just to be safe, though, we removed our Allied analysis, the BancLab report, and my TheStreet.com article from our Web site. We thought it was a shame, but we did not want to invite extra attention as the world looked for bear market scapegoats after three tough years.

■ ■ ■

We held our seventh annual partner's dinner on January 21, 2003. This dinner was unusual because instead of enjoying meeting with our partners, I spent much of the cocktail hour off to the side on a borrowed cell phone answering a series of pointed questions from David Armstrong, a reporter from *The Wall Street Journal*. I had never spoken to him before, but I knew who he was. He had recently written an article about hedge funds shorting retailer JCPenney that caused a minor uproar in the fund community for its heavy-handed, anti–short-seller slant. The story blamed short-sellers for causing a decline in the stock by working with class-action lawyers. Armstrong's story failed to broach the possibility that JCPenney's stock might have fallen because it twice announced disappointing earnings during the period in question.

We had recently hired Abernathy McGregor, a public relations firm, to help with the media relating to our buyout of Greenlight's original partner, Jeff Keswin, at the end of 2002. With Abernathy's help, and Greenlight's lawyer's input (he happened to be with me at the dinner), I answered Armstrong's questions about Allied, MBIA, and Greenlight's relationship with Gotham. Armstrong thought Gotham was a large investor in Greenlight and implied that Gotham's wind-down would cause it to redeem its investment in Greenlight and put Greenlight at risk. That was not true—Gotham wasn't an investor in Greenlight. He also asked if I had heard from Spitzer's office or the SEC. I hadn't heard from any regulators. He wouldn't say why he asked.

I have no idea how I got through my hour-long presentation to our partners and another half hour of questions that evening. I worked into the presentation my views of regulators looking into investors sharing ideas and noted that we received a related press inquiry. When I got home that evening, I checked *The Wall Street Journal*'s Web site and saw that there was an article set to appear in the next day's paper. Armstrong and two other reporters wrote that the SEC and Spitzer would look into Gotham Partners Management Co., Tilson Capital Partners, the Aquamarine Fund, and Greenlight to see if we conspired to manipulate stock prices by publishing research and asking critical questions on conference calls. While I knew Gotham well, I had met Whitney Tilson only briefly and had never even heard of Aquamarine.

I knew we hadn't done anything wrong and believed it appropriate to share investment analysis and opinion, positive or negative, about companies and ask challenging questions on conference calls. Everything we said or wrote about Allied was a combination of fact and good-faith belief. I had even asked Allied in writing to identify factual errors and promised to publicly correct any mistakes. How could it be manipulative to tell the truth?

With that in mind, I began to wonder how Armstrong knew about the investigations. I believed then and do now that the story started with a leak from Spitzer's office. Spitzer may have accomplished many good things as attorney general; however, his office was well known for leaking the subjects of its investigations to the press prior to finding actual wrongdoing, a practice at odds with the grand jury system and prosecutorial ethics that enables the authorities to investigate possible criminal activity without the identities of the subjects becoming public until an indictment is delivered. Under this system, if the investigation does not turn up a crime, reputations are not harmed. In this case, I believe Spitzer sought headlines to bolster his image as a crime fighter—now taking on hedge funds—before he determined whether any crime had been committed.

The next morning, many of our partners began calling to find out what was going on. Some were nervous, but there wasn't much more we could tell them because we didn't know more than what the newspaper reported. No regulator had contacted us, and we had no way to know if we would hear from them. So we decided we had to adopt a "no comment" policy. We knew that we had done nothing wrong, but we didn't want to update some partners and not others. The right way to update everyone would have been in writing. However, written correspondence has a way of getting into the media, and development-by-development updates could begin to spiral out of control. A fraction of a percent of our partners asked for their money back, but many called to express support. We had always been open with our partners on almost any topic other than what we were currently buying or selling. The "no comment" policy was tough on us, and it was tough on them. However, minimizing the media circus was in our mutual interest.

Allied, however, went running to the press. *Bloomberg* reported that Allied requested the investigation the previous week. Abernathy released a statement from me, saying, "We wish companies would address valid business issues, rather than attacking investors who raise them. We stand by our research on Allied Capital and would welcome a meaningful discussion with management on the facts."

I raised the subject of a discussion with management because Allied's management no longer even pretended to engage in the discussion. Management had recently come to New York for a "road show." These are a series of one-on-one and group meetings for investors, often sponsored by investment banks. Some road shows are in connection with a securities offering, while others are called non-deal road shows. At its recent road show, Allied refused to permit us to attend. Even more, they refused to allow *any* hedge funds to attend. They were only willing to meet with long-only investors. Putting aside the issue of fair access to information, Allied quite simply didn't want to be faced with any pointed questions. Over the subsequent years, Allied has maintained its policy of refusing to meet with hedge funds. In fact, one time it announced a one-day road show to be followed by an overnight stock offering led by Citigroup. Citigroup was unaware of Allied's policy and scheduled management to come to our office and then to another hedge fund's office. When Allied's management saw the schedule, they canceled both meetings. Other times, various brokerage firms have hosted group events for Allied to meet investors. As a client of the brokerage firms, we have been invited to attend—only to be turned away at the door at the direction of Allied management.

On Friday, January 24, 2003, two days after *The Wall Street Journal* article, we received a letter from the SEC addressed to Greenlight Capital, LLC, referencing "In the Matter of Federal Agricultural Mortgage Corp." (Farmer Mac). The SEC advised us of an informal inquiry and asked us to produce our research on Allied, all contacts we made to third parties about Allied and our research file on Allied. They also wanted all of our trading records, organization chart, contact information for all Greenlight employees and all documents to describe our compensation structure, a list of our bank and brokerage accounts, and our telephone records. They wanted all this information going back to January 1, 2002. The letter requested voluntary production of the information by the following Friday. Greenlight's lawyers worked with the SEC to get more time, and we produced the information as promptly as we could.

The *Journal* article not only hurt my company's reputation, but it also affected my wife. About a week after the article appeared, Cheryl was fired from her job as a writer and editor at *Barron's*, the weekly financial magazine owned by the *Journal's* publisher. Her boss told her that they had huddled with the company lawyer, who suggested that they part ways with Cheryl until the investigation was over. He told Cheryl that they were worried about appearances. "It's difficult to be married to someone in the investment business," he told her. She had worked there for about ten years. It was a bad few days. It is never a good thing to get your spouse fired.

■ ■ ■

Lanny Davis appeared on CNBC's *Kudlow and Cramer* on January 30, 2003, to suggest shareholders directly sue short-sellers. Echoing Allied management's wording in the Davis-scripted conference call the previous June, Davis talked about short-sellers spreading the "Big Lie" about his clients. Jim Cramer asked Davis, "Why don't the companies sue the short-sellers, and if the stuff—you know the libel laws—if it's reckless disregard of the truth, sue the entities that are printing it on behalf of the shorts?"

Davis answered, "Actually, Jim, I've looked at that in several instances where I've been able to demonstrate to my own satisfaction, to a flatly false statement damaging to the company's share value. Where we gave notice to the short shareholder, to say this is false, please correct. And afterwards, the retraction was not actually printed, but further the falsehood was repeated. The problem in a defamation action is that you have to prove damage to the company. And a shareholder is the one that could really bring that suit more than the company." This seemed like a not-so-veiled suggestion to Allied's shareholders to sue us, despite the fact that a shareholder probably would not have standing to bring such a suit. Allied probably would have liked for us to be sued, but the company was probably too scared about letting us have legal discovery into the company's business records to risk starting a lawsuit itself.

Davis continued by calling for Congressional action to impose additional rules on short-selling. Larry Kudlow asked, "It's not really personal. It's about—these research reports are presumed to be just business. It seems to me that if you can show a conspiracy, both for positive stock research or negative stock research, you've got a case for fraud or criminal legality. But if there's no conspiracy, Lanny, I don't understand it. It's just one person's opinion—why prosecute?"

Davis responded, "Well, first of all, it's a crime for one person to put out false information, manipulating the market by doing so, and then profiting. But the conspiracy that I believe that Attorney General Spitzer and I believe others are looking at, are when short-sellers and publications engage in spreading misinformation. And I have evidence in the case of several clients, where false information has been spread. And they are cashing out and making a profit, I think, based on misinformation. Now, the bar is very high, Jim and Larry, to prove that case, and I would not want any of my clients to make that charge unless we can demonstrably prove that there has been false information put out." I wondered whether Davis would agree that management should be similarly prosecuted if it said anything that was false.

■ ■ ■

News of the investigations also caused the former BLX executive to stop replying to my e-mails. One of the last things he told me was that Keith Hohimer from the Office of Inspector General of the SBA contacted him to inquire about BLX. He questioned whether the investigation was serious, because Hohimer complained about the amount of work a thorough investigation would require. Nonetheless, at least something was happening.

On February 4, 2003, Allied announced two significant transactions at BLX. First, it purchased $122 million of performing SBA loans from Amresco Independence Funding. Adding a group of performing loans enabled BLX to mask the high delinquency and loss rates in its existing portfolio. Allied increased its investment in BLX by $50 million and converted $43 million of its subordinated debt investment in BLX to equity. Apparently, BLX needed an equity infusion and a debt-to-equity conversion to keep going. Nonetheless, Allied did not reduce the carrying value of its investment in BLX. Second, BLX changed its own corporate structure to an LLC, "for tax purposes and greater flexibility, should the company default," as Allied management explained on its earnings conference call held the following week.

On that same call, I was allowed to ask another question. Since Allied had a habit of not disclosing bad news until forced to, I decided to put them on the spot, querying, "Could you comment at all relating to the

Office of Inspector General in the SBA that I understand has been calling around to people close to Business Loan Express? What do you think they are looking into, and is there an investigation, and, if so, what do you believe the status to be?"

After a pregnant pause, Sweeney responded, "Yes, David, I don't know. I mean, clearly, BLX is a regulated entity by the SBA. I know that the Office of Inspector General typically works with the SBA looking at its lenders. It is usually a routine, they are usually routine inquiries, if there is an inquiry. So that's about all I can say. We don't know the nature of any sort of inquiry. So, you know, again this happens routinely in the SBA lending markets."

In March 2004, we discovered that Sweeney's "play dumb" answer came only days after she had personally signed an agreement to shift defaulted loans from BLX to Allied. The SBA had determined that the loans were improper, demanded, and received a refund of over $5 million. Yet, she claimed to have no idea about this when I asked her about it.

Later that afternoon, after Allied's conference call, I got a call from the SEC Division of Enforcement, asking me what my basis was for asking the question on the conference call. Obviously, Allied had the ear of the regulators and had complained. It impressed me that the SEC was following up the very same day. The questions they asked implied a concern that I created a phony issue to scare other participants on the call, rather than get an answer from the company. I explained what I knew of Carruthers' work and the subsequent follow-up calls from Hohimer to the former BLX employee and to me. The SEC lawyers seemed satisfied that I wasn't making this stuff up.

■ ■ ■

In early March 2003, we received a subpoena from Attorney General Spitzer's office dated February 28, 2003. I was requested to appear on April 15 "to testify in connection with the offer and sale of securities including, but not limited to, false statements, fraud, and efforts to manipulate the market." We were to provide an even more exhaustive list of material, including records relating to several companies on which Gotham published research, a list of all of our investors, communications with several other hedge fund managers, and communications with several journalists, including my wife.

On March 25, we received a subpoena from the SEC. The case had been recaptioned *In the Matter of Gotham Partners Management Co., L.L.C.* The attachment showed that on February 11 the SEC upgraded it to a "formal investigation." This gave it subpoena power. I was asked to appear in Washington, D.C., on April 15 and 16. The investigation sought to determine whether Gotham and other hedge funds used false or misleading statements or engaged in manipulative trading to depress these stocks. The investigation related to Farmer Mac, MBIA, Allied Capital, and American Capital Strategies. American Capital Strategies was one of Allied's competitors, which we had not shorted or criticized. In fact, we owned it in 1998–1999. It had the same business model as Allied, so some believed that our criticisms applied to it as well. In fact, most of our critique had nothing to do with the business model. I don't believe there is anything inherently wrong with business development companies. Greenlight's criticisms are specific to Allied Capital, its accounting and corporate behavior.

On April 4, the SEC sent a subpoena for documents to be produced by April 11. Was it a coincidence that these notices kept arriving on Friday afternoons? Now they wanted information on other companies, information on trading credit derivatives (we don't trade these), our client list, client redemption requests, and our correspondence with several other hedge funds. As we turned over documents and prepared to meet the government, I was not at all worried that we were in trouble or had done anything wrong. But I found it irritating to have to hire lawyers to sift through e-mails and was frustrated that the government was investigating the wrong party. It seemed as though they were looking through the wrong end of the binoculars at the wrong (very small) person—me. I hoped that when we met, I could convince them to retrain their sights on Allied.

■ ■ ■

A couple of weeks later, a federal judge in New York dismissed the class-action suit against Allied over its accounting that had been filed shortly after my speech. The judge ruled:

> Since Allied's accounting policies were publicly disclosed in some detail in each of its SEC filings, the basis of plaintiffs' theory of fraud must be either that the stated policies led to hidden overvaluations

of specific investments, or that Allied did not adhere to its publicly stated policies. Because plaintiffs have not alleged sufficient facts to either theory, they have failed to plead that defendants made fraudulent or misleading statements.

First, plaintiffs have not sufficiently pled that Allied's valuation policies resulted in its overvaluing some of its investments. The complaint simply states plaintiffs' opinion that various valuations were inappropriate, and sometimes a brief reason for that opinion, but fails to allege what plaintiffs contend was the true valuation.

A few pages later, the ruling continued:

Even if plaintiffs had pleaded sufficient facts to support an inference that Allied may have overvalued some of its investments, plaintiffs have not alleged the extent of any such overvaluation. In order to plead fraud with particularity, plaintiffs must state by how much Allied overvalued the investments. . . .

Because plaintiffs have not alleged the amounts by which Allied allegedly overvalued the questioned investments, plaintiffs have not pleaded any facts that would permit a rational jury to conclude that a reasonable investor would have viewed the overvaluation as significant.

In other words, it was up to the plaintiffs to show the judge what the true valuations were. This was a Catch-22, because the lawsuit was dismissed prior to discovery. Since most of Allied's investments were to private companies, where only Allied held the confidential information required to ascertain a precise valuation, plaintiffs were in a tough spot to show the true valuations without access to the information.

The judge was not worried by this, because he came to the questionable conclusion that "Allied's actual valuation policies were public, as was all adverse information about the companies in which Allied had invested. . . ." Where did the judge think Allied disclosed all this adverse information?

The judge found:

. . . Even when plaintiffs provide a reason that an investment's value should have been reduced, such as the company's bankruptcy, they do not explain why that factor should have been accorded significance or allege that Allied's policy did not take that factor into account. Therefore, the complaint establishes nothing more than that the plaintiffs disagree with some of Allied's investment valuations—but given the difficulty of valuing illiquid securities, and the multitude of factors that may appropriately be taken into account, alleging disagreement with some of Allied's valuations does not equate to alleging fraud. . . .

Because the case was thrown out before the plaintiffs were able to take discovery, the plaintiffs were never able to take testimony, see Allied's books and records, or see how Allied justified its valuations. In other words, the case was dismissed before the plaintiffs could get their hands on the Allied documents that would have shown the fraud the judge said he couldn't see.

I didn't see the judge's ruling as an important development. No one had looked at Allied's valuations and related evidence. The procedural ruling to dismiss the case under such circumstance could not vindicate Allied's accounting. But it did show that Allied had talented lawyers.

CHAPTER 17

A Tough Morning

When I arrived to testify at the SEC on May 8, 2003, I went through endless security, and then I was led to the basement. There, in a stark, white room with a bare floor and bare walls, I sat next to a court reporter and across from the SEC lawyers set to grill me. The room temperature felt like eighty-five degrees. There wasn't much ventilation, and there was no drinking water. For that, there was a vending machine down the hall. The only amenity was a red fire alarm box attached to a pipe. The environment was unsettling. It was supposed to be that way. Perhaps the austerity foreshadowed what might happen if your case didn't go well.

My testimony went well, at first. I brought along three lawyers to advise me, and for a half hour the SEC lawyer, Kelly Kilroy, asked me basic questions about Allied and Greenlight. She asked me a lot of biographical questions. It was an easy back and forth.

A second SEC lawyer, Mark Braswell, walked in and took over the questioning, almost in mid-sentence. The gist of his questions was: When did you start manipulating Allied stock? He was baldly aggressive and

157

157

became incredulous over my answers. We would get into debates and he'd get angrier and angrier. I could see he was the "bad cop." He obviously wanted to establish that I was in league with other fund managers to manipulate the market.

"Have you ever met regularly or irregularly with a group of fund managers that would include Whitney Tilson [of Tilson Capital Partners] and Bill Ackman [of Gotham Partners]?" he asked.

"Well, Bill Ackman was in the Richard Shuster group for a period of time," I said, referring to an informal quarterly "idea dinner" of money managers, which I sometimes attend. Richard Shuster ran a small hedge fund called Arbor Partners and organized the dinners. Idea dinners are commonplace. Some, including Richard Shuster's, are self-formed, while institutional salesmen or the investment banks sponsor others. Generally, at an idea dinner each participant presents one or two investment ideas and gets grilled by the group. "He hasn't come for a while, maybe several years," I responded.

"Was Mr. Tilson part of the Richard Shuster group?"

"I don't think so."

"What about Guy Spier [of the Aquamarine Fund]?" Braswell asked.

"I don't think so."

"David Berkowitz? [Bill Ackman's partner at Gotham]"

"I really don't know."

"Are there any other forums, organizations, or informal groups that you participate in that also include Mr. Ackman?"

I said I couldn't think of any.

Kilroy jumped in with a bunch of similar questions.

"How do you know Mr. Ackman? Do you know David Berkowitz as well? Did you meet Mr. Ackman before you met Mr. Berkowitz? And do you recall when you met Mr. Berkowitz? And can you describe your relationship with Mr. Ackman? Are you social friends or just acquaintances? What about Mr. Berkowitz? Do you know one of them better than the other?"

I basically answered that, yes, I know these guys. We went out to dinner once. I knew Ackman better.

A few minutes later Braswell asked, "Mr. Einhorn, have you ever compensated Gotham Partners, Mr. Berkowitz, and Mr. Ackman for providing you with an investment idea?"

"Except in-kind, no," I answered.

"Have they ever compensated you for providing them with an investment idea?"

"The same answer."

Then one of Greenlight's lawyers, Bruce Hiler, jumped in.

"Can I have a minute?" We went into the hallway. I had made a mistake. I needed to make it clear that there was no financial compensation. While it is true that I share investment ideas with other fund managers, this works best as a two-way street. No one likes a freeloader. So as a general matter, I share more ideas with others who share back. I don't keep score about who shares what with me, and the practice is quite informal. My first answer was incorrect, as there is no "compensation" arrangement.

I re-entered the room and answered the question again.

"I think the more correct answer to your question is that there's been no compensation for the ideas."

"Are there any other relationships between you and/or Greenlight and Mr. Ackman and/or Gotham Partners?" he asked.

"I don't think so."

"Let me ask you the same question about relationships that you and/or Greenlight have with Whitney Tilson?"

"I don't know of any."

"What about Mr. Spier of Aquamarine Fund?"

"I don't think so."

Soon, the questioning switched to Allied Capital. Kilroy asked me how I first heard about the company. I said other fund managers introduced me to the idea.

"And when did you first have discussion with those individuals about Allied?"

"I think it was around last March."

"And what was the substance of those discussions?" she asked.

"They thought this was something of merit, and they wanted to get our view on it also, thought this was something we should look into, and they came over to our office and told us what they thought they knew and maybe provided us with some materials of their analysis."

Braswell wanted to hear about my Allied speech.

"Had Greenlight already taken its short position in Allied prior to the May 15th speech?" Braswell asked.

"We were short Allied at the time of the speech."

"And you said the purpose of focusing or talking to them about Allied in this presentation was because you wanted to share one of your better ideas at the charity event. Was another purpose of your speech about Allied to inform others of your thoughts in the hopes that it would put downward pressure on Allied stock?"

There it was: Was I manipulating?

There were ten other speakers that day. Needless to say, the SEC wasn't going to call Bill Miller in to ask if his recommendation to buy Nextel stock, of which his fund was a large owner, was an effort to create upward pressure on that stock. The difference appears to be that *saying something* that makes a stock go up is unquestionably accepted, but the opposite is potential manipulation.

"I disagree with the second part of what you said. Definitely inform others."

"Did you not anticipate that others, other fund managers and Wall Street types who were at this dinner, would short Allied in response to your presentation?"

"I would have thought that based on what I said at the conference, people would have looked into Allied, and I think given what I said and what I believed the facts to be that people very well could have decided to sell or sell short Allied . . . on the basis of the merits of the situation at the time."

"Okay," Braswell said. "Isn't it a true statement that you had a reasonable expectation that other participants at that meeting would either short Allied based on the idea they heard from you or exit a long position?"

Then Hiler, Greenlight's lawyer, interrupted. "I think he already testified to that. Now you're asking him something that has 'reasonable expectation' in it and I don't know if you're trying to get at some legal standard or not, but he's answered your question as to what he thought. People could decide that he's all off base and buy more, too, once they heard him. So people could make their own decisions, and I don't know what the 'reasonable expectation' standard is you're trying to put on here."

"Well, I'm not referring to a particular legal standard, Mr. Hiler, but I am asking the witness a different question," Braswell responded.

"He said what his expectation was."

"No," Braswell said. "He said that other people might do their research."

"Well, he didn't—he didn't adopt your answer. That may be the answer you want, but he did say what his answer was to your question of what did he expect people to do."

This went on for a bit more until the SEC got into the issue of the active Blackberries during my speech.

"Mr. Einhorn," Braswell said, "the record reflects from our investigation that there were people sitting at that dinner and as you spoke, they were on their Blackberries shorting Allied at that very moment."

"Then they must have found what I said to be persuasive."

"And did you have any anticipation that people would do that?"

"No. I heard those stories, too, and I was surprised when I heard that. I wouldn't have expected people to be calling from the conference."

"So in making this presentation," Braswell asked a few minutes later, "you had no intent to try to convince the listener that your analysis was in fact correct?"

"I thought my analysis was correct. And I thought I gave an analysis that I thought was correct, and I attempted to tell people things that I thought were correct."

"And so isn't it reasonable to say that you intended to—"

At that point, Hiler had had enough.

"Look, I really think, if you want him to say he was trying to move the stock, he's not going to say that," Hiler said.

"No, that's not what I'm asking him."

"You're going over this question six times. This witness has said that this was a charitable event that he was asked to attend and give an idea on a stock. He wanted to give a good idea, he said, because he felt people there deserved it because it's a charitable event.

"He's not saying he worked backwards from 'let me intend to do this,' and go forward to the speech. He's told you as much as he can," Hiler said. "'I went in there to give them what I thought was a good idea and to give them my thoughts on that. They can decide whatever they want to decide.' And that's all."

"I am not asking this witness to jump in the mind of anyone who was listening to that speech," Braswell said. "I am simply trying to understand"

"He has told you what his intent was, what his purpose was, and what he did," Hiler finished.

"Actually, Bruce, you've told me more of what his intent was than the witness has. And I would appreciate it if you wouldn't testify."

"I'm not testifying, but I do not want this witness badgered because this has been gone over six times," Hiler said. "It's obvious you want some answer you're not getting, and I think we should be done with this topic."

Braswell persisted, "Did you have any intent that your speech would have an effect on the market price of Allied securities?"

I answered, "That was not the purpose of the speech."

"That was not the purpose. Did you have an intent?"

Now, I was confused, "What's the difference between a purpose and an intent? . . . My intent was to do what the organizers of the charity asked me to do. . . ."

Then Braswell got back to the Blackberries.

"While you were giving the speech, did you witness people in the audience using their Blackberries?"

"I did not witness that, no."

"When did you first hear that others had been trading Allied securities during the course of your speech?"

This wasn't correct. My speech occurred after the close of trading. The Blackberry messages were requests to borrow shares in anticipation of shorting them the following day. I answered, "Some weeks later I had a meeting at Goldman Sachs and they told me that they were receiving questions during the meeting about the availability to borrow Allied shares, that that had happened during the meeting."

Then suddenly we broke for lunch. I was dizzy and sick to my stomach. I felt that my testimony was not going well. Braswell was confrontational, and I didn't know how many more arguments over the difference between *purpose* and *intent* I could stand. I was not looking forward to going back into that depressing room. They were hammering at me, and I knew I had to somehow get through the rest of the day and the following day. I had already made a mistake ("in-kind compensation") and I was worried about making more as they wore me down.

After lunch, though, and for the rest of the next day of testimony, the questioning became gentler. It was as if Kilroy had told Braswell to cool it. When we returned, the SEC lawyers went through all the main issues that Allied was sensitive about: the press, my supposed dealings with class-action lawyers, and my relationship with David Gladstone, Walton's predecessor and the CEO of Gladstone Capital, in which Greenlight had held a small position. Actually, the SEC seemed very interested in Gladstone.

"And what were your discussions with Mr. Gladstone at that time?" Kilroy asked.

"We asked him about things that were on our mind and what his opinion of those things were," I replied.

"What sorts of things were on your mind at that time?"

"We were concerned with some of the valuation processes, some of the individual valuations that Allied was doing, some of the what we would call the intercompany relationships and so forth, and I think we posed a variety of questions to David Gladstone."

That obviously wasn't enough for Kilroy, and she kept coming back to Gladstone. Even though my answers were always the same, she asked me repeated questions about him throughout the session, fishing for something that just wasn't there.

"How did you meet Mr. Gladstone? Did you remain in contact with Mr. Gladstone since the time that you met him, or did you came back into contact with him when you started looking at Allied? How did you start speaking with him about Allied? What was the substance of your dialogue? Did he assist you with your research or serve as a sounding board? What was the nature of your discussions?"

I believe the SEC was focusing on Gladstone because Allied had advanced a conspiracy theory that I was a shill for Gladstone and our true purpose in criticizing Allied was to advance the prospects for Greenlight's minimal holding in Gladstone Capital, which we sold in the second quarter of 2002.

Allied seemed so concerned about Gladstone that after *Forbes* ran an article where Walton called me a "predator," Allied approached the author with a juicier story. On September 2, 2002, *Forbes* published "Hit Man," which said Gladstone had been fired from Allied for hitting a female employee and suggested that a vengeful Gladstone had been badmouthing Allied's accounting. I believe Allied did this as part of its campaign to attack the messenger when they couldn't attack the message and to gain sympathy as a victim of another imagined conspiracy.

During my SEC testimony, the lawyers also asked repeated questions about my speech and why I had issued a written report a month later.

I answered, "Allied had several conference calls and several press releases and was saying various things to the media and so forth. And I felt that a lot of what they were saying was untrue. I felt a lot of what they were saying was misleading. I felt that some of what they were saying was defamatory, and I felt that they were misstating what we had said. I felt that they were mischaracterizing our analysis, and they were accusing us of a whisper campaign. And I felt it was important to set the record straight and to say what we thought the facts were and see if we could put some real facts out there to clarify things."

Periodically, Kilroy asked softball questions, possibly because she may have seen merit in Greenlight's criticisms, which allowed me to defend myself easily and even turn the question back toward Allied. For example, "Were you more often than not able to ask questions on [Allied's conference] calls or did you get a sense that you were being screened out of their calls?"

Near the end of the first day of testimony, Kilroy asked me a question, the answer to which had become obvious: "At the time that you made the speech, did you anticipate that your position on Allied would become so public, or was it your thought that you would give this speech, say what you thought about the company, and then that would sort of be it, and what would happen to the stock would happen to the stock?"

"If what you're asking is did I feel that the reaction was much, much greater than I would have anticipated? The answer is *yes*."

CHAPTER 18

A Spinner, a Scribe, and a Scholar

On the morning of my second day of testimony, *USA Today* ran a feature on Lanny Davis, headlined, "Crisis Lawyer Tackles New Target: Hedge Funds." According to the article, Davis had put together a crisis management team to represent companies that were embroiled in scandal. Davis indicated that he had worked for several dozen firms since 1999 and only a couple of times had his name surfaced as part of his work. The article told how Davis took HealthSouth CEO Richard Scrushy "on a tour of corporate governance experts" to help the company form "an ethics oversight board." Scrushy left HealthSouth and was acquitted of the securities fraud charges in 2005. In 2006, he was convicted of bribery, conspiracy, and mail fraud and sentenced to almost seven years in prison in 2007. According to the article, Davis "broke off his relationship with HealthSouth." The article explained:

> Davis goes on and off the record with such frequency that a newcomer to the game can easily suffer spin vertigo. [Now, Davis was]

165

busy assembling the Full Disclosure Coalition, a group of corporate clients who are pressing Congress to enact legislation that would require investors who sell stocks short (making bets that they will fall) to meet the same disclosure rules as [long investors].

I believe the point of asking short-sellers to disclose who they are is to intimidate them. As I had seen, Allied made great effort to refer to Greenlight's criticisms as "the short attack" and to undercut our credibility by harping on Greenlight's financial motive. Allied personified me as the villain to appeal to investors to make a choice: Either they were with Allied or they were with the manipulator. That way investors didn't need to pay attention to the substance of what we said or critically judge the adequacy of Allied's responses.

The *USA Today* article continued by describing Allied's "campaign" against me:

> "Allied Capital has launched a very unusual and very aggressive shoot-the-messenger campaign," Einhorn says. "I suspect it's because they don't have adequate answers to serious questions about their business and accounting."
>
> Davis shoots back: "Allied has answered every assertion Einhorn's made. Einhorn has a record of using innuendo as a surrogate for facts."

Now, Lanny Davis wanted the ability to launch similar campaigns against others. As Jim Chanos, a prominent short-seller, observed, the sponsors of the Full Disclosure Coalition have insisted on *anonymity*—an Orwellian twist too rich for fiction. Allied may or may not have been its largest financial backer. However, aside from the *USA Today* article, I never saw another public reference to the Full Disclosure Coalition. A recent Google search for "Full Disclosure Coalition" only showed twelve results, including the *USA Today* article and a couple of short-sellers commenting on the story.

To my relief, my second day of SEC testimony was less stressful than the first. We went through the parts of Greenlight's published report where Allied disagreed. I almost enjoyed getting to explain why the PIK income forced Allied to raise capital to support its tax distribution; how I determined Allied mismarked 35 percent of its investments; why Allied's ability to exit certain investments at their carrying value didn't prove Allied valued the portfolio properly; how Allied changed its business model and accounting; why Allied's relation to BLX was analogous to Enron's relation to its Raptor partnership; why Allied had no reasonable basis for its valuation of BLX; and how Allied designed the rights offering to manipulate the market. These were all easy topics for me. They asked some more questions about Gotham and our short sales of Farmer Mac and MBIA. Finally, they asked about Todd Wichmann of Redox Brands, who had told us of Allied's bad behavior with his company.

At the end of the day, they asked me if I wanted to add anything to the record. At the time, the SEC was considering regulating hedge funds in an effort to curtail fraud. I said that I couldn't see how hedge fund regulation could be effective when the SEC allowed an already regulated investment company, Allied, to complete additional public offerings prior to the SEC fully investigating and resolving the issues we brought to its attention.

We were done. We even finished before lunch. I left feeling like I had just gotten out of class on the last day of school. I went back to New York and waited for the fallout and my turn with Spitzer. His office set up dates for interviews twice, but canceled both times. Since then, we've heard from neither the SEC nor the New York attorney general's office about investigating us.

We did hear again from David Armstrong, one of *The Wall Street Journal* reporters who had written the article about regulators investigating Greenlight. He said he wanted to write the Allied/Greenlight story, I suspected at Allied's suggestion. So James Lin and I sat down with him. Armstrong had already met with Allied and came armed with questions. Like the SEC lawyers, Armstrong asked questions on topics that were upsetting Allied, and James and I answered them all. We watched the video of the charity speech together. Armstrong remarked that it didn't seem like a big deal. When we were through, I thought Armstrong believed we had the stronger argument and raised some good points about Allied's valuations and accounting practices. He seemed to leave with an understanding of our criticisms of Allied.

The *Journal* soon published a multipart series on hedge funds. The series graphically depicted hedge funds with a pair of fuzzy dice. The series didn't contain a positive word about anyone in the field. I suspect Armstrong targeted his work with us to fit into that anti–hedge fund series, but *couldn't* because the facts were on our side. I believe this ran contrary to his purpose and personal bias in working on the subject. Rather than writing a story that supported our view, he wrote none at all.

We next heard from Professor Perold from Harvard Business School, who completed his case study of Allied. I was surprised because he hadn't contacted us since I spoke to his class in October 2002. Though he had not yet shown it to us, he'd given the case study to his students and already taught from it. The case study was also "in the market," because a mutual fund called to inquire about it.

The study read like Lanny Davis wrote it. I was dumbfounded. Why would a professor at the Harvard Business School, who seemed like an intelligent guy, write a case study that resolved everything in Allied's favor? The study was full of errors and told only Allied's side of the story. The study described many of our arguments as false and having been "refuted." It misunderstood Allied's accounting, how the company treated BLX on its books, and implied that the company's critics were involved in a conspiracy against it. The case study accepted Allied's contention that it did not change its accounting in 2002 and had been consistent all along. The study even repeated Allied's claim that we barely spoke to management before I made the speech.

I worried that this study could become the "history" of the event from Allied's point of view, but with Harvard's name on it! Perold completed the report on July 3, 2003, and sent us a PDF version by e-mail. We asked if he would send us a version in Word so we could intersperse comments into the text of the document. He refused, so I had to have an assistant retype the whole case study so we could note the errors to send Perold. James Lin and I followed up with a phone call to walk through our comments, point out errors, and express our concerns.

Perold promised to make things right, and we spoke for more than two hours as we went over the study point by point, telling him about the mismarkings, Allied's lies, and the problems at BLX. It was a long, exhausting phone call.

"I warned you this was going to take some time," I told him when we were about halfway through.

Perold expressed his willingness to continue the discussion and his enjoyment trying to sort out the contradictory claims.

I told him that I also had a problem with the study's habit of calling this a short attack, which is Allied's often-used terminology.

"We think this is inflammatory," I said.

"Oh, go on," he said, amused. "What the hell else is it?"

"It's not an attack. We raised issues. We shared our research."

Perold laughed. "Oh, God," he said, sounding exasperated. "You didn't sell the shares hoping the stock would go up."

"That's not an attack, that's an investment," I said.

He agreed to change it.

By the end of the call he agreed to take my points to Allied for its response. I asked if he would offer the similar courtesy to show us Allied's response so we could comment on it before he published again. He declined. He indicated that it was customary in Harvard case studies to give the subject company involved a chance to comment. I pointed out there were two subject companies—them and us. It made no difference—this was a one-way street. Perold would offer only Allied the opportunity to comment in advance.

Yet, a larger problem still remained: that Perold had already distributed the first draft of the case study. I asked Perold if he could reclaim the erroneous copies from his students. Perold said he would try his best and would tell everyone that the study in its current form was just a draft, a work-in-progress. That process repeated itself a few months later when Perold released another faulty version of the case study to his students prior to soliciting Greenlight's comments. We pointed out the errors and complained about the process. In each version, he incorporated many of our changes, while ignoring others.

I was still mystified as to why this process was so difficult. Then, out of the blue, one of Perold's students informed me that Perold's research assistant on the case study worked at the investment firm Capital Research and Management (CRM) the previous summer. *CRM was Allied's largest shareholder.* After graduation, the research assistant rejoined CRM. I asked Perold to disclose the conflict or even the appearance of conflict in the report. He refused. When I pressed him, he could offer no other reason than it was his case study. The final version came out in early 2004 and was fairer.

CHAPTER 19

Kroll Digs Deeper

While all of this was going on, Kroll was making significant progress in its investigations into American Physicians Services (APS) and BLX. While Allied revealed nothing about the nature of APS, Kroll discovered APS was a "physician practice management company." In the late 1990s, Wall Street thought companies that purchased doctor practices and provided back-office services, including scheduling, supply purchasing and billing, were the future of medicine. The problem was that most of these companies didn't really improve the doctors' lives and interfered a lot, which caused relations between the doctors and the corporate owners to deteriorate. Once companies got a bad reputation from the doctors, it became harder to acquire additional doctors to meet growth plans. As a result, the stock prices fell, which eliminated any remaining ability to use stock to acquire more doctors. The doctors, who accepted stock up-front to sell part of their practices, became even unhappier. Ultimately, most of these companies, including the industry leader, Phycor, failed. As discussed in Chapter 4, we had seen this happen at Orthodontic Centers of America.

Kroll found that APS fit into this bucket. TA Associates, a well-regarded venture capital firm in Boston, backed APS's start-up, and Allied provided a subordinated loan. Kroll found that the majority of doctors and former executives interviewed did not believe APS would ever be successful or that Allied would recover its investment. A number of physicians interviewed were unhappy with their relationship with APS, using such words as *incompetent, dishonest,* and *crooked* to describe management.

Kroll concluded that ongoing losses due to the shrinking number of doctors would require Allied to continue to inject capital to keep the company afloat. Subsequent to Allied's initial investment, results severely deteriorated and the number of doctors with the company declined from about one hundred at its peak to thirty-five in 2003. Kroll doubted APS generated profits. The company was in such bad shape that its bank lenders dumped its loans in June 2001 to Allied for about fifty cents on the dollar. TA Associates walked away. Despite purchasing the senior debt at a discount and equitizing some of the senior debt, Allied did not mark down its own junior debt investment in APS.

Instead, when Allied bought out the senior lenders, it took over APS and put Sweeney in charge. However, the business continued to crumble. Still, Allied carried its original loans to APS at full value on its books. It put the loan on "non-accrual" in April 2002, but didn't begin to write-down the investment until December 2002, and then by only a small amount. Allied gradually wrote-down the value during 2003, before taking a large write-down in March 2004 just before APS went bankrupt. Allied had to take further write-downs through the balance of that year (see Table 19.1).

In a September 2004 *The Wall Street Journal* article, Allied claimed that it was optimistic about APS until late 2003, when APS lost a malpractice lawsuit and then received bad publicity after one of its patients died in early 2004. Kroll's work showed that APS was in deep trouble long before that.

Kroll's investigation of BLX was trickier. It turned out that Jock Ferguson, the investigator working on the project, knew Jim Carruthers, the partner at Eastbourne Capital who was doing a lot of digging into BLX on his own. As a result, the two crossed paths on several occasions. I instructed Kroll to cooperate with Carruthers but not reveal it was Greenlight that had retained the company. I was not interested in word getting into the market, the media, or to Allied that we hired Kroll—until

Table 19.1 American Physicians Services

Date	Debt Investments		Equity Investments		Comment
	Cost	Value	Cost	Value	
December 31, 1999	14,388	14,388	1,476	1,476	Initial investment
March 31, 2000	14,404	14,404	1,476	1,476	Increase may be PIK
June 30, 2000	14,661	14,661	1,476	1,476	Increase may be PIK
September 30, 2000	14,792	14,792	1,476	1,476	Increase may be PIK
December 31, 2000	14,809	14,809	1,476	–	Write-down of equity; debt at cost
March 31, 2001	15,090	15,090	1,476	–	Increase may be PIK
June 30, 2001	39,405	39,405	1,000	100	Recapitalization; buy-out of Sr. debt; no Jr. debt write-down
September 30, 2001	39,580	39,580	1,000	100	Increase may be PIK
December 31, 2001	40,194	40,194	1,000	100	Increase may be PIK
March 31, 2002	40,780	40,780	1,000	100	Increase may be PIK
June 30, 2002	41,362	41,362	1,000	100	Placed on non-accrual; no write-down
September 30, 2002	40,643	40,643	1,000	100	
December 31, 2002	40,662	38,492	1,000	–	Equity investment is written down to zero
March 31, 2003	40,662	38,492	1,000	–	Gradual write-down
June 30, 2003	42,162	36,239	1,000	–	Gradual write-down
September 30, 2003	43,062	36,793	1,000	–	Gradual write-down
December 30, 2003	40,812	32,185	1,000	–	Gradual write-down
March 31, 2004	43,512	19,300	1,000	–	Gradual write-down
June 30, 2004	44,730	16,750	1,000	–	Gradual write-down
September 30, 2004	34,987	4,663	1,000	–	Gradual write-down
December 30, 2004	4,801	4,225	–	–	A $32.9 MM realized loss

Note: Dollars in thousands

Kroll completed its work. This led to several awkward conversations I had with Carruthers in which he informed me that someone hired Kroll and the Kroll investigator was quite experienced and was doing a great job. I sheepishly listened and encouraged Carruthers to share with Kroll, but to make sure it was a two-way street.

Carruthers developed several former BLX employees as sources. One of them gave him an internal August 2001 delinquency report that detailed $135 million of delinquent loans, or about 20 percent of the company's portfolio. Allied had consistently said that BLX delinquencies were less than half this amount. Kroll used the delinquency report as a road map to the troubled loans. They talked to banks, brokers, former employees, and some of the borrowers.

In August 2003, Kroll completed a twenty-three-page report on BLX, with two binders of source document exhibits each six inches thick. Kroll found "a series of loans originated by BLX that appear to be frauds against the SBA." Kroll wrote, "Further audits of BLX loans could uncover violations of SBA loan issuing rules and regulations and lead to the possible recovery by the SBA of many tens-of-millions of dollars from BLX."

Kroll confirmed and documented BLX's misconduct as the former employee who had contacted me had outlined and as Carruthers had discovered. BLX made loans that could never be repaid. Kroll found that in numerous cases BLX flouted many SBA underwriting requirements. The SBA provided the same type of lax governmental oversight that contributed to the savings-and-loan crisis in the 1980s.

What's more, Kroll discovered that BLX issued new SBA loans to borrowers to pay off existing SBA loans, a clear violation of SBA eligibility rules. Kroll found cases where BLX did not confirm that borrowers made the required equity contributions; let borrowers take fees from loan proceeds; did not verify details in loan applications; and failed to properly assess a borrower's credit history, capitalization adequacy, repayment ability and collateral. Kroll also found that BLX accepted inflated real estate appraisals. As SBA rules summarize, "The lender must analyze the borrower's proposal as to whether it is a reasonable and appropriate undertaking for the business." Kroll found that BLX violated this principle and many other more technical SBA underwriting requirements.

Kroll said that BLX focused on generating a high volume of new loans and said it heard indications that loan officers were not encouraged to be careful. BLX made its money based on loan volume and left most of the credit risk to U.S. taxpayers under the SBA program. This caused them to emphasize the quantity rather than quality of loans.

Kroll found that several borrowers received their loans and never even made a single payment. BLX relied on independent loan brokers to generate volume. Kroll reported that former BLX employees, who worked as loan underwriters, said that most loan approval decisions were based solely on the information in the loan application paperwork provided by the loan broker without verification.

Kroll found possible fraud in loans originated in Michigan, New York, South Carolina, Georgia, and Virginia, where Matthew McGee, the convicted felon I discussed in Chapter 11, ran (and still runs) the Richmond office. Kroll said McGee was obviously overstepping SBA restrictions limiting his responsibilities after he was released from prison in 1997. Kroll said many of the loans out of the Richmond office defaulted.

When BLX hired McGee, the SBA approved the hire, provided that McGee not be involved in the financial affairs of the company or have credit approval responsibility. Kroll found that McGee routinely exceeded this authority by overseeing the acquisition, processing, and underwriting of all SBA loans in the Richmond office, often personally presenting them to the loan approval committee. Once approved, he would oversee the issuance of the new loans. Separately, the SEC had banned McGee from affiliating with an investment company. As Allied is an investment company, it appears that McGee violated his SEC ban because we have seen no evidence that Allied obtained an SEC waiver.

The fraudulent loans were pervasive and seemingly blatant. In one case in Georgia, BLX extended a $1.6 million SBA loan to Magnet Properties LLC, a motel company that operated a Howard Johnson Express Inn owned by Mangu Patel, who had already defaulted on another SBA loan in 1998. (Indeed, over the years, BLC/BLX would make several SBA-backed loans to Patel, many of which flouted agency lending rules and many of which defaulted. Kroll found that Patel himself often acted as the broker on some of these loans.) The new loan soon went into default, and BLX lost more than $1 million, three-fourths of which the SBA reimbursed on the taxpayer guarantee.

Kroll detailed problems with a number of other fraudulent motel loans in the South and a number of fraudulent gas station loans in Detroit and

New York. Kroll found a motel loan where a month before the transaction the property had been "split," separating the motel from the adjacent restaurant, administrative building and parking. BLX funded a loan based on the entire property, but had collateral for only the main motel. The owner put up a makeshift wooden fence to divide the property and sold the separated property free and clear.

In another example, BLX loaned $1.35 million in 2001 to Ryan Petro-Mart LLC, naming Amer Farran as the borrower and incorporated by Abdulla Al-Jufairi, a loan broker who brought many deals to BLX. We later learned that Abdulla Al-Jufairi (also spelled Al'Jufairi in some documents) and Pat Harrington, the head of the Detroit BLX office, were business partners. The tax assessment for the property was only $443,000, about $900,000 below the loan amount. Only one partial payment was made on the loan before it went into default a few months later.

BLX also made a $1.35 million loan to Farmington Petro-Mart, another Detroit-area gas station, and again listed Farran as the borrower. When interviewed by Carruthers, Farran said he knew nothing about the gas stations or the loans. He said he worked as an engineer at the Ford Motor Company. He implied that he was related to Al-Jufairi (we later learned he was a brother-in-law), who was listed as the contact person on this loan. "I guess I have a call to make to Abdulla, don't I?" Farran said. The loan, of course, went into default.

Al-Jufairi was also listed as the incorporator of Golfside Petro-Mart LLC, which borrowed about $1.3 million from BLX, a loan that defaulted, as did a $1.35 million BLX loan to the Jefferson Fuel Mart. Al-Jufairi brokered that loan, and the records indicated it was a sham transaction between related parties at an inflated value financed by BLX. Also, $200,000 of the loan proceeds went to Hussein Chahrour, who pled guilty and received two years' probation in a cigarette smuggling ring. He received a light sentence in exchange for testimony against other members of the ring, which used some of the smuggling proceeds to finance the Lebanese terrorist group, Hezbollah. Kroll said it was evident that the Detroit office of BLX barely reviewed the loan applications created by Al-Jufairi, again flouting SBA requirements. Including the Al-Jufairi loans, a total of eleven BLX gas station/convenience store loans in the Detroit area went into default for a combined $11.2 million.

In Norfolk, Virginia, Kroll found that BLX made a loan to the Town Point Motel, which the police closed just months later, claiming the motel was a center for the local drug trade. The owner of the motel stopped making loan payments and the city of Norfolk eventually tore it down.

Colleton Inns was a motel in Walterboro, South Carolina, where BLX held a junior loan. After it failed, a senior officer at Walterboro Bank (which held the senior loan) told Kroll, "I sold the motel on the courthouse steps for a little more than the total owing on the first mortgage. . . . BLX walked away with nothing, losing at least $1.1 million."

Kroll found that since the beginning of 2000, there had been more than one hundred bankruptcy filings on loans issued by BLX. As with Al-Jufairi and Patel, Kroll found that delinquent borrowers often had ties to the independent loan brokers used by BLX. Sometimes the borrower and the broker were the *same person*. Some banks told Kroll that so many BLX loans went into default that the company earned a reputation of being the lender of last resort in the Preferred Lending Provider world.

BLX was pretty much getting away with this fraud, but occasionally regulators noticed. The early default of the $1.6 million loan to Magnet Properties LLC in Georgia triggered an audit in 2002 by the SBA's Office of Inspector General (OIG), which found numerous lending violations (see www.sba.gov/ig/2-35.pdf). The SBA audit said that "the deficiencies in the subsequent loan application package of (Magnet) were concealed" and the loan did not meet agency eligibility criteria. The audit found that Patel paid himself $170,000 from the loan proceeds and used the loan to refinance the earlier SBA loan. This was a clear violation of SBA rules, which state, "No proceeds of a PLP [Preferred Lending Provider] loan may be used to either refinance or pay off an existing SBA loan."

The OIG concluded that BLX's actions "were egregious acts and warrant SBA action to seek civil fraud remedies against the lender." The company's failure "to follow prudent lending practices, and materially comply with SBA requirements, undermined the integrity of the Section 7(a) business loan program." The OIG recommended suspension of BLX's PLP status in the Georgia District Office "due to its failure to comply with SBA regulations, policies and procedures for originating loans." In addition, BLX had to repay the nearly $750,000 reimbursement to the SBA. Ultimately, the SBA did not pursue civil fraud remedies or suspend

BLX's license in Georgia. As we would see many times, the SBA has been strangely forgiving of BLX's misdeeds.

Even some former BLX employees whom Kroll interviewed were amazed at how the company conducted its business. "It was appalling how BLX operated," one former BLX executive told Kroll. "They had poor underwriting talent, no proper training (and), because there was no regulator overseeing them, they assumed the SBA would never look at them. They were pure sales people who never saw a bad loan deal. It is a recipe for disaster."

Former BLX employees also indicated that the company rushed to produce loans because the compensation of senior executives was tied to the volume of new loans. They also said that BLX would keep impaired loans that were in foreclosure or bankruptcy on its books so they wouldn't have to be written off. "It is clear that BLX is hiding its actual loan losses from Allied shareholders," a former BLX employee told Kroll.

Around this time, another of Carruthers's sources told a story from his tenure at BLX. The ex-employee believed that BLX should take a $10 million write-down for bad loans. BLX didn't want to do it. The employee approached Robert Tannenhauser, BLX's CEO, and advocated the write-down and said the appraisals didn't support the carrying values.

Tannenhauser's response: "F**k the appraisals."

CHAPTER 20

Rousing the Authorities

Greenlight's law firm, Akin, Gump, Strauss, Hauer & Feld LLP, arranged meetings in August 2003 with the SBA, the SEC, and New York Attorney General Spitzer so that Kroll could share its report. At the SBA meeting at its office in Washington, D.C., Jock Ferguson, who led Kroll's field effort; Rich Zabel from Akin, Gump; and I met with David R. Gray, counsel to the inspector general of the SBA; Robert Seabrooks, assistant inspector general for auditing; Mark R. Woods, assistant inspector general for investigations; and Garry Duncan, with the Atlanta field office.

As we laid out a number of fraudulent transactions, they seemed drowsy.

"Do you have the SBA loan numbers for these loans?" one of them asked.

"No, we don't," Ferguson said. BLX's delinquency report was not indexed by SBA loan number. The legal records supporting Kroll's research didn't contain them either.

One of them asked, "Do you know how we could get those?"

Was the SBA really asking outsiders how to obtain its own loan numbers? Apparently, giving them the borrower's name and address wouldn't do.

I wanted to scream, "Send them a subpoena!" Instead, I said, "Why don't you ask BLX?"

Ferguson walked through the loan frauds and pointed out the lack of equity injections. One of the SBA guys said, "We see this all the time; what is special about these?" It was as if they were well aware that no one actually follows the rules.

This wasn't a group of government investigators likely to work overtime. The meeting's high point was when they bragged they actually recovered about $5 million from Allied for bad loans earlier that year. Obviously, that was news. I had no way to know that half a year later this nugget would resurface.

I was naïve enough to expect that the SBA would actually take an interest. Here, we had spent private resources and laid out an easy road map to show an ongoing fraud that was costing taxpayers at least tens of millions of dollars in guarantee payments on loans that should never have been made and served no purpose other than to line the pockets of crooks. The SBA has limited resources; we were offering free help and were obviously willing to provide additional help, if asked. Most perplexing—the folks we were meeting with had presumably chosen careers in public service to root out *exactly* this sort of misconduct, yet seemed unwilling to do anything to stop it.

Ferguson told them that he had a list of sources that could help them in their investigation. We suggested that someone from the SBA follow up by calling Ferguson to obtain the list. No one ever did.

Ferguson followed up with one of the SBA officials. He learned that the SBA agreed with Kroll's assessment of the Mangu Patel loans. In April 2004, Ferguson sent us this update of one conversation with an SBA official:

> The OIG [Office of Inspector General] has had difficulty obtaining internal SBA computer records on all the loans listed in BLX's Delinquent Loan Report dated August 8, 2001.
>
> The loans in the 113-page BLX document did not have SBA loan numbers attached to them and it became impossible for the

OIG to find them in the SBA computer database. Then the SBA discovered that the database for August 2001 was no longer available.

Recently a former SBA loan officer has been hired by the OIG to investigate the status of BLX delinquent loans. That person has begun two different investigations of BLX loan records, the SBA source said.

She is looking at the current status of BLX loans to assess whether or not the SBA is being properly notified of the loan status once it becomes delinquent.

In addition, the same person is looking at all the loans in the BLX August 2001 Delinquency Report to determine what the SBA was told about their status and when.

One of the early findings by the SBA is that proceeds of the delinquent loans were improperly used. "We are finding a lot of problems," the SBA source said.

At this stage, there is only one OIG staff member investigating the BLX loan portfolio status because of a shortage of personnel.

Putting a person on it and finding a lot of problems was a good sign. Perhaps the SBA was slow—a turtle to our hare—but would get there eventually. However, if the investigators were having trouble with the SBA loan numbers and that particular delinquency report, why didn't they call BLX and ask it to send over every monthly delinquency report for the past couple of years? And further, ask BLX to index the reports to the SBA loan numbers?

The lack of resources was not a trivial concern. The SBA is more than fifty years old. It was created during the Eisenhower administration with the passage of the Small Business Act in 1953. Its goal is to help small businesses compete.

Under the SBA, loans would come from private lenders, not directly from the government. Instead, the government acts as the loan guarantor. It charges a guarantee fee on each loan, which it uses to pay the majority of the losses on the loans that default. However, if the losses run in excess of the guarantee pool, taxpayers are on the hook.

The SBA 7(a) lending program is the SBA's largest business loan program. At the onset of the program, SBA rules required it to approve every loan before it was issued. In an effort to speed things up, the agency created the Preferred Lender Program (PLP) in 1984 to delegate much of the SBA's decision-making authority regarding loan approval, loan servicing, and liquidation activity to lenders who have demonstrated thorough knowledge of the requirements. In 2003, the 7(a) program guaranteed $10 billion of loans to 60,000 businesses.

While the PLP made the lending process quicker, more efficient, and less costly to the taxpayer, the government, in effect, turned over its underwriting pen to private enterprise. One would think that the SBA would dedicate *some* of the resources it saved by not having to review every loan to ensure it doesn't get ripped-off. Not so.

The majority of the 7(a) loans are made in the PLP. As part of its oversight function, Congress had asked the United States General Accountability Office (GAO) to evaluate the SBA's lender oversight. In December 2002, the GAO reported that the SBA contracts with outside firms (inappropriately paid for by the lenders being reviewed) to evaluate the PLP lenders. The GAO found that the evaluations do not make a qualitative assessment of the lenders' decisions but, rather, are only a cursory review of lenders' processes and documentation maintained in a sample of the lenders' loan files. According to the GAO report, the SBA does not adequately measure the financial risk PLP lenders pose to its portfolio. The report indicated that the SBA lacks resources to properly monitor lenders. The office of lender oversight had only twelve staff members overseeing over four hundred preferred lenders, one of them being BLX. There was only one staff member assigned to portfolio analysis and reporting in the entire SBA program.

The GAO report observed that "PLP reviews are not designed to evaluate financial risk, and the agency has been slow to respond to recommendations made for improving its monitoring and management of risk—posing a potential risk to SBA's portfolio. PLP reviews are designed to determine lender compliance with SBA regulations and guidelines; however, they do not provide adequate assurance that lenders are sufficiently assessing eligibility and creditworthiness of borrowers."

The SBA reviews lenders through a questionnaire and checklist that generally reviewed the presence or absence of documents in the lender files. Reviewers "are only required to review loan files for completeness and required documentation. Review staff rely on the lender's attestations rather than independent assessment of loan file documentation." In short, it's a check-the-box review without any substance.

"SBA officials said that lender review staff focus on the lender's process for making credit decisions rather than the lender's decision. SBA officials said that it is unlikely that the review would result in a determination that the loans should not have been made. An SBA official stated that review staff would not perform an in-depth financial analysis to assess the lender's credit decision and that a lender's process would only be questioned in the case of missing documentation. . . . This official said additional training would be required for lender review staff to make more qualitative assessments of loan documentation during the review process." The report concludes, "Without a more substantive method of evaluating lender performance, this approach does not provide a meaningful assessment."

Allied touted that BLX routinely received the highest ratings in its PLP audits. Apparently, this equated to good filing technique and the ability to attest to compliance when the poorly trained, government-contracted reviewer came calling. Even if it stumbled onto a problem, the GAO found that the SBA hadn't even established procedures to suspend or revoke PLP authority. In fact, there were no follow-up procedures for PLP lenders that received poor reviews. Because the SBA wants to encourage lenders to participate in the PLP program, it chose to "work out problems with lenders, and therefore rarely terminate PLP status."

With this regulatory framework, it wasn't hard to see how a team of bad guys could bilk the government and taxpayers for big dollars. As Kroll noted, "Senior BLX executives know they can flout SBA rules because there is no effective oversight or regulation of PLP lender practices. In effect, the SBA has no idea of the quality of the loans that BLX is originating, whether BLX is in compliance with SBA rules and regulations or how its loan portfolio is performing."

After our discouraging meeting with the sleepy-eyed SBA in the morning, we proceeded to the SEC's headquarters that same afternoon. We met with two SEC enforcement officers, Charles Felker and Walter Kinsey. They walked into the meeting with blank legal pads and let us lay everything out. They took a lot of notes and seemed engaged in the presentation. As we moved from the wrongdoing at BLX to how Allied used BLX to inflate its own financials and made false and misleading statements to confuse the market, Kinsey asked for a *written summary*. He became frustrated that

I didn't have that information with me, and I promised to provide it in a follow-up package.

That the SEC meeting was better than the SBA meeting was a low hurdle cleared. As with the SBA, the SEC officers didn't seem interested in obtaining the supplemental list of people with whom to follow up. Indeed, there was no evidence they followed up on anything from our meeting. When I returned to the SEC the following spring (as I will describe in the next chapter), the SEC had an entirely new set of lawyers, who expressed no knowledge of this prior meeting.

To complete the regulatory trifecta, we met Attorney General Eliot Spitzer on August 14, 2003, the day of the Northeast blackout, which shut New York City down shortly after we left. Spitzer took no notes, though he was attentive. He asked good questions, asked for a copy of the Kroll report, and promised to review it and get back to us. We left with some optimism that someone within a governmental office would jump on this. To my surprise, we never heard from Spitzer's office again.

■ ■ ■

I sent the SEC a thirty-nine-page follow up letter and supporting analysis in October 2003. The letter covered a litany of our initial accounting criticisms and the change in Allied's accounting. We included a statistical analysis to test Allied's contention that it used a consistent valuation method. By comparing the percentage of investments that Allied changed in valuation from one quarter to the next, we were able to show, almost without a doubt, that Allied had indeed changed its portfolio valuation methodology.

For the statistically minded, the data in Table 20.1 showed a 99.9 percent confidence level, a correlation of 0.95, an R-squared of 0.9, and a t-statistic of 8.8. For the non–statistically minded, that is about as certain a conclusion as you can have in statistics.

On the July 29, 2003, Allied conference call, notably, Houck, the Wachovia analyst, asked Allied whether the increased number of mark-ups and mark-downs in the most recent five quarters indicated a change in the valuation methodology. "You know, actually I think it's more related to the economy than anything else. The valuation practice is the same as always," Sweeney fibbed.

Table 20.1   Write-ups and Write-downs Recognized Each Quarter

Date	# Write-ups	$ Write-ups	# Write-downs	$ Write-downs	Total changes	
December 31, 2000	8	6,349	3	(1,851)	11	
March 31, 2001	9	27,806	8	(17,400)	17	Pre-speech
June 30, 2001	9	6,325	9	(6,330)	18	Pre-speech
September 30, 2001	1	28,250	14	(12,472)	15	Pre-speech
December 31, 2001	14	24,462	10	(32,057)	24	Pre-speech
March 31, 2002	3	13,794	6	(15,251)	9	
June 30, 2002	15	98,681	32	(80,267)	47	
September 30, 2002	18	12,194	26	(30,277)	44	
December 31, 2002	18	70,545	44	(57,422)	62	
March 31, 2003	17	6,533	29	(22,937)	46	
June 30, 2003	20	63,532	35	(59,729)	55	
September 30, 2003	22	23,057	39	(43,296)	61	
December 31, 2003	27	71,984	32	(40,557)	59	
March 31, 2004	24	11,983	36	(50,624)	60	
June 30, 2004	31	43,425	35	(26,112)	66	
September 30, 2004	33	27,010	37	(30,910)	70	Post-speech
December 31, 2004	39	56,876	38	(79,086)	77	Post-speech
March 31, 2005	35	116,767	38	(57,873)	73	Post-speech
June 30, 2005	30	122,837	45	(46,054)	75	Post-speech
September 30, 2005	42	113,693	29	(88,498)	71	Post-speech
December 31, 2005	41	354,455	32	(54,853)	73	
March 31, 2006	48	85,325	24	(56,460)	72	
June 30, 2006	41	49,587	35	(75,128)	76	
September 30, 2006	39	139,714	38	(115,028)	77	
December 31, 2006	49	140,489	32	(155,295)	81	
March 31, 2007	49	152,674	43	(76,167)	92	
June 30, 2007	62	114,779	34	(88,485)	96	
September 30, 2007	45	84,634	49	(242,806)	94	

Note: Dollars in thousands

We did another statistical analysis demonstrating that Allied smoothed its investment performance rather than independently valuing each of its investments. The amount of investments written up each period correlated with the amount written down each period. (The correlation was 0.93, R-squared was 0.86, the *t*-statistic was 7.4, and the confidence level was 99.5 percent.) The relationship grew even stronger in the five quarters after

Allied changed its accounting in June 2002. (The correlation was 0.99, the R-squared was 0.98, the *t*-statistic was 13.4, and the confidence level was 99.9 percent.) This meant that Allied artificially "managed" its write-ups and write-downs.

Write-ups and write-downs should be negatively correlated, or inversely related, because shifts in the economy and capital markets occur in only one direction per period. As Allied's portfolio investments were positively correlated with the economy, the values of write-ups and write-downs themselves should be negatively correlated. In a strong economy, there should be many write-ups and fewer write-downs. Conversely, in a weakening economy, there should be many write-downs and fewer write-ups. Our analysis showed that Allied did the opposite in order to fabricate smooth performance: Allied wrote-down its problem investments *gradually* over time and matched them with offsetting gains as they developed.

We did a third statistical analysis that showed a serial correlation between current and subsequent changes in the value of Allied's investments. The data showed a 99.9 percent probability that initial write-downs of investments are disproportionately followed by further write-downs of the same investment. If management were marking the portfolio fairly, then future adjustments should be independent of prior adjustments. No pattern should exist and write-downs should not beget further write-downs. Just as we saw in Sirrom years before, the only conclusion to make was that Allied was slow—intentionally slow, profitably slow—to account for bad news.

That was more than just bad behavior. It is *illegal* for investment companies to smooth their performance by matching winners to losers and belatedly recognizing problems. This inflates the earnings and the balance sheet. Allied's practice of delaying write-downs enabled them to dilute the eventual impact of the losers by repeatedly selling additional equity in the interim. Also, it gave investors a false impression that the investment results are smoother, more stable and less risky than they really are. The statistical analyses showed that this was not a case of a few isolated anecdotes of inflated valuations, but a broad, systemic pattern of reporting manipulated and misleading results. Some frauds are more obvious than others. Because this one seemed too sophisticated for regulators to catch, we tried to give the government a statistical analysis, which would make it clear, even to them.

Along with the statistical analysis showing how Allied illegally smoothed its portfolio performance, my SEC follow up letter contained a lengthy discussion of BLX, noting Allied's high purchase price of BLC Financial (Allied paid four times book value, and an unusually large premium to the pre-deal trading price) and pointed out that even as Allied reported interest and fees from BLX, the subsidiary burned cash. The money path was circular: Allied extended additional investment to BLX each quarter. Allied began to disclose some summary financial information for BLX in the June 2002 quarter and had then made a full year of those disclosures, which showed that BLX's loans did not have the cash economics that Allied promised at its investors' day in August 2002. Cash premiums on loans sold averaged only 4.3 percent, rather than 10 percent. Residuals grew $56 million in the year, compared to earnings before interest, taxes, and management fees (EBITM) of $44 million, meaning 126 percent of its EBITM was non-cash. This meant that BLX generated no cash to pay Allied: All of Allied's "revenues" from BLX were funded by Allied putting more cash into BLX.

Even as origination volume and EBITM hadn't changed much and Sweeney insisted on the July 29, 2003, conference call that Allied valued BLX using the same valuation process, Allied increased BLX's enterprise value to $465 million as of June 30, 2003, from $390 million the previous year.

Allied recognized "unrealized appreciation" of $50 million in its BLX investment that quarter. Since Allied reported $59 million of net income that quarter, the BLX mark-up was most of Allied's earnings. The write-up more than offset sizeable write-downs from four other investments: $14 million from Executive Greetings, $10 million from ACE Products, $8 million from Color Factory, and $7 million from Galaxy American Communications.

Allied explained that part of the increase in BLX's value came from an increase in the multiples of comparable companies. The multiples did expand in the June 2003 quarter from the March 2003 quarter, and on the second-quarter conference call Allied cited the higher public multiples to justify the enormous write-up of BLX's value—even though its operating results had not improved. However, in the September 2002 quarter, comparable company multiples had fallen an average of 32 percent and conveniently that decline did not cause Allied to write-down BLX. All told, the multiples in June 2003 were lower than in June 2002. We didn't know how Allied changed its valuation methodology for BLX, but certainly it did.

The following quarter, Allied disclosed that it changed the comparable companies it used in its analysis. Allied dropped DVI, Inc., which went bankrupt, and replaced it with additional companies that used portfolio lending accounting, including HPSC Inc., GATX Corp., and Capital Source. This was the first time that Allied identified the publicly traded comparable companies in an SEC filing. Allied said on the conference call that the comparable group was "about the same," but it had actually changed dramatically.

Finally, the letter to the SEC discussed Allied's other investments in Hillman, GAC, Startec, Fairchild, Powell Plant Farms, Drilltec, the CMBS portfolio, and Redox Brands. We reminded the SEC about the experience of Todd Wichmann, the Redox chief executive, who said Allied asked him to falsify his company's financial statement to avoid problems with the senior lender. We also summarized Kroll's findings about American Physician Services.

"Simply put," I wrote, "in our view, Allied continues to engage in valuation and accounting fraud, and then attempts to disguise its valuation practices through the dissemination of misleading statements. This practice is repeatedly demonstrated in investment after investment."

The letter continued, "Through such practices, Allied has presented to the public a completely inaccurate view of the strength of the company and its investment portfolio. This fraud allows Allied to grow continually—as its most recent stock offerings demonstrate." Since my speech in May 2002, Allied had raised about $470 million from issuing roughly 22 million shares, or 20 percent of the company.

I concluded the letter by urging the SEC to be more aggressive toward Allied: "Allowing Allied to persist in this behavior is fundamentally unfair both to investors and to competing investment companies that keep honest books and fully disclose negative information concerning their investments. We request that you investigate Allied's practices and take appropriate action promptly and publicly to correct Allied's misleading disclosures and overstated financials."

■ ■ ■

Then, like always, we waited. While we were waiting, Allied announced that BLX had a bad third quarter in terms of loan originations and profits. For the quarter, BLX's origination volumes declined 21 percent and earnings before interest, taxes and management fees fell 53 percent to only $6 million, compared to $12.9 million the previous year. On the conference call announcing the results on October 28, 2003, Allied management began by trumpeting that BLX obtained PLP status from the SBA in all markets, including Puerto Rico and Guam, before explaining that, to improve its securitization execution, it needed to diversify its industry concentration. It appears BLX's loans were too concentrated in gas stations and motels. This "strategic shift" to reduce the overconcentrations caused the decline in origination volumes and profits. Management thought the problem would persist as the "diversification efforts will take some time." Notwithstanding this obvious bad news that the company admitted would persist for a while, Allied further expanded the enterprise valuation of BLX from $465 million to $476 million.

These were important numbers. As discussed in Chapter 12, Allied's initial description of how it valued BLX was absurd. Now, with Allied's announcement of the enterprise value, we could compare that old valuation of BLX to this new, even more fanciful one.

As Table 20.2 on page 190 shows, originations and operating profit before management fees (EBITM) had fallen over a full year. BLX incurred more bank debt. Even so, Allied dramatically increased the valuation of its own investment. The valuation multiples, which we believed to be unreasonable a year earlier, expanded dramatically. Allied's expansion of BLX's multiples, even as the results deteriorated, reached absurdity.

We were also able to follow the circular money trail between Allied and BLX. Allied recognized more in fees, interest, and dividends than BLX generated in EBITM, none of which was cash. We pieced together all the SEC filings and found that BLX burned through $32 million in cash before paying Allied anything the previous year. BLX borrowed this money from its credit line, which Allied co-signed. BLX then "paid" Allied $39 million in interest, fees, and dividends. That money showed up on Allied's books as income, boosting its earnings per share. Allied used it to pay its distribution. At the same time, Allied invested an additional $39 million in BLX. It was a spinning circle of money.

■ ■ ■

Table 20.2   BLX Valuation Comparison

	Sept. 02	Sept. 03	Growth
Most Recent Quarter Originations	153.7	121.4	−21.0%
Most Recent Quarter Revenue	25.7	24.9	−3.1%
Most Recent Quarter EBITM	12.9	6.0	−53.5%
Last 12 Months Originations[1]	624.5	564.3	−9.6%
Last 12 Months Revenue	94.0	108.3	15.2%
Last 12 Months EBITM (as reported)	47.0	37.5	−20.2%
Last 12 Months EBITM (as adjusted)[2]	47.0	42.1	−10.4%
Bank Debt Outstanding	96.9	129.5	33.6%
ALD's Investment in BLX[3]	254.3	344.9	35.6%
Enterprise Value[4]	351.2	474.4	35.1%

Multiples:	*Sept. 02*	*Sept. 03*
Enterprise Value/Orig. Volume[5]	0.57x	0.98x
Enterprise Value/Orig. Volume (Last year)	0.56x	0.84x
Enterprise Value/EBITM[6]	6.8x	19.8x
Enterprise Value/EBITM (Last year as reported)	7.5x	12.7x
Enterprise Value/EBITM (Last year as adjusted)	7.5x	11.3x

Note: Dollars in millions

[1] Excludes $121.5 million of loans purchased from Amresco in 2003.
[2] Allied suggested adjusting BLX's EBITM for various non-recurring expenses.
[3] At Allied's carrying value.
[4] For simplification, this is Bank Debt plus Allied's carrying value of its investment.
[5] Most recent quarter annualized.
[6] Most recent quarter annualized.

On November 18, 2003, I asked Walton about BLX's cash flow at an investment conference sponsored by Merrill Lynch. He responded, "It is generating enormous amounts of cash" and "is generating great cash flow, great earnings and pays a dividend." Walton's statement was a gross mischaracterization of the facts. As shown in Table 20.3, Allied's SEC disclosures indicated that BLX actually burned cash, since 63 percent of revenues and 181 percent of EBITM were non-cash. BLX required additional bank loans and further direct investment from Allied to fill the hole.

We were able to estimate that BLX recognized revenue of approximately 15 percent on every loan it originated. How could loans with a

Table 20.3   BLX Noncash Revenue

Total Revenues	108.3	(A)
% Cash Including Cash from Residuals	83%	(B)
Cash Revenue Incl. Cash from Residuals	89.9	(C) = A * B
Cash from Residuals	49.3	(D)
Cash Revenues	40.6	(E) = C – D
Noncash Revenues	67.7	(F) = A – E
EBITM	37.5	(G)
Noncash Revenue/Total Revenue	63%	(H) = F / A
Noncash Revenue/EBITM	181%	(I) = F / G

Note: Dollars in millions

four-year average life and an interest rate cap of prime plus 2.75 percent be worth 15 percent more than the face value of the loan? Here's how: The SEC filings revealed that BLX achieved average origination fees and premiums of about 6 percent for selling the guaranteed pieces, plus BLX booked approximately 9 percent of non-cash residuals on every loan. Considering that BLX sold the most valuable portion—the guaranteed piece—it was not reasonable to book the smaller, riskier, unguaranteed piece, and the servicing, at such a high value. BLX could only achieve this through the magic of gain-on-sale accounting supported by super-aggressive assumptions.

■ ■ ■

While we waited for the SEC to act, Steve Bruce from Abernathy McGregor, Greenlight's public relations firm, suggested we meet with Kurt Eichenwald from *The New York Times.* Eichenwald had a reputation as an intelligent bulldog, unafraid of investigating crooked companies, and was in the process of writing *Conspiracy of Fools* about the Enron fraud.

Eichenwald invited us to Dallas, where he worked, to meet. Bruce, Jock Ferguson of Kroll, and I flew to Dallas to meet Eichenwald in October 2003. We met at the Crescent Hotel in Dallas for about five hours. We presented the Allied and BLX stories of fraudulent loans and accounting. Ferguson went through the Kroll report with Eichenwald, and we also gave him a copy of some of the SEC letters and the BancLab report.

"Take me through this," he asked Ferguson. "How did this work?"

Eichenwald seemed interested in the drug den motel loan and the Detroit gas station frauds. He wanted all the details. Eichenwald's questions were excellent. He had seen this before and knew how to report this kind of story. He was energized and intrigued. Sitting on the couch reading the documents, he was animated. "This is unbelievable," he said. "Wow. This is great. I love this."

"What is the SEC doing about this? Why can't they figure this out? Why didn't *The Wall Street Journal* jump all over this?"

By the end of the meeting, he said, "I'm going to do it, but I want an exclusive."

"Sure," I said. "That's not a problem."

He told us that reporting this sort of story takes a long time, but promised that if the facts checked out, he would definitely write it. I left the meeting thinking that we would see something in about six months.

Months went by . . . nothing. At Eichenwald's request, we kept sending more documents and updates as the story progressed, and he kept enthusiastically expressing that he wanted all the information. Eichenwald claimed he was working on it, but none of the sources we'd suggested he contact said he had called. Not a good sign.

CHAPTER 21

A $9 Million Game of Three-Card Monte

Sometimes, revealing events come from the most insignificant places. Jim Brickman, the retired real estate developer from Dallas who had continued to independently research Allied and BLX, found one of those places in early 2004.

He had been digging through court records of the bankruptcy proceedings of bad BLX loans. In the bankruptcy of a convenience store called Trilogy Conifer in Colorado, lawyers for Allied, rather than BLX, had oddly showed up in court to collect on the loan. Allied told the judge that it owned the loan and submitted the proof to the court. It was a short, but revealing, document: Allied told the court that BLX assigned Allied ten loans, including this one, with balances of $9,062,489, in exchange for Allied forgiving the same amount of BLX's debt to Allied. The document, dated February 3, 2003, was signed by Sweeney for Allied and by Tannenhauser for BLX. Why would Allied accept a defaulted loan from BLX for full value? Were the other loans in similar shape?

Brickman and I tried to get information on the ten loans. Several appeared on BLX's August 2001 delinquency report. We were able to find nine of them and all defaulted long before BLX assigned the loans to Allied in February 2003. A look at the court records clearly showed that these were not only troubled loans, but that there was no way anyone other than Vito Corleone could have expected repayment.

Why did Allied accept these loans? My first instinct was to believe they did it to mask BLX's deteriorating situation. As Allied valued BLX at a minimum of eleven times earnings, a $9 million loss at BLX translates to a $99 million valuation loss for Allied. So shifting the loss from BLX to Allied enabled Allied to value BLX $99 million higher. In contrast, if Allied owned the loans, it would only be a $9 million loss on its books. Table 21.1 lists the transferred loans.

In the Trilogy Conifer bankruptcy in 2002, the company already owed Allied $1 million on a promissory note from December 1998. As of August 2003, Allied was owed $1.2 million, but was second in line to BLX, which was owed about $1.1 million plus legal fees and costs on an apparently separate loan.

In a legal proceeding Trilogy filed against Allied, Trilogy claimed that Allied's representative prepared projections that "overstated revenues and understated expenses, with the result that the unachievable debt service was made to appear reasonable and achievable." According to Trilogy's complaint, Allied increased the 1998 loan amount by another $135,000 on

Table 21.1   Bad Loans Transferred to Allied

Company	Amount
Au Gres Pinewood Inn, Best Western Pinewood Lodge	$1.0 million
Avant-Garde Enterprises	$0.4 million
Dibe's Petro Mart	$1.0 million
Farmer House Foods and XTRA Foods and Orchard Food Center	$1.0 million
Federal One Stop and William Grossi	$1.0 million
The Kelfor Companies	$1.1 million
The Learning Center at Birch Run's Playpark	$1.0 million
The Links at Birch Run's Playpark	$1.0 million
Trilogy Conifer	$1.0 million
1750 Woodhaven Drive and the ATS Products Corporation	$0.5 million

August 16, 2000, at a time when "it knew or should have known that the projections of profitability were not possible." The complaint further adds, "[t]he loan balances were far in excess of a reasonable debt load for such a convenience store operation." The complaint alleged, "Allied purposefully pursued a pattern and practice of making loans to gas station proprietors that it knew could not service the heavy debt." Allied later settled the case on undisclosed terms.

The other loans each had its own story—all bad. Most were in bankruptcy, but some had been discharged from bankruptcy; that is, there wasn't anything more to be done to collect on them. *Yet, Allied paid BLX full value for them.*

Meanwhile, Allied's stock had performed strongly since April 2003, reaching $31 a share in February 2004. When Brickman posted these findings about the loans and links to the source documents on the Yahoo! message board, Allied stock quickly fell a few percentage points. Allied, as far as I could tell, did not disclose this transaction to shareholders. I found no mention of the loan transfers in any of Allied's filings with the SEC.

■ ■ ■

Allied's poor investments continued to pile up. Two more companies to which Allied loaned money filed for bankruptcy protection. Each bankruptcy filing provided a fresh example of Allied's failure to mark down loans as they deteriorated.

Executive Greetings filed in December 2003. Allied invested $16 million in subordinated debt and warrants in 1999. In early 2002, Executive Greetings either stopped or reduced its interest payments to Allied. Despite this, Allied carried the investment at cost through September and continued to accrue non-cash or PIK income throughout 2002 (see Table 21.2). According to Executive Greetings' plan of liquidation, the company lost one-third of its revenues and more than half its earnings between 1999 and 2002. Plainly, the lack of interest payments and deteriorating results were evident long before the end of 2002. According to the bankruptcy records, Allied held a junior loan that would receive "little or no distribution."

In February 2004, Garden Ridge filed for bankruptcy. In 1999, Allied had invested $28 million in subordinated debt and equity in the retailer. Allied's 2003 10-K indicated it held a debt investment of $27.3 million,

Table 21.2 Executive Greetings

Date	Debt Investment		Equity Investment		Comment
	Cost	Value	Cost	Value	
December 31, 1999	15,825	15,825	360	360	Initial investment
December 31, 2001	15,938	15,938	360	360	Increase may be PIK
March 31, 2002	16,658	16,658	360	360	Stops or reduced payments; no write-down
June 30, 2002	17,327	17,327	360	360	Increase may be PIK
September 30, 2002	18,061	18,061	360	360	Increase may be PIK
December 31, 2002	18,830	16,500	360	–	First write-down
March 31, 2003	18,830	14,315	360	–	Value supported by possible bid by Allied
June 30, 2003	18,830	–	360	–	Allied abandons buyout
September 30, 2003	18,830	50	360	–	
December 30, 2003	18,830	50	360	–	Files for bankruptcy
June 30, 2004					$19.3 MM realized loss

Note: Dollars in thousands

while Garden Ridge's financial statements reflected only a $25.3 million obligation. We suspected Allied might have recognized an extra $2 million of PIK income that didn't even appear on Garden Ridge's books. Garden Ridge's bankruptcy records indicate that, from 1999 to 2002, comparable store sales fell by 16 percent, and earnings before interest, taxes, depreciation, and amortization (EBITDA) fell from $24.8 million to –$18.3 million. From the time Allied invested—after which its deterioration shortly began— Garden Ridge lost about $45 million. Nonetheless, Allied carried all of its debt and equity investment in Garden Ridge at cost through September 2002. In December 2002, it belatedly wrote down the equity to zero and the debt to 95 percent of cost. Allied took incremental modest write-downs nearly every quarter through the end of 2004 (see Table 21.3 on page 198).

■ ■ ■

A few months earlier, around the turn of the year to 2004, I had discussed our Allied investment and the government's lack of responsiveness with one of our long-time partners. She was aghast at the story and said she knew SEC Chairman Bill Donaldson socially. She offered to pass our information directly to him. I wrote her a two-page summary, to which she attached a personal note. A couple of weeks later, she received a form letter thanking her for her letter. A couple weeks after that, four SEC enforcement officials called her to find out if she had more information on Allied. Apparently, the SEC finally formed a team to investigate our concerns. Now, I was the one aghast that this is what it took to get the SEC off the dime.

Brickman wrote to the SEC about the $9 million loan transfer. The SEC called Brickman and invited him to Washington for a meeting to discuss it. Brickman asked the SEC if I could join him. We scheduled the meeting for April 27, 2004.

Brickman also called Houck, the analyst at Wachovia. Houck initiated coverage of Allied with a "Strong Buy" at $23.20 per share two days after my speech and aggressively argued his bullish view with me. But since then, he repeatedly lowered his opinion of the company. He cut his rating to "Buy" in July 2002 at $22.40 per share after Allied announced the disappointing second-quarter results. In January 2003, he lowered the rating to "Market Perform" at $23.55 per share citing "valuation considerations." Finally, he lowered his view to "Underperform" in April 2003 at $21.22 "due to

Table 21.3 Garden Ridge

Date	Debt Investment		Equity Investment		Comment
	Cost	Value	Cost	Value	
December 31, 1999	26,537	26,537	1,743	1,743	Initial investment
December 31, 2000	26,537	26,537	1,743	1,743	Deteriorates; no write-down
December 31, 2001	26,948	26,948	1,743	1,743	Deteriorates; no write-down
March 31, 2002	27,006	27,006	1,743	1,743	Deteriorates; no write-down
June 30, 2002	27,070	27,070	1,743	1,743	Deteriorates; no write-down
September 30, 2002	27,133	27,133	1,743	1,743	Deteriorates; no write-down
December 31, 2002	27,198	25,667	1,743	–	First write-down
March 31, 2003	27,264	25,712	1,743	–	
June 30, 2003	27,271	25,000	1,743	–	
September 30, 2003	27,271	25,000	1,743	–	
December 30, 2003	27,271	20,323	1,743	–	
March 31, 2004	27,271	20,323	1,743	–	Files bankruptcy
June 30, 2004	27,271	18,300	1,743	–	
September 30, 2004	27,271	16,500	1,743	–	
December 30, 2004	27,271	12,722	1,743	–	
March 31, 2005	27,271	12,722	1,743	–	
June 30, 2005	22,500	14,985	–	–	$7.1 MM realized loss on bankruptcy exit
September 30, 2005	22,500	16,935			Restructured debt at 7% interest rate
December 31, 2005	22,500	22,500			Worth par
March 31, 2006	22,500	15,369			Not worth par
June 30, 2006	22,500	8,455			Not worth par
September 30, 2006	22,500	13,630			Not worth par
December 31, 2006	22,500	22,500			7% debt, worth par, again
March 31, 2007	22,500	22,500			
June 30, 2007	22,500	22,500			
September 30, 2007	20,500	20,500			

increased dependency on capital gains to support the current dividend, anticipation of two consecutive years of declining NOI/share (Net Operating Income), increased risk of a dividend cut in 2004, continued deterioration in credit quality metrics, and valuation considerations."

Houck lobbied Allied to provide better disclosure, including the secret gain-on-sale assumptions at BLX. When they refused, he wrote, "Given the relative size of BLX, we believe management should provide audited financial statements for BLX." Houck completed a transition from optimistic to pessimistic about the company and published several critical research notes. In October 2003 he wrote, "We continue to struggle with Allied's disclosure and lack of transparency with respect to their private finance portfolio. In our opinion, it is difficult to assess the reasonableness of the management's portfolio company valuations . . ."

He also challenged the valuation of BLX. He said: "We have specific concerns regarding the valuation of BLX. Without disclosures on BLX, it is difficult to assess the appropriateness of management's valuation of the portfolio company. Specifically, in order for investors to gain comfort with valuations, they need to be able to compare the original assumptions used to calculate gain-on-sale at the time of BLX's securitizations versus the actual experience (e.g., loss rates, prepayments, discount rates). An increase (decrease) in loss rates or prepayment speeds versus original assumptions can result in a decrease (increase) in the carrying value of the residual asset that is created at the time of securitization. For companies that securitize loans on a regular basis, industry standard is to report monthly loss and prepayment experience on a static pool basis (i.e., AmeriCredit, Capital One, Providian). In the case of BLX, Allied reports aggregate data only on a quarterly basis, and the data is limited in its utility because growth and acquisitions can mask the underlying trends. In addition, we also believe that in Q2 2003, Allied changed the composition of the peer group used to value BLX, which, in our opinion, further obfuscates the valuation of BLX. On its Q2 earnings conference call, Allied management noted that the peer group for BLX had changed but declined to discuss the composition of the peer group at that time. Management indicated that the peer group used to value BLX would be identified in the subsequent 10-Q filing. However, the composition of the peer group for BLX was not identified in the 10-Q."

Brickman informed Houck about the dubious $9 million loan transfer. Houck called Allied, which informed him that it was just one bad loan.

Houck relayed this to Brickman, who indicated that it was ten bad loans. Houck went back to Allied. Allied said it fully disclosed the transaction in its SEC filings.

In Allied's SEC disclosures, under a footnote titled, "Supplemental Disclosure of Cash Flow Information," Allied wrote, "Non-cash operating activities . . . included . . . receipt of commercial mortgage loans in satisfaction of private finance loans and debt securities of $9.1 million." Calling these loans, which had defaulted and, in some cases, been discharged, "commercial mortgage loans" was quite a stretch. Though the transaction occurred in February 2003, Allied did not refer to this deal in the March 31, 2003, 10-Q. Instead, it made its first reference in the June 30, 2003, 10-Q, which identified a $9.9 million transaction. Allied amended the amount to $9.1 million, which matched the repurchase agreement, in its subsequent filings. Though the June 30, 2003, 10-Q had pages of disclosure about BLX and, in fact, references "BLX" more than one hundred times, Allied chose not to reveal that this transaction involved BLX or describe the defaulted status of the "commercial mortgage loans" when it accepted them. This disclosure was about as non-disclosing as a disclosure can be.

Sweeney told Houck that BLX sold the loans to Allied pursuant to a *put agreement*, where BLX would have a contractual right to assign the loans to Allied at a particular price. Houck relayed this to Brickman. Brickman asked Houck to find out where Allied disclosed the put agreement.

Once more, Houck called Sweeney. This time she asked Houck whether he had been reading the Yahoo! message board on the company. Houck said he hadn't, but heard there were concerns. Houck asked about the disclosure of the put agreement. Sweeney said that there isn't anything in writing, just an oral agreement to buy back loans made at the time of the merger between Allied Capital Express and BLC Financial, Inc. to form BLX, and said Tannenhauser wanted to keep this clean for the SBA. Apparently, these were fraudulent loans that Allied transferred from its books to BLX as part of the merger. Tannenhauser didn't want his reputation tarnished by these loans. She couldn't talk about what loans they were, because of Regulation FD, but agreed that many of the loans were worthless.

FD stands for Fair Disclosure. The regulation requires companies to disclose material information simultaneously to all market participants.

Allied would later claim that the transaction didn't need to be disclosed because it was "immaterial." Obviously, if it were immaterial, Regulation FD didn't apply. Alternatively, she could have discussed what loans were involved in the put agreement, provided she disclosed it to the whole marketplace.

Oral business agreements are sometimes made because somebody doesn't want someone else to know about them. Taking Sweeney at her word to Houck, that someone was the SBA, a federal agency. Perhaps there were others as well. Did Sweeney want the put agreement concealed from Allied's auditors, investors, rating agencies, and, possibly, even its own board of directors? Surely, a binding put agreement should have been disclosed in Allied's financial statements. It wasn't.

The actual document where BLX assigned the loans to Allied did not reference a put agreement. Instead, it explained that BLX wanted to "prepay" its debt to Allied.

Houck concluded that this was fraud, but didn't want to write a detailed explanation of what he understood. "Given who these individuals are and how they act, to me I don't want a personal stake in this," he told me. I empathized with Houck: I never wanted a *personal* stake in this, either. I viewed my speech as professional, but Allied responded with personal attacks. I understand why Houck didn't want a similar experience.

Another problem was that Houck's bank, Wachovia, had a strong relationship with BLX. Indeed, they underwrote a number of BLX's securitizations. Houck decided to run his concern up the chain of command. Rather than write a detailed report, Wachovia and Houck decided to simply cease covering Allied. In a brief published research note, on April 26, 2004, the day before our scheduled meeting with the SEC, Houck discontinued his coverage of Allied. He wrote: "We believe the financial statement disclosure for the company is inadequate and the fundamental information provided with respect to ALD's largest portfolio company, Business Loan Express, lacking. Our concern includes questions related to a repayment and assignment agreement dated February 3, 2003, between ALD and Business Loan Center. In our opinion, management's response to our requests for additional financial disclosure has been unsatisfactory."

"With BLX representing a significant portion (13% at Q4 2003) of ALD's investment portfolio, and hence book equity, we believe additional disclosure for valuation purposes is warranted. Without additional disclosure/information on BLX, we lack a reasonable basis to value Allied Capital and the cash flows associated with the investment."

After he dropped coverage, Houck explained to me, "I think the larger point here is that [it] wipes out a lot of earnings for Allied as a whole. And all the while they are selling stock. So this is securities fraud. If you want to take it to an extreme, how can you sell stock when BLX's earnings were clearly inflated? Even if there was a put agreement, if it was in writing, it still is a scheme to inflate earnings."

We then discussed Allied's refusal to disclose BLX's gain-on-sale assumptions. Houck said that Sweeney told him the reason for this refusal was that BLX generates so much cash and Allied didn't want people to see how good it was. Houck agreed that BLX didn't generate any cash and added, "If you tell a big enough lie, maybe people will believe it." After discussing other problems in Allied's portfolio, Houck concluded, "You start to see a pattern of fraud at an organization, you tend to think it is cultural."

Allied, as it said about me, whispered that Houck just didn't understand the company and how it did business. It claimed Houck insisted they violate regulation FD, and when it wouldn't, Houck retaliated. Houck wasn't able to defend his view or answer Allied because Wachovia told him to make no further comment.

I also told Kurt Eichenwald at *The New York Times* about the secret $9 million loan transfer. Houck's dropping coverage of the company spurred Eichenwald to, at last, write something. The next day, April 27, 2004, the *Times* published his article about the transaction and Houck, headlined "Allied Capital Under Scrutiny Over $9 Million Transaction." Eichenwald wrote:

> The reason for the concern about the documents was simple: defaulted and troubled loans are not worth their full value; indeed, under most lender accounting, a defaulted loan must have its value reduced in the company's books. That decline in value is then usually accounted for by a reduction in the lender's profits.
>
> In other words, by counting the loans at full value, the transaction raised concerns among some investors both that the income of BLX had been manipulated upward—raising dividend payments to Allied—and that it may be a signal of other undisclosed related-party transactions.

After explaining the oral agreement between Allied and BLX, the article continued: "'The management of BLX did not want the loans. So they were placed with BLX under an oral agreement that they could be shifted back to Allied if their credit quality deteriorated further,' she [Sweeney] said." The original transfer caused BLX to owe Allied the face value of the loans. Ultimately, BLX invoked the oral agreement and transferred the questionable loans back to Allied, which forgave the related debt, according to the article.

This, at least, answered one question I had long had. I had always wondered why Allied paid such a hefty price for BLC Financial. Now I had a new theory: Allied Capital Express held a bunch of improper SBA loans on its books. In 1999, the SBA had conducted an audit and determined that a number of Allied's SBA loans failed to meet SBA standards. At some point, the SBA would ask Allied to reimburse any losses on those loans. Rather than disclose the bad audit and write-down the loans in 1999, Allied purchased BLC Financial in 2000 (at a high price) and shifted the problem off its books by parking the loans at the newly formed BLX. Apparently, neither company took a write-down for the disqualified loans. Over time, some of the loans performed, while others deteriorated to the point where the SBA demanded a refund. In early 2003, Allied and BLX unwound the parking arrangement for the bad loans and repaid the SBA $5.3 million relating to these loans. This was the repayment the SBA bragged about in our meeting in August 2003.

During the time Allied parked the loans on BLX's balance sheet, Allied raised almost half a billion dollars of fresh equity. The combination of some of the loans performing, which reduced the potential liability to the SBA, and Allied's much larger size, meant that the loss was less material to Allied's financials in 2003 than it would have been if Allied had properly recognized the loss when the initial problem surfaced years earlier.

Sweeney tried to distance Allied from the blame. As she told the *Times*, "These were loans that were originated by a prior management team, and we had agreed to take them back." According to Allied's description of Sweeney's biographical information in its SEC disclosures in 2000, "Ms. Sweeney also has direct responsibility for the small business lending operations through Allied Capital Express." Prior management, indeed.

Eichenwald also reported that federal regulators started an informal inquiry into the transaction. Allied issued a press release in response, saying it knew of no such inquiry "into this immaterial transaction that had a negligible effect on Allied Capital's balance sheet or on BLX's value."

Steve Bruce, our public relations adviser, thought Eichenwald's article was the first shot of his planned exposé. Eichenwald told Bruce that he couldn't believe the number of hostile e-mails he received from Allied shareholders in response to the article. For a reporter, this is a good sign—he is on to something. He said shareholders were really angry with him for reporting that the SEC would investigate the company. They thought he made it up. Bruce thought the reaction of Allied and its shareholders would inspire Eichenwald to finish the job and report the larger story. We had not told Eichenwald about the SEC's recent interest or about our pending meeting with the SEC, because we didn't want to anger the agency. He had his own sources.

■ ■ ■

On the day the article was published, Brickman and I met with the SEC. It was the first time I met Brickman in person. He was just as he seemed on the phone and via e-mail: irrepressible.

Unlike my previous meeting at the SEC, this one was in a much nicer conference room on the main floor. They had four people there including Kilroy, the "good cop" investigator who had questioned me nearly a year ago. Kilroy indicated she would not be involved going forward, but was there to help the others with the history and to transition the work. The SEC staffers asked us to go through all our current concerns about Allied and BLX. They were engaged, polite and inquisitive. They even brought an accountant with them. The enforcement lawyers asked what kind of documents they should request from Allied and whom should they interview there. Basically, they were asking us to be their cartographers.

■ ■ ■

Three weeks later, on May 12, 2004, Allied held its annual shareholder meeting. At the end of his prepared remarks, CEO Walton came at the short-sellers once again:

Now I would like to switch gears. I think any people who read the [*Washington*] *Post* probably are aware that we have some people in the market who don't necessarily agree with everything we do. I guess that's part of being public. It is a phenomenon, which not only affects us but I think many public companies.

But in our case, two years ago we became the target of a misinformation campaign, which we believe was initiated by short-sellers attempting to profit by putting downward pressure on the stock through the use of such misinformation.

In the last several weeks that campaign has once again manifested itself. This seems to be part of a standard playbook used by people who call themselves event-driven investors who distort or, in some cases, simply make up information to manipulate the market. The pattern is pretty clear—take short positions and then do anything in their power to engineer an outcome in their favor. This manipulative activity harms shareholders and ultimately harms the whole capital market.

We've watched this activity for the last couple of years. We've watched this not only with us, but we believe it has been used with hundreds of companies. There's a pretty clear pattern to this game. Let me tell you what we see are the ten steps in the short sellers' playbook. Not quite David Letterman's Top Ten, but it's somebody's top ten.

Anyway, you *first* identify a company which is highly regulated or complicated. We happen to be complicated and we are regulated.

Second, find some fact. It doesn't matter if it is material or not. Find a way to take the fact out of context or distort it so it has little or no relationship to the truth and make it sound sinister and quite material.

Third, take your short position.

Fourth, search out what we call research analysts, regulators, long investors and the press and tell them something bad is afoot. And, oh, by the way, don't call the company to get the real story. Nobody has called us . . . I mean not in any material way and call the company. Don't call the company to get the story. It will only get in the way of the distortion.

Fifth, attack the credibility of management in anonymous chat boards is the usual way to do this.

Sixth, create the illusion of a groundswell of concern. Get the short-sellers in a syndicate, call the SEC, research analysts, long investors, and press, and repeat your lies and distortion. If you do it enough and do it well, you can marshal powerful tools to bring about your outcome. Unknowingly, they become part of the game.

Seventh, get a class-action lawsuit. More sure to follow.

Eighth, go on the road and get every short-seller to pile on and pressure the stock down.

Ninth, keep reminding everyone that the shorts uncovered Enron. They are the smartest investors in the world, and if the company fights back, it must have something to hide.

Tenth, if everything goes according to plan, the stock goes down and you profit. And, as an added bonus, and this is their favorite part, if people figure out this is a game, go long and you ride it back up. And we have seen people coming out of our stock over the past two years who have played this game several times.

But we think the game has gone on long enough and it has got to be exposed for what it is. We believe our shareholders have been harmed, and it has interfered with our business. When we started this two years ago, or when this started two years, we believed that if we continued to correct the record and run the business we were doing the right thing for our company and the shareholders, but the manipulation has continued.

Let's understand where, who is behind this. These event-driven investors manage large pools of capital funded by wealthy investors, and their activities are completely unregulated and undisclosed. It's undisclosed and we believe it is damaging the investment savings of retail investors whether you invest directly or whether you invest through a fund. There's no transparency as to this trading activity and the financial motives. You can freely manipulate or freely execute the manipulation game without detection.

The most recent attacks, the well publicized $9 million BLX loan transfers generated a profit for those short the Allied story. Our accounting and disclosure surrounding this transaction were completely appropriate.

Sooner or later, the facts and the truth will prevail over the misinformation and innuendo. We proved that two years ago, and we will continue to provide proof through performance. But we are also going to work to expose the market manipulation activity whenever it occurs, and we're looking at every option available to us to protect the company and your shareholder value. We have a great company and a great future ahead of us.

■ ■ ■

In the two years since the speech, Greenlight had its own good performance. We survived a real bear market in 2002, with the S&P 500 falling 22 percent and the Nasdaq an even more vicious 31 percent, and we came out with a positive 7.7 percent return. The Allied short generated a 21 percent return on capital, and we made all our profits that year on our short sales. It was the first year we were not profitable on both longs and shorts. Eleven of our fifteen most profitable investments were shorts, as the short portfolio returned 65 percent on its capital invested. We needed them because we suffered large losses in long positions, particularly WorldCom and Tenet Healthcare.

The market turned up in 2003 and Greenlight returned 36.8 percent, with all the top fifteen winners being longs and the top seven losers, headed by Allied, being shorts. Our five largest longs heading into that year each went up at least 78 percent, which made Allied's 38 percent rise manageable. In fact, Allied went up slightly less than the rest of the short portfolio. It was a broad bull market with the S&P 500 advancing 28 percent and the Nasdaq rallying 50 percent. We ended the year with $1.8 billion under management.

■ ■ ■

As the months passed, we realized that Eichenwald had not made progress on a larger story. He was focused on his Enron book, and although he told us that he remained interested in the Allied/BLX story, we asked him to free us from the exclusive. He agreed, saying that he wasn't going to get to the article anytime soon. That was a big disappointment because we had given him a valuable exclusive for eight months.

We decided to approach *The Washington Post*, because the story of Allied, as a Washington, D.C., company abusing a federal agency, seemed natural for the newspaper. Steve Bruce, Jock Ferguson from Kroll, and I met with the reporters Jerry Knight and Terrence O'Hara. I had spoken to Knight three years earlier about Computer Learning Centers, another local company. He remembered, and I thought that would help me get the benefit of the doubt. Both had written about Allied previously. We met in a conference room next to the newsroom and spoke for about three hours. Ferguson and I made the same presentation that we made to Eichenwald and gave the reporters supporting documents.

Unlike Eichenwald, though, they didn't seem interested in reading anything. Actually, they were politely dismissive. Their message to us was, "Grow up—fraud at the SBA happens every day. Why should anybody care?" It seemed odd to me that *The Washington Post* would be so dismissive of a government-related fraud conducted by a local company. This seemed to be their beat.

"Do you know if the SBA is going to do anything?" O'Hara asked.

"We've given them the same information we've given you," I said. "Hopefully, they're going to pursue it."

As it turned out, this was the first of a number of meetings we initiated with a "Who's Who" of the financial media. Each declined the story in one of three ways. Some were like *The Washington Post*—that is, if we could show them that the government was cracking down, that would be news. Otherwise, they weren't interested. The second group would indicate that so much had been written about Allied and Greenlight that they didn't see what was new. We would respond that all the previous coverage was "he said, she said" and invited them to spend some time, independently research the facts—for which we could provide a road map—and determine for themselves and their audience whether Allied had acted badly. The third group would act as Eichenwald did initially. "I can't believe this. How could everyone else turn this down? We need to do more stories like this!" For this last group, months would pass. Inevitably, we would hear that they would get to it after they completed some other project. They never got to it.

Certainly, one of the biggest things I have learned from the Allied experience is the surprising reluctance of the media to dig into complicated financial stories. Even if the story is served up on a silver platter, there is not much interest. We needed someone able to do more than talk to us, talk to Allied, he said, she said. This story required investigative journalism. When Allied and we disagreed, someone needed to be willing to spend time, do the work, and come to an independent view on this complicated debate. There was simply nobody in the business press willing and able to do this.

On June 23, 2004, David Armstrong from *The Wall Street Journal* left me a message late in the afternoon, after I left for the day. He also called Bruce. By the time Bruce located me, it was too late to reach Armstrong before his deadline. It turns out that Allied had been notified it was under investigation by the SEC after all. Rather than announce the bad news themselves, again, they gave Armstrong, crusader against hedge-fund evil, the story. It was no surprise that Armstrong didn't reach out to me until after business hours. Armstrong's story positioned the announcement of the investigation as regulators paying heed to some noisy short-sellers who had been attacking the company for years. It was almost positioned as good news for Allied to have an opportunity to achieve vindication.

Allied put out a release confirming the SEC investigation. According to Walton:

> Over the last two years, we have consistently refuted frivolous allegations made by short-sellers based upon false and misleading information and distorted facts. We welcome the opportunity to fully cooperate with the SEC, provide all the facts, and demonstrate once and for all that the short-sellers' allegations are false. Allied Capital is a great company and as the facts are understood we expect to put this short attack behind us.

O'Hara covered the story in the next day's *Washington Post*. Again, the coverage made us the focus of the news. The story began:

> Allied Capital Corp.'s stock price fell 10 percent yesterday after the Washington financial services company disclosed a Securities and Exchange Commission inquiry involving its small-business lending affiliate. Allied officials said the agency's investigation was triggered by accusations made by short-sellers, who enter into risky agreements which make money only if a stock price falls. It was the second time in two years that Allied has become

embroiled in a public struggle with short-sellers, particularly New York's Greenlight Capital LLC and its manager David Einhorn. (©2004, *The Washington Post*. Reprinted with Permission.)

This was an SEC investigation, not a public struggle with short-sellers. I couldn't believe that "risky" nature of short-selling made it into the lead of the story. The article discussed the $9 million loan transfer and Allied's explanation that it wasn't a big deal. The article then reported we had investigated BLX and reported our findings to the SBA and quoted me explaining why the $9 million transaction was fraudulent, undisclosed, misleading and led to BLX and Allied inflating their results.

Walton was quoted in the *Post* discussing the short-sellers, "They've learned how to play the fiddle, and we want to break the strings." Rather tough talk from a guy who just received news that his company was the subject of an SEC investigation.

PART FOUR

How the System Works (and Doesn't)

CHAPTER 22

Hello, Who's There?

Later in the summer of 2004, Herb Greenberg, a reporter who had written several critical articles about Allied for TheStreet.com and CBS Marketwatch.com, called and asked if I paid my phone bill online.

"No," I said. "Why?"

"You should check to see if someone has opened an online account to get your phone records," he told me.

"How would I do that?"

Greenberg explained, "If someone else opened up an online account, if you try to open one yourself, it won't let you and will say that an account is already open."

"Why are you asking about this?"

Because it happened to him—he was calling his sources to see if the same thing had happened to any of them. I agreed to check, and when I tried to open an account at Verizon, my local phone service provider, there was no problem. In light of that, I forgot all about it.

About a week later, Jim Carruthers of Eastbourne called me at home. He asked me the same questions as Greenberg, telling me, "My cell phone and home phone records have been taken," he said.

Now, I was curious. While Carruthers held on our call, I checked my cell phone account. Again, no problem. Then I tried AT&T, my long-distance provider. It denied me access—someone had already created an online account. I asked my wife, Cheryl, about it. Nope, it wasn't her. Since we hadn't opened the account, someone else did. Whoever that "someone" was had obtained access to our entire calling history.

"Wow. I'm amazed that somebody would actually do this," I told Carruthers. I doubted anyone wanted to know how many times my wife calls her sister.

A couple of days later, Greenberg told me that Charles Gunther, a research analyst with Farmhouse Equity Research, who issued a report with a "Sell" rating on Allied, also had his records taken. I asked others at Greenlight and other people I knew to check. I found that Ed Rowley, who had been quite involved in the Allied matter working with Steve Bruce of our public relations firm Abernathy McGregor, had his cell phone records taken the same way. During my testimony, the SEC had asked me to identify Rowley and his role. In all likelihood, Allied complained about him. Brickman said that he already paid his phone bills online, so it wasn't possible for someone else to open an account for him, but said his bank notified him that someone had accessed his bank records using his Social Security number. I had never spoken with Gunther, but knew that Brickman had. The only thing connecting Greenberg, Gunther, Carruthers, Rowley, and me was Allied Capital. Equally indicative was the fact that none of Greenberg's sources on other topics reported phone records being taken.

Why might Allied might want our records? First, the company alleged various conspiracies among short-sellers, class-action lawyers, the media (in particular Greenberg), and Allied's former CEO, Gladstone. Additionally, I believe Allied was surprised at how much information we were able to gather about its investments and wondered whether it had a leak from the inside. Finally, Allied might have been looking for information about our personal lives so it might extort us or intimidate us into silence.

Was this what Walton meant when he promised shareholders at Allied's annual meeting in May 2004, "We are also going to work to expose the market manipulation activity whenever it occurs, and we're looking at every option available to us to protect the company and your shareholder value?"

Cheryl called AT&T. She learned that on December 7, 2003, a woman calling as "Cheryl Einhorn" used Cheryl's Social Security number to open an online billing account for our home phone. The records were sent to up4repo@aol.com. AT&T noted that they received a "bounce-back message" from that e-mail account on May 28, 2004.

Greenberg had already called his local FBI office in San Diego. The rest of us reported the incident to the agent assigned to Greenberg's case. It took the FBI a long time to make progress. The agent, Tedd Lindsey, was enthusiastic and diligent, but he needed to subpoena each of the phone companies for the records. It took seemingly forever to receive responses and compile the information. Eventually, Greenberg became frustrated by the lack of progress. He decided to write an article about the experience. In a February 2005 column, he wrote, "The only thing any of these people appear to have in common—me included—is that they've all been snooping around Allied Capital," referring to the other people whose records were stolen.

In this column, Greenberg said that someone opened his online phone account on July 8, 2004. Greenberg wrote that it happened only "six hours (coincidence of coincidences) after I wrote a piece headlined, 'Is Allied Capital's Dividend Vulnerable?' The piece quoted Farmhouse Equity Research analyst Charles Gunther, who had initiated coverage of Allied with a 'sell.'"

Greenberg also wrote that he had no evidence that Allied was involved. However, he wrote, "Joan Sweeney, Allied's chief operating officer—and normally its chief spokesperson—didn't return two calls I placed to her in recent weeks, even though she was in the office both times. The most recent call, last week, included a voicemail with an explanation of what had happened and several questions. It was followed by an e-mail." Greenberg expected this to become a national story. It didn't. The media did not take interest in a story about one of their own being spied on by a subject of critical articles.

Meanwhile, David Armstrong from *The Wall Street Journal* tried to re-engage us. But this time we chose not to help—too much water under the bridge. As mentioned previously, he had ambushed us in January 2003 before publishing the news that we would be investigated; failed to write an article a few months later after spending hours with us (possibly because he couldn't bash us); and ambushed us again the night before he wrote that the SEC was investigating Allied, but focused the article on short-sellers rather than the investigation. Now, he asked about someone's hiring Kroll to investigate Allied. We wanted no part of him.

Armstrong also contacted Carruthers for his article. His firm, Eastbourne Capital, was also wary of Armstrong and would accept questions only in writing. Armstrong's questions made Carruthers suspicious. In particular, he was bothered by a question about his relationship with a former BLX employee, who had become his key source. Shortly after Carruthers noticed that his phone records had been taken, the former BLX employee, who until that time had a pleasant relationship with Carruthers, called and was extremely angry with Carruthers. Plainly, BLX got to him. But how did BLX know he was talking to Carruthers? How did Armstrong know to ask about this relationship? Someone had stolen Carruthers' phone records. Things were getting curiouser and curiouser.

Armstrong also was strangely suspicious about Brickman's communications with Gunther. Brickman decided to engage him, despite the evidence of Armstrong's bias. Not only did Brickman believe he was right, he thought he could convince others. Not only does he think it, he's done it: I believe he convinced Houck to change his mind and approach Allied about the SBA loan parking. Now, Brickman took on Armstrong.

That made Brickman the subject of a front-page article in *The Wall Street Journal* on September 24, 2004. The article, with the headline "A Retiree in Texas Gives a Firm Grief with Web Postings," identified Brickman as having made over 2,000 postings on Allied's Yahoo! message board under the moniker *tellmeitsnottopsecret*, having provided information to the SEC and convincing two securities analysts to turn negative on the stock. In response to Brickman's claims of management dishonesty, Armstrong wrote, "Ms. Sweeney says she and Allied have always been truthful."

Walton was quoted as saying, "Brickman works in concert with short-sellers led by David Einhorn to spread false or misleading information about Allied Capital." The article said that Eliot Spitzer began looking into whether Greenlight had manipulated Allied's shares in early 2003. No charges had been brought, but the inquiry "is still open," the article said. That part really upset me, because we hadn't heard from the attorney general's office for more than a year, and it hadn't really been much of an inquiry in the first place.

The article also retold the story of the SBA loan-parking arrangement. While BLX CEO Tannenhauser said the company agreed to the loan shift after Allied said it would buy back any loans that went sour, Sweeney offered a new story. Now, she said Allied hadn't promised to buy back any bad loans, only to *consider* doing so. I suspect she realized that having a secret *put agreement* that isn't taken into account in the financial statements was a problem.

In addition to Brickman's being a regular poster on the Yahoo! message board, Allied seemed to be keenly aware of Yahoo! In our initial call with Suzanne Sparrow from Allied's Investor Relations department in April 2002, I thought it was odd for her to lead off with a discussion of how she carefully watched the Allied message board on Yahoo! It is unusual for managements to express interest in anonymous message boards. Sparrow added, "We have a policy that we are not permitted to chat, and I think it has probably served us well." I told her that I didn't spend time reading message boards.

Shortly after my speech in May 2002, several people told me that a lively discussion emerged on the Allied message board. There were way too many posts to read them all, but a few were brought to my attention. One poster identified himself as "Dave Einhorn." This was not me, but I give the guy credit because he had an excellent sense of humor. At one point, the fake Dave Einhorn even suggested that my Allied speech was the result of a bar bet. If the fake David Einhorn is reading this, feel free to contact me. I will take you out for a beer.

Based on Sparrow's initial comments and my observations of the board immediately following my speech, I suspect Allied or its agents were also posting on the Yahoo! message board. Certainly, they were focused on it, because Walton routinely complained about the board. One poster under the name "stop_theft2002" posted repeated requests for investors to agitate for the SEC to act against Greenlight. They read as if a lawyer wrote them. The posts were headed, "How to suggest SEC look at Greenlight," "SEC: Bring Sunlight to Shorts," "SEC: Did Greenlight Manipulate?" "Tell SEC about Greenlight" and "SEC: Investigate Greenlight." Though the postings had different headings, the message was repeated verbatim many times between May and October 2002. It read:

We wonder whether Greenlight's actions (speaking engagements, publishing white papers, issuing press releases regarding issuance of their white papers, etc.) were designed to manipulate the price of

Allied Capital stock. If you would like to suggest to the SEC that they investigate the possible market manipulation by Greenlight Capital, I suggest that you use the following addresses. A simple letter or email suggesting that the SEC should investigate the possible manipulation of Allied Capital's stock by Greenlight Capital, and perhaps giving a few facts, should be adequate.

The message closed with detailed instructions to best reach the SEC and ended with "Thank you." It lacked the individuality, humor, sarcasm, personality or lunacy of most personally posted messages.

■ ■ ■

In the fall of 2004, Sydran Foods, another Allied investment, filed for bankruptcy, and court records revealed that the company began its decline in 1999. The records stated, "By the end of 2000, significant declines in sales at the Debtors' Burger King restaurants caused a liquidity crisis and defaults under the Debtors' agreements with their principal lenders and under the leases with the Holding Companies." On November 13, 2001, Sydran completed a restructuring wherein Allied exchanged debt for equity. Nonetheless, Allied carried its investment in Sydran at cost through June 2002. Over the following year, Allied gradually wrote the investment towards zero (see Table 22.1). This was another example of Allied taking its write-downs gradually and too late.

■ ■ ■

On December 27, 2004, I got a phone call from our trader alerting me that Allied just announced that the U.S. attorney for the District of Columbia had launched a criminal investigation of Allied and BLX. The company once again blamed short-sellers for the news. Allied issued a statement that said the investigation "appears to pertain to matters similar to those allegations made by short-sellers over the past two and one-half years."

However, this time there was no reason to blame us. We had not contacted the U.S. attorney. The SEC is a civil regulatory agency and can commence civil investigations and actions. However, it has no criminal prosecution authority. If it finds evidence of criminal behavior, it may refer the

Table 22.1 Sydran Foods

Date	Debt Investments		Equity Investments		Comments
	Cost	Value	Cost	Value	
December 31, 1998	11,881	11,881			Initial investment
December 31, 1999	11,674	11,674	266	266	Deteriorates; no write-down
March 31, 2000	12,642	12,642	266	266	Deteriorates; no write-down
June 30, 2000	12,652	12,652	—	—	Deteriorates; no write-down
September 30, 2000	12,973	12,973			Deteriorates; no write-down
September 30, 2001	12,973	12,973			Deteriorates; no write-down
December 31, 2001	12,973	12,973	3,909	3,909	Recapitalization; added money; no write-down
March 31, 2002	12,973	12,973	3,909	3,909	Deteriorates; no write-down
June 30, 2002	12,973	12,973	3,909	3,909	Deteriorates; no write-down
September 30, 2002	12,973	12,973	3,909	—	First write-down
December 31, 2002	12,973	9,949	3,909	—	Gradual write-down
March 31, 2003	12,973	9,949	3,909	—	
June 30, 2003	12,973	6,646	3,909	—	Gradual write-down
September 30, 2003	12,973	50	3,909	—	Almost complete write-down
December 31, 2003	12,973	50	3,909	—	
December 31, 2004					Bankruptcy; $18.2 MM realized loss

Note: Dollars in thousands

matter to the U.S. attorney's at the Justice Department. We didn't know what the SEC found in its investigation, but whatever made them pass this to the U.S. attorney we considered it to be a good sign.

While Allied's press release announcing the SEC inquiry had read, "We welcome the opportunity to . . . demonstrate once and for all that the short-sellers' allegations are false," Allied's release announcing the criminal investigation did not include a similar "welcome."

Over on the Yahoo! message board, the most aggressive poster in defending Allied's views and attacking me personally posted as *sharonanncrayne*. This poster, claiming to be an individual investor, made 1,370 posts between May 20, 2002 (five days after my speech) and November 17, 2004. Many were quite vicious, and I suspected from their detail that they came from an Allied insider, trying to walk a fine line about providing inside information. Once the criminal investigation was announced, *sharonanncrayne* never appeared again. While we can't know for sure, it made sense that she was an insider acting outside the lines and would stop at the sound of a criminal investigation.

Finally, two years after my speech and immediately following the criminal investigation announcement, a major media outlet actually looked at the debate between Allied and us and picked our side. *USA Today* posted on its Web site an article by Thor Valdmanis with a headline that read, "Is Allied Capital Just Another Victim of Unscrupulous Short-Sellers?" The Web site indicated that the article was intended for page 1B of the paper's December 30, 2004, edition. The article talked about the recent investigations and Allied's blaming us for "a vicious disinformation campaign." The article cited a person with knowledge of the Allied case, pointing out that it isn't unusual for the SEC to initiate a probe and then ask for Justice Department help.

"Businesses often go to their graves blaming short-sellers," Valdmanis wrote, before concluding that "short-sellers, who often produce the best Wall Street research, can be the market's first line of defense against corporate fraud." After seeing the story online the night before, the next morning I bought a *USA Today*. The article wasn't on page 1B. It wasn't anywhere in the business section. It wasn't in the main section. In fact, it wasn't anywhere. I went back to the paper's Web site—the article was gone.

In writing this book, I contacted Valdmanis, who left the paper shortly after the story was pulled, and asked him what happened. He said, "I can't remember my editors ever explaining why the story was zapped from the Web site (and didn't run in the print edition). But it is fair to say that kind of thing almost never happened. All I know is that Lanny (Davis) was working extremely hard at that time behind the scenes to burnish Allied Capital's image. And we all know Lanny can be very persuasive—particularly in the face of uncomfortable facts."

CHAPTER 23

Whistle-Blower

The federal government doesn't like being ripped off—or at least doesn't like the humiliation that comes with discovering it is being ripped off. The government was certainly humiliated during the Civil War, when many war contractors were overcharging it for inferior goods. So Congress passed the False Claims Act during the war, which is commonly known as the whistle-blower law. It allows people who discover fraud against the federal government to report it, and, if wrongdoing is found, to share in the money the government collects. The law also protects whistle-blowers from retribution.

Most false claim suits involve either Medicare or defense contractor fraud. The *qui tam* (the Latin abbreviation for "Who sues on behalf of the king as well as for himself") provision of the law would allow Greenlight to file suit against Allied/BLX on behalf of the federal government and to share in any money that it recovered from BLX's fraud. Whistle-blowers can receive from 10 percent to 35 percent of the recovery.

Between Kroll's work and our own, we had a well-documented case of fraud at BLX. Under the False Claims Act, the case is filed under seal, which

223

would prompt the Justice Department to investigate it and decide whether to intervene. If it intervenes, it takes over the case. If not, we would have the option to pursue the case ourselves. As we were preparing to file a case, Brickman was updating me on his latest discoveries of fraud at BLX and venting his frustration with the government, when he said, "I'm going to file a whistle-blower case." He hired a lawyer to pursue it.

That was a problem, because there could be only one case. Under federal rules, you have to be the first case to file or your case gets dismissed. Rather than have a competition to see who would file a suit first, Greenlight's lawyer indicated it was permissible to have multiple whistle-blowers in the same suit. I called Brickman back, admitting we were pursuing the same thing and suggested that we team up. Happily, he agreed.

Brickman researched dozens of additional apparently fraudulent BLX loans. To detail them all would be frighteningly tedious. However, here are a few lowlights:

- In Michigan, there were a number of loans to affiliates of Imad Daeibes (whose name is spelled differently in various documents). One of the bad loans in the loan-parking arrangement had been to Dibe's Petro Mart. In pursuit of collecting on that bad loan, Allied took legal action and obtained a judgment in June 2002. Daeibes failed to show up for a creditor's exam, and an arrest warrant was issued. Notwithstanding this history, BLX extended at least five additional loans in transactions that involved Daeibes. For example, on December 8, 2003, Daeibes purchased a gas station for $350,000 and resold it the same day to Tawfiq Alfakhouri for $1.2 million. BLX financed the inflated purchase. This was an obvious sham transaction called a property flip. Several of the other loans appeared to be related to similar property flips.
- There were several additional fraudulent loans involving Abdulla Al-Jufairi in additional property flips and in "piggyback" loans, where the SBA was placed in a subordinated position. Brickman also found evidence of loans where the borrower didn't make the required equity injection. The SBA requires equity in its loans to ensure that the buyer has "skin in the game." In one court record, Daryoush Zahraie was asked about a $240,000 down payment. He said it wasn't made due to a verbal agreement at closing. In the same case, Zahraie testified that "Pat Harrington [BLX executive vice president in Detroit] and Al'Jafairi were sometimes business partners and had perpetrated

fraudulent mortgage transactions in the past where Al'Jafairi greatly profited by the transactions and where the price of the transaction in question, including this one, was inflated because of his wrongful dealing with Plaintiff executive, Pat Harrington."

- In New York, the EPA cited White-Sun Cleaners for major environmental violations on April 12, 2001. The next month, BLX issued an SBA guaranteed loan for $1,330,000 for the property. Initially, 34th Street Associates owned it. The U.S. Department of Labor had sued one of 34th Street's general partners for mob connections and breach of duty as trustee of Teamsters Union 363. In August 2001, 34th Street Associates sold the property to White-Sun Cleaners, the tenant. BLX issued a replacement loan to finance the purchase. In August 2003, BLX assigned the note to the SBA because White-Sun Cleaners defaulted.

- In Illinois, BLX issued a $990,000 SBA loan to Inter Auto Inc. to bail out Witold Osinski, a borrower already in default on a $280,000 first loan to a local savings association. This violated SBA policy by transferring a credit loss from a private lender to the government. The loan was supposedly made to a body shop. Inside was an insurance scam. In 2004, Mr. Osinski was indicted for paying people to stage false auto accidents and submitting fraudulent claims to insurance companies. He reached a plea agreement with the U.S. attorney's office, agreeing to cooperate on another case in return for a reduced sentence. He received up to 71 months in prison. Ingrid Osinski, his wife, pled guilty to one count of Frauds and Swindles and was ordered to pay $450,000 in restitution and sentenced to thirty-three months in prison.

These were just a few examples of Brickman's discoveries. In January 2005, Kroll had a follow-up conversation with the SBA. Kroll reported that the Office of Inspector General's (OIG's) investigators, along with SEC investigators, were working together and had looked into many of BLX loan files and found many problems with its operating practices. The probe was focused on origination fraud, rather than accounting fraud. The OIG interviewed two former BLX loan origination employees, who provided good evidence of improper loan origination practices. The head SBA investigator met with the U.S. attorney in Washington, D.C., in early December to discuss their findings.

■ ■ ■

I thought Allied's board should be made aware of our findings, so I wrote its directors a letter in March 2005, informing them that BLX engaged in a huge fraud against the SBA and United States taxpayers. I said that BLX maintained its loan origination volume by repeatedly flouting SBA lending regulations, including using inflated appraisals, failing to verify equity injections, permitting impermissible property splits and property flips and committing other violations. Allied used the fraud to receive income from BLX and increase its valuation of BLX. I also wrote the directors about my stolen phone records and reminded them of their obligation to investigate and ensure that those engaged in this sort of misconduct don't serve in a management capacity in a publicly traded company or engage in this conduct at the company's direction.

I explained to the directors how management had established a pattern of dishonesty. Walton and Sweeney were charismatic and I considered it possible that they had deceived the directors as they had Allied's shareholders and others. Now that the company was under investigation, board members might begin questioning management. Perhaps they would now take our charges more seriously, and my letter was an attempt to open a dialogue with them.

I pointed the directors to Sweeney's comments in the February 2003 conference call denying that she knew why, or even if, the SBA was gathering information about BLX. She had said that only days after she personally executed the agreement to unwind the loan-parking arrangement, while BLX simultaneously reimbursed the SBA $5.3 million in related guarantee payments for the parked loans. I noted the shoddy disclosure relating to the whole circumstance by saying, "This raises serious issues about the honesty of management with its shareholders and perhaps with the board. As the board of directors could not have sanctioned such public misrepresentations, the question you need to ask is, are they lying to you as well?"

A week later, Brooks Browne, the chairman of Allied's Audit Committee, sent me a dismissive letter. The board said it asked Allied's management and outside counsel for a response to Greenlight's claims of misconduct. According to Browne, the information from Allied's management did not support our accusations. Moreover, the letter didn't mention any of the specific concerns I raised, including the theft of my phone records. Instead, it noted Greenlight's short position against the company, implicitly attacking my credibility. The letter said if I could "provide (the board) with specific information upon which you base your allegations" then the Audit Committee could "determine whether further action is warranted." I thought my letter was rather specific. It sure didn't sound like they were terribly interested in getting to the bottom of the matter.

In Allied's first SEC quarterly filing (for the first quarter of 2005), after receipt of my letter, the company dramatically reduced the summary information about BLX's performance that it had provided since the middle of 2002. There was still enough information to track how much income Allied recognized from BLX and how fast BLX's debt grew. However, Allied stopped disclosing origination volumes; revenue; earnings before interest, taxes, and management fees (EBITM); net income; the size of the loan portfolio; and the amount of residuals, among other things.

■ ■ ■

Brickman wrote a lengthy letter in June 2005 to Janet Tasker, the SBA associate administrator for lender oversight. Tasker was responsible for renewing BLX's preferred lender status. The letter detailed many dubious loans and said that to protect the SBA and taxpayers from further losses, BLX's preferred lender status should not be renewed. Despite the evidence, the SBA renewed the license for another six months. This was unusual because renewals were usually for one or two years.

Meanwhile, Brickman continued digging into BLX's loans. He discovered a large number of dubious shrimp-boat loans. In fact, the company became the major lender of SBA guaranteed loans in the shrimp-boat industry. The data showed that BLX made no shrimp-boat loans in 1998, but made 20 percent of all such loans in 1999. That number climbed to 58 percent in 2000 and 75 percent in 2001 and 2002.

The sudden and rapid increase in the percentage of loans was particularly suspicious because cheaper shrimp from fish farms, foreign competition, higher fuel prices, and falling shrimp prices hurt the industry operating out of the Gulf of Mexico. Moreover, SBA rules required shrimp-boat loans to have a certificate from the National Marine Fisheries Service (NMFS), indicating that the NMFS declined to provide assistance to the borrower but had no objection to the SBA's providing a loan. However, the NMFS determined that it would not provide certificates due to the overcapacity of the industry.

Brickman obtained a representative letter from the NMFS to BLX, which read, "My management also expresses the opinion that none of the fisheries in the country needs additional capacity and no Government agency should be extending financing which increases harvesting capacity. In this regard, we will be unable to provide you with documentation of our consent to the proposed financing." While other lenders responded by abandoning the industry, BLX stepped into the void and issued loans, despite the missing certificate. Over 70 percent of BLX's shrimp-boat loans eventually defaulted, and most of these loans came out of the Richmond office of the convicted felon McGee.

Brickman found one case where BLX made a $1.1 million boat loan in 2002 to Hung Vu. Hoa Nguyen witnessed the loan. Hung Vu defaulted in 2004, and BLX bought the boat with a "credit bid" of $1,000. Brickman's work indicated that the real value was about $300,000. BLX then made a $750,000 loan to Hoa Minh Nguyen on the same boat. The second loan allowed BLX to delay recognizing a loss and increased the liability to the U.S. taxpayer. (In an interview, Hung Vu indicated that he was a mechanic and never made any equity injection. In fact, the boat belonged to two of his uncles who already had financial problems on other boat loans.)

Brickman also found that BLX made a $480,000 SBA-backed loan to Master Chase Enterprises for two old shrimp boats in 2001. When the loan showed strain, BLX tried to defer the problem by making a second SBA-backed loan for $40,000. After the boats' owners filed for bankruptcy in 2003, BLX repossessed the boats and sold them for a total of $60,000 in January 2004. Brickman estimated that once fees and other costs were figured in, the loans had a loss of about $500,000. He also noted that the SBA had not taken a charge-off on the $480,000 loan as of the end of 2006. This was typical of BLX: delay charge-offs in order to manipulate SBA lender statistics.

Brickman generated detailed and well-documented write-ups for every defective loan he found. He discovered abundant evidence of impropriety. He concluded that BLX violated many SBA policies, including making loans to borrowers who were already in default on debt to other lenders; not verifying equity injections; inflating collateral values; and using false or doctored bills of sale to support fictitious transactions.

Even when the SBA happened to find problems with BLX, it favored a "lender-friendly" approach. On November 4, 2004, SBA's OIG provided

BLX with a list of "paid in full" loans that had been improperly paid off with the proceeds of a new SBA loan. BLX responded on November 15, and conceded that the loans were ineligible and volunteered to repay the government for two of the loans. The SBA Loan Programs Division responded that it ". . . appreciated the lender's offer to repay the guaranties . . ." but that it was imposing too harsh a penalty on itself and recommended a "repair" instead.

In one of the loans, Yogi Hospitality purchased a Ramada Inn in Petersburg, Virginia, from Host and Cook, Inc. in December 2000. The SBA loans to both entities were originated in BLX's Richmond office, headed by McGee. In the documentation, BLX had failed to identify the loan as a change-of-ownership transaction or that there was an existing SBA loan to the seller. In response to the SBA's suggestive e-mail, BLX decided not to reimburse the SBA for that loan and claimed the borrower had made all principal and interest payments for three and a half years until March 2004, when the borrower ran into financial difficulties.

In contrast, a subsequent report by the SBA's OIG found that six months after funding, BLX granted a deferment so the borrower made no principal payments from June 2001 to July 2002 and during other periods. Further, "the lender also neglected to mention" that the loan was a $1.33 million second mortgage behind a $1.6 million first mortgage held by Richmond Bank, and also failed to mention the property had been appraised at $3.6 million at origination, but had been reappraised to only $940,000 in August 2004. The SBA loan was a complete loss.

■ ■ ■

Brickman and Greenlight filed a "whistle-blower" suit relating to the shrimp boat loans in December 2005 under seal, as required, so that the government can conduct a confidential investigation before notifying the defendants. Due to the fact that this litigation is currently on appeal, there are some aspects that I am not permitted to discuss at this point. As a result, I have limited the narrative and excluded parts of the chronology, documents, and interactions with the government. I don't believe any of the excluded material is exculpatory to Allied or BLX in any way. But it is important for you to know that this discussion is not quite the full story.

Greenlight's lawyer and I flew to Atlanta (where the case was filed) to meet with Justice Department lawyers and an investigator from the

SBA's OIG. Under the False Claims Act, it is standard protocol for them to meet with the "relators," as the whistle-blowers are called. They met with Brickman a few weeks later. After some basic questions about me (they wanted my resume), what we do at Greenlight and our relationship with Brickman, I walked them through our problems with Allied and the company's long campaign of attacking us. I gave them the whole history. The meeting lasted for about an hour and a half.

A month after our meeting, our lawyer heard from the Justice Department lawyers, who, after consulting with the SBA, were under the misimpression that the entire loss from BLX across the entire program was only $3 million! That figure made no sense—it should have been in the tens or even hundreds of millions of dollars. The Kroll report alone found more fraud than that, and those were only a small percentage of the company's loans. The fraud was certainly more prevalent and damaging to taxpayers than $3 million. Dissatisfied with this figure, Brickman found out the losses. It took him a while, but paperwork, government bureaucracy, and time have never hindered him. He filed a series of Freedom of Information Act (FOIA) requests to the SBA relating to BLX defaults.

Greenlight also filed a few FOIA requests. We asked for access to BLX's regulatory filings. The SBA denied this request because release of the information "may pose harm to the lender." In contrast, banks and insurance companies also must make regulatory filings. These filings are public documents. As a result, Greenlight appealed to the SBA and argued, "[We] believe that there is a public interest in releasing this information that outweighs any potential harm to this particular lender, as [we are] investigating whether this lender has committed fraud against the SBA." The SBA denied our appeal.

In 2003, the SBA had announced that it would create risk-ratings to monitor individual lenders. So now we requested that the SBA release the risk-rating and related analysis for BLX. The SBA denied our access again, for the same reason. It also denied our appeal.

Eventually, the SBA provided Brickman with access to BLX's loan history. It took him months to get clarifying information. He also found a database of SBA loans at the University of Missouri School of Journalism. We were able to extract the BLX loans and sorted them by year of origination and status. What we found was even beyond what we expected (see Table 23.1).

Table 23.1   Includes Loans Originated by Allied Capital SBLC, BLX Financial Services, Inc. and Business Loan Center

Loan Approval Date	Loans Issued	Defaulted Loans	As % of Issued	Defaulted Loans in Liquidation	As % of Defaults	Loans Outstanding	As % of Issued	Charge-Offs	As % of Issued
1999	$ 237,002	$ 57,109	24.1%	$ 32,065	56.1%	$ 68,968	29.1%	$ 9,584	4.0%
2000	317,830	82,957	26.1%	55,213	66.6%	143,729	45.2%	11,051	3.5%
2001	498,276	97,273	19.5%	79,471	81.7%	249,797	50.1%	6,226	1.2%
Subtotal	1,053,107	237,339	22.5%	166,750	70.3%	462,494	43.9%	26,861	2.6%
2002	567,991	83,281	14.7%	69,786	83.8%	304,619	53.6%	4,789	0.8%
2003	371,588	35,059	9.4%	31,421	89.6%	238,512	64.2%	920	0.2%
2004	304,334	12,079	4.0%	10,536	87.2%	252,488	83.0%	414	0.1%
2005	327,913	3,597	1.1%	2,401	66.8%	304,930	93.0%	1,195	0.4%
Total (1999–2005)	2,624,933	371,355	14.1%	280,894	75.6%	1,563,042	59.5%	34,179	1.3%

Note: Dollars in thousands

SBA guarantee: 75% = $278 million

Lower defaults due to lack of seasoning

Most defaulted loans linger "in liquidation"

Small charge-off's due to non-resolution of defaulted loans

Sixty days after a loan becomes delinquent, the SBA honors its guarantee by "purchasing the guarantee." The "Purchased Loans" column shows the loans where the SBA did that. The SBA only has to pay on the guaranteed portion, so its actual outlay is generally 75 percent of the purchased loans. After the SBA purchases the guarantee, BLX continues to try to collect on the loan. During that period, the loan is in a limbo status called "liquidation." When BLX resolves the loan, it remits 75 percent of whatever it recovers after expenses back to the SBA. At that point, the SBA charges-off any remaining balance.

The SBA data showed that in BLX's oldest loans (1999–2001), the SBA paid up an average of 22.5 percent of the time. The "Outstanding Balance" column shows that from those years 43.9 percent of the loans remained outstanding. The high purchase rate combined with a significant amount of remaining balances suggested that the eventual default rate could eventually reach 30 percent or more. The data showed that in more recent years, there have been fewer defaults, probably because there has been less time for defaults to develop. Since 1998, the SBA has paid out almost $280 million (75 percent of $371 million) in loan guarantees on BLX loans. That's almost *one hundred times* more than the Justice Department found or was told by the SBA.

We suspected that the SBA's inaccurate claim of small losses might have come from the agency's not regularly charging-off the loans that went bad, but it also might have been someone within the SBA trying to protect BLX. About 75 percent of all the BLX loans where the SBA paid the guarantee had not been charged-off on the agency's books. The loans instead remained in liquidation. It was up to BLX, not the SBA, to determine when it had completed every effort to collect. Of course, many bankruptcies take time to resolve. It can take years to resolve a complicated disaster like Enron, satisfy all the creditors, and handle all the things needed to reorganize or liquidate a company. However, these SBA loans are much simpler loans to convenience stores, gas stations, car washes, and motels. They are generally backed by a single property and a personal guarantee. When the loans default, it shouldn't be a long process to foreclose on the property, hold an auction, and pursue the personal guarantee. It's hard to see why this should normally take more than a year.

The simple matter was that the SBA wasn't making its lenders charge-off the loans. This allowed the SBA to defer losses on its books—making the entire program look better than it was. Standard government accounting procedures would require the SBA to book its losses when it pays out on the guarantee. The SBA doesn't report the results of its program on that basis. I suspect if it did, Congress would better see the enormous risk the program creates for taxpayers.

The effect of the SBA's policy is that unscrupulous operators like BLX can defer losses on their own books for years. As long as BLX claimed it was trying to collect, it accrued annual servicing fees that it would get to eventually deduct from any recovery it passed back to the SBA. Carruthers heard from a former BLX employee that the company would sometimes create an inflated appraisal for the file to justify its carrying value and then hold the defaulted asset indefinitely, sometimes leasing it for "rental income" instead of liquidating it. Worse, Brickman found loans where the borrower filed and exited bankruptcy and even though the SBA debt was discharged, the loans remained classified as "in liquidation" rather than charged-off. It is hard to see how either the SBA or BLX was following its respective accounting rules.

By leaving the defaulted loans in the purgatory status of "liquidation" indefinitely, BLX was able to claim it had a low "loss rate," which it touted to regulators, the securitization market, and investors as evidence that its portfolio performed adequately (recall that BLX claimed to have less than a 1 percent average annual loss rate). BLX also structured its securitizations to permit it to repurchase defaulted loans out of the collateral pool, reducing the reported losses in the pools, but leaving the defaulted loans on BLX's books. Not only that, but on the few loans that it did charge-off, BLX had a relatively high recovery rate. This could easily have been a voluntary decision by the company, where loans with a good recovery were posted and resolved, while those with little chance of recovery lingered. Some of the good recoveries may have come by engineering property sales to new buyers financed by fresh loans.

The SBA measures success by how many loans it originates, how many businesses it helps. Every year it puts out a press release proclaiming the amount of support it provides. The SBA also is often criticized when it doesn't make enough loans fast enough, such as after Hurricane Katrina. I believe the SBA took a "lender-friendly" attitude toward BLX because the company, by pumping out the loans, was making the agency look good. It also didn't hurt that Allied, BLX and/or their high-priced lawyers aggressively lobbied the agency to ignore complaints from profit-motivated short-sellers, as we heard repeatedly from many regulators.

When we demonstrated that the losses far exceeded $3 million, the Justice Department continued its investigation into our *qui tam* complaint. The department has ninety days to decide if it will intervene, but it commonly asks for extensions, which it did with us several times in order to complete its investigation. We could have rejected their request, but that would mean we would have to pursue the case on our own. So we gave them more time.

After Brickman tabulated the SBA data on BLX's loan performance, he sent a second letter to Janet Tasker, the SBA lender oversight administrator, in December. The SBA set benchmarks for the maximum amount of delinquent loans (11 percent), defaults (9 percent), and loans in liquidation (7 percent) that a lender could have to remain in the program. Brickman estimated, using SBA's definitions and methods, that the delinquency rate exceeded 17 percent, the default rate exceeded 13 percent (and could be closer to 17 percent under some assumptions) and the liquidation rate also exceeded 13 percent.

BLX was far worse than other SBA-backed lenders. Brickman calculated that about 13 percent of the SBA's guarantee payments on defaulted loans nationwide were on BLX loans in 2004, despite BLX having less than a 4 percent share of national originations. Nonetheless, the SBA, again, renewed BLX as a preferred lender at the end of 2005. We passed the data showing BLX's astronomical default rate to Jesse Eisinger at *The Wall Street Journal*. He wrote about it on December 28, 2005. Eisinger reported that Allied said that Brickman's numbers were "wrong." However, they weren't materially different from Allied's figures, which showed a default rate of 11.25 percent, a level still far in excess of the SBA's 9 percent limit, even though the rate was depressed by including many recently originated loans that hadn't had much time to default.

Eisinger reported that the SBA renewed BLX as a preferred lender by excluding the loans originated by Allied Capital Express, supposedly because Allied, rather than BLX, originated them. The agency also excluded the shrimp-boat loans, supposedly due to an industry-wide slump. As Eisinger put it in his article, "BLX also worked the refs, and the SBA kindly moved the goal post closer."

■ ■ ■

I went to Atlanta in March 2006 and further discussed the shrimp-boat fraud with a larger group of Justice Department lawyers. (Brickman, again, went down separately in May.) The SBA also sat in on the meeting. I once again needed to explain who I was, what Greenlight was, and how BLX defrauded the SBA.

At the meeting, the investigator for the SBA's OIG, Kevin Kupperbusch, asked me how we obtained so much detail on the shrimp-boat loans. He asked if we had the loan records. "No, we don't have the loan files," I said. The detailed information came from a variety of other sources. "You have to match stuff up," I said, explaining that they needed to sit down and match up the loans to our allegations of specific lending violations. Our suit contained a laundry list of ways BLX flouted SBA rules: fraudulent appraisals, not properly collecting on the loans, making multiple loans to one borrower, not verifying the equity injections, and so forth. We included a disclosure statement with all this information when we filed the lawsuit, so the government had it. They just didn't have it in the room we were sitting in.

As for the lack of a certificate from the National Marine Fisheries Service, Kupperbusch speculated that it might not be a problem, because he thought that the SBA decided in 1998 that a certificate was no longer required for a loan. Though the SBA's standard operating procedure specifically required the letter, Kupperbusch implausibly suggested that, perhaps, the error was that no one bothered to change the regulation on the books.

Of course, BLX had been by far the largest originator of SBA shrimp-boat loans since that time. I wondered whether this might be just another SBA stonewall. Afterward, Brickman sent a FOIA request to the SBA asking for any records indicating the agency had changed the rule. The SBA's response was that there were no records of any changes.

At the meeting, I tried to draw their attention to the pattern of abuse. BLX made many of the loans to Vietnamese-Americans. "There are forty-five loans to Nguyen at a particular address in Biloxi," Kupperbusch said. "One of the things I have run into is that Vietnamese families often live on their boats and their address is the pier. They all use the same address. The SBA is very familiar with Na Nguyen. She had an insurance company there also. She is one of the few who are bilingual, and since the shrimpers may be out for a month at a time, when the lenders need to contact the boat operators, she is the intermediary." Kupperbusch said the SBA officer he talked to said they don't believe the Vietnamese fleet is one business, but rather a cluster of families. However, Kupperbusch acknowledged that there were multiple loans that went to the same Social Security number. He said he believed "that this was a good, solid allegation that may lead to criminal fraud."

The meeting lasted for about an hour and a half. After it was over, the lead Justice Department lawyer walked me to the elevator and said that the SBA was pushing back hard against our complaint in a manner she's never seen from a government agency. I asked her if the pushback was potentially corrupt. She said she didn't think so, but the SBA sees itself as a "lender-friendly" agency.

Then she reminded me that the SBA was actually *her client*, but she was clearly bothered by its pushback.

As I left, she said, "As a taxpayer, this boils my blood."

Mine, too.

■ ■ ■

In early September 2006, we received news that the Justice Department declined to intervene in our whistle-blower suit. It didn't say why. I speculated that the SBA "pushback" had won the day. Although we were frustrated by this decision, we believed that the evidence was overwhelming that BLX violated the False Claims Act and caused tens of millions of dollars in damages to taxpayers. So we decided to continue the suit on our own.

The complaint was unsealed a few weeks later, and the judge ordered us to serve it on the defendants by the end of the year. Ordinarily, the statute gives 120 days, but the judge said that it had been on her time clock since 2005 and she wanted more progress. Our lawyers prepared an amended complaint, and with leniency from the judge, we filed and served it in January 2007 on the defendants Business Loan Express LLC, Robert Tannenhauser, Matthew McGee, George Harrigan, and (John) Does 1–100. Actually, it was hard to serve it on Tannenhauser. He avoided the process servers for several days and failed to meet them, even though he agreed on the phone several times to do so. Then, he took off on a vacation to Indonesia.

CHAPTER 24

A Naked Attack

On August 11, 2005, Patrick Byrne, the CEO of the Internet retailer Overstock.com, called Greenlight to speak with me. I was out of the office at a meeting, so the call was passed to Alexandra Jennings, our analyst who covered Overstock, although we had been out of the stock for months by then. We briefly held a small short position in Overstock that we closed out at a profit in January 2005.

When Jennings heard she had a call from Byrne, her antennae went up. About an hour before, Overstock had issued a press release announcing it was suing Rocker Partners LLP, a hedge fund that was short Overstock, and Gradient Analytics, an independent research boutique that published critical research about Overstock. Overstock claimed there was an improper relationship between the two. The announcement said there would be a conference call and Webcast the next day to discuss the suit.

Byrne introduced himself and asked for me. Jennings told him I was out of the office for the day.

"Do you follow us?" Byrne asked.

"I do."

She didn't elaborate, and Byrne seemed to stumble, waiting for her to say more, but she was too smart for that.

"Ahh, okay, well, just let David know I called. And he can call my cell if he has anything to talk about."

"All right, I certainly will," she said, and hung up.

That was an odd way to put it, saying if I had anything to talk about with him that I should call. He called me, so he obviously had something on his mind. If I had anything to ask Byrne, I would have called him myself.

He and Jennings spoke for only thirty seconds. Jennings had researched Overstock, including doing some "comparison shopping" on the site and building a spreadsheet, where she modeled Overstock's performance. She performed financial analysis, including comparing the stock value of Overstock, which was a large number, with Overstock's profits, a negative number. The spreadsheet also identified rising customer acquisition costs, which is not good. But she didn't tell Byrne any of that.

I probably would have called him back, but I didn't have a chance that day, and after hearing about the conference call the next morning, I decided to steer clear of him. So I never did call him.

But I did decide to listen to the conference call and could not believe what I heard. Byrne went on a bizarre tirade. He made a flurry of charges against so many people and organizations that it would be funny except it was really sad, because he actually *meant it* and some folks actually thought he was right.

"Even hardened denizens of Wall Street were shocked by a conference call that Patrick Byrne, the CEO of the retailer Overstock.com, held on August 12," *Fortune* reported. "'I want to get something off my chest,' Byrne announced. Then he launched into a rant about a 'Miscreants Ball' in which he mentioned hedge funds, journalists, investigators, trial lawyers, the SEC, and even Eliot Spitzer."

This book shows that this is the opposite of how it works. Nobody has cooperated with Greenlight.

According to Byrne, the conspiracy is run by someone he called the "Sith Lord," in reference to the villain in the *Star Wars* movies. In Byrne's own words:

> As this went on I started realizing that there was actually some more orchestration here being provided, by what I'm calling here is the Sith Lord or the mastermind. Now, can I tell you who that

designated bottom feeder was who was supposed to end up with our company? Can I tell you? I can. But I'm not going to today. The Sith Lord is, can I tell you who that is? Well, I could tell you it's a name that everybody on the phone, every single person on the phone would recognize this person's name. He's one of the master criminals from the 1980s, and he's back in business. But I'm not going to. I'll just call him the mastermind today.

A few moments later, Byrne continued, "The man I've identified here as the Sith Lord of this stuff I just say, you know who you are and I hope that this is worth it, because if the feds catch you again, this time they're going to bury you *under* the prison. And I'm going to enjoy helping."

Though we were not part of his lawsuit, as Byrne went through his list of "miscreants," first my name came up and a few minutes later my wife, Cheryl, joined the "Ball." Byrne's bringing me up in his public harangue was out of all context, except for one: Allied. Our fight with Allied had become so public that Byrne lumped me in with a cast of who he considered evildoers trying to undermine perfectly good companies and ruining America.

"David Einhorn runs a fund in New York called Greenlight Capital," Byrne said in about his only truthful statement about me. "Greenlight, I've been in Greenlight, and they told me sort of a founding myth of Greenlight, which was that David Einhorn was a Cornell guy who found some arb and traded it from his dorm room and that turned into Greenlight over time," he continued.

Byrne had never been "in" Greenlight. I didn't find an "arb" in college or trade it from my dorm room. This does sound like the story of Ken Griffin, founder of Citadel, who did just that at Harvard. It seemed that Byrne conjured up various stories and stereotypes about hedge fund managers and depicted me as an amalgamation of a bunch of them.

He next turned to Cheryl. "Then there's *Barron's*," Byrne said. "And *Barron's*, anybody on the 'Street' understands *Barron's* more or less as just being a group of quislings for the hedge funds. . . . There has been until recently an editor there named Cheryl Strauss, married name Cheryl Strauss Einhorn, wife of David Einhorn. And if you trace the articles around, which I'm going to talk about in a minute, you'll see that both entered these very odd relationships."

This did not take a lot of detective work. At *Barron's*, Cheryl always wrote and published as "Cheryl Strauss Einhorn." Byrne went on to say that if people checked, they would find that a reporter who had recently written a negative article about Overstock in *Barron's* probably knew Cheryl. That was probably correct, but so what? It was hard to tell because all he had was Joe McCarthyesque innuendo. Possibly, he wanted listeners to believe Cheryl fed a story to the reporter on our behalf at a time we weren't even short his stock. In Byrne's paranoid view of the world, reporters blindly accept assignments from former colleagues.

He also saw a conspiracy between Kroll and me. I guess Allied told him Greenlight had hired Kroll to investigate Allied and BLX loans. Now, according to Byrne, Kroll was investigating him. That's all the evidence he needed to think this was my doing.

Byrne continued, "Kroll has been investigating me for a number of months, trying to come up with dirt on me. The general—well, I had trouble nailing that down until I discovered the personal relationship between Jules Kroll and David Einhorn."

Though we retained the firm to investigate Allied, I have never met or spoken with Jules Kroll, the founder. Byrne seems to have made the connection because Kroll went to Cornell about twenty-five years before I did and also lives in the same town as my family.

Enter Jim Carruthers.

Byrne said:

Jim Carruthers is an interesting fellow. He's up at Eastbourne Capital, north of San Francisco. Eastbourne has an "E" at the end. It's funny because there's a fellow holding himself out in a nearby location by the name of Jim Karruthers, with a slightly different spelling, holding himself out as a private investigator from Eastbourn Investigations, no "E" at the end. I know that couldn't be this Jim Carruthers, because that would be a felony for a person to hold himself out as a PI when he's not. And that PI has a very interesting relationship with a certain lawyer in Detroit, who has some very odd practices that maybe we'll have time to get back to.

I suspect the part about the lawyer in Detroit referred to Carruthers's getting information about the fraudulent BLX loans in Detroit. Plainly, Byrne spoke with Allied.

Before the show ended, he put my picture up on the screen next to a picture of David Rocker under the heading "Short-sellers."

David Einhorn is the guy who is, of course, obsessive about his [security] concerns. They literally told me in Greenlight how he's got six cell phones and swaps SIM cards and takes a different route to work. And when I was in Greenlight, they were explaining how you can't even, I couldn't even go into this part of the office and see him. He's extremely shy and careful, won't be seen in public, have pictures taken, anything like that. So if you ever see this man in public, do not take his picture because he's evidently extremely concerned about it being known or on the Internet.

Again, Byrne has never been "in" Greenlight, nor has anyone at the firm met him. Obviously, there is no secret part of Greenlight where I hide. I own only one cell phone and didn't know what a SIM card was until I asked someone after the conference call. Most days, I take a train to work, though I admit I don't always come in at the same time. Pretty tricky of me. I was also unaware of an unmet demand or interest from people I don't know to have my picture. I had no problem with Byrne having one, though.

I know all about CEOs of troubled companies lashing out at critics. I've had firsthand experience, but Byrne attacked anyone and everyone. It was a spectacularly bizarre performance.

■ ■ ■

Since then, Byrne has been on a crusade. Overstock.com even refers to it as the "CEO's Crusade" on the Web site. Byrne's big complaint is about what he calls "naked shorting." Incidentally, his lawsuit against Rocker and Gradient has nothing to do with naked shorting. Presumably, in response to Byrne's complaint and the related publicity, the SEC jumped into the fray to investigate these claims. The case made significant news when the SEC tried to force journalists to reveal their sources. The journalists refused and, ultimately, the SEC dropped the investigation.

Naked shorting is selling short shares that have not been borrowed. Byrne has made a big to-do about this by accusing hedge fund "miscreants" of driving good companies out of business. According to Byrne, a naked short is the equivalent of creating counterfeit shares and selling them on the market, thereby driving down stock prices. The SEC has listened to Byrne and other critics of the practice, eventually adopting rules in June 2007, making it harder to naked short. According to SEC Chairman

Christopher Cox, naked shorting is a "fraud that the commission is bound to prevent and punish."

The primary evidence of naked shorting is the large number of trades that don't properly clear. These are called "failures to deliver." I doubt there is a lot of naked shorting in the market. The practice is probably more widespread among market makers, who are permitted to short without borrowing the stock, and short-term traders, who plan to hold the position for such a short time that they will cover before the initial trade is due to settle. I don't believe that research-driven short-sellers, who often hold positions for long periods, engage in much naked shorting. It simply doesn't make sense, and the clearing brokerages don't permit it.

However, there is an alternative explanation for the large number of failures to deliver. Suppose a shareholder lends his shares to a short-seller. The short-seller sells the shares to a new owner. The trades clear, and everything is fine. Now suppose the original holder sells his shares. His broker has to recall the lent shares to deliver them to the new owner. When the clearing broker for the short-seller gets the recall notice, instead of forcing the short-seller to immediately repurchase the shares in the market, the clearing broker looks for a new lender of the shares. It may take time to secure those shares. Perhaps the clearing broker has also lent shares and decides to solve the problem by recalling those shares. While the clearing broker looks for new shares to borrow or waits for his recall notice to be honored, time passes and the system can back up—creating failures to deliver.

When you extrapolate this over numerous brokerage firms that are each borrowing, lending, and recalling shares from one another as the underlying shares switch owners, often rapidly, the clearing system can get behind and a good pile of failures to deliver can develop. This can happen without anyone naked shorting, manipulating or creating counterfeit shares and so forth. This happens more in stocks where there is a great interest in selling them short, because it is harder for the clearing brokers to find substitute shares to borrow when faced with a recall request. If there is a problem in the system, Byrne should point his finger at someone other than "miscreant" hedge funds.

His real beef, though, is that some hedge funds figured out that his business model was no good and his stock overvalued. He has made a huge effort to force the shorts to cover. Overstock's stock price was $43 on August 11, 2005, the day he announced his lawsuit. The stock hasn't seen that price since and fell to $13 by November 2006. Too bad we weren't short.

Byrne professes to have no issue with "legal" shorting or hedge funds. Sure. It burns Byrne that short-sellers have made money betting on his failure. The Byrne performance reminded me of something Warren Buffett once told me about the difficulty of shorting the stocks of companies run by crooks, because they'll fight dirty to save themselves. "The crook's life depends on it," Buffett said. While I am not calling Byrne a crook, his made-up rant about me indicates his dishonesty.

■ ■ ■

In September 2005, nine months after Allied announced the criminal investigation, the U.S. attorney's office in Washington, D.C., invited us to share our information about Allied to assist their investigation. I went to Washington in October to present the federal prosecutors with a fifty-page slide show. In a cramped conference room, I met for eight hours with Assistant U.S. Attorney Jonathan Barr and another prosecutor and three FBI agents. It was plain that they had done a fair amount of work and were well prepared. At various points, they even referred to my testimony to the SEC. They asked devil's advocate–type questions, repeating what Allied's lawyers were obviously telling them in defense.

We went through all Greenlight's problems with Allied, including its numerous false and misleading public statements, the history of ten separate investments it valued without reasonable basis, how it changed its accounting, and how its valuations still lacked any reasonable basis. We also discussed BLX's fraud, the loan-parking arrangement, and the oral agreement. We went through Kroll's findings and Allied's various attempts to manipulate the market through the rights offering and other efforts. We finished with a discussion of my phone records and a few other Allied misdeeds.

Several months earlier, the FBI agent in San Diego told me he had discovered who obtained my phone records, though he could not tell me who it was. Now, I learned the Department of Justice transferred the investigation to Washington, D.C., where it was in the hands of the team investigating Allied. I could draw my own inferences about who obtained my phone records. The prosecutors and agents took notes and seemed smart, serious, and capable. I left feeling optimistic.

CHAPTER 25

Another Loan Program, Another Fraud

BLX's loan fraud didn't stop with the SBA 7(a) program. The U.S. Department of Agriculture (USDA) guarantees Business and Industry Loans. The USDA's Rural Business-Cooperative Service runs the loan program, which guarantees about 75 percent of the loan value. The loans are intended to help develop rural areas and increase employment, improving the economic and environmental climate in rural communities. Like the SBA, the USDA allowed unscrupulous lenders to abuse the program and does not provide enough oversight to catch them.

BLX underwrote a $3 million B&I loan to Bill Russell Oil in June 2000. Like Bill Walton of Allied, the Bill Russell referenced is not a retired basketball star. (Brickman is still looking for a Kareem Abdul-Jabbar loan fraud.) The company, an oil-and-gasoline distributor in Rector, Arkansas, operated gas stations in southeastern Missouri and northeastern Arkansas. By June 2000, it already had about $1 million in loans to other creditors. The EPA cited Bill Russell Oil for numerous violations concerning fuel storage and ordered a cleanup. Bill Russell Oil was supposed to use some of the proceeds of the BLX loan to correct the violations. The company had weak collateral and virtually no prospects of paying the BLX loan back or even making interest payments. In November 2000, BLX made a fresh $400,000 SBA 7(a) loan to the company. Almost a year to the day after BLX made the USDA loan, the USDA paid out its guarantee. The SBA paid on its guarantee on the smaller SBA loan in November 2001, though the SBA data indicates that the agency was eventually repaid in full.

Bill Russell Oil ignored the EPA demands to comply with its environmental rules and did not return the agency's phone calls. The Justice Department eventually filed a complaint. In April 2005, the District Court for the Eastern District of Arkansas granted a judgment against the company for $83 million. This triggered an audit of BLX's loan by the Office of Inspector General (OIG) of the USDA.

In September 2005, the USDA issued a forty-page audit recommending that BLX repay the guaranteed amount of the loan and be kicked out of the Business and Industry Loan program. (The audit at www.usda.gov/oig/webdocs/34099-07-TE.pdf does not name BLX or Bill Russell Oil. Instead, it refers to them as the "lender" and the "borrower," respectively.) The audit report describes the kind of behavior that Kroll, Carruthers and Brickman found on many of BLX's SBA loans. In particular, the auditor found that BLX misrepresented the value of the borrower's property. For example, when the borrower obtained an appraisal of the collateral, the appraiser noted that the Environmental Protection Agency (EPA) had closed several of the stations and that the agency had required upgrades at the properties. When the appraiser asked the company to provide documents to better determine the value of the properties, the borrower said it could not because its records were destroyed in a fire. The appraisal in March 1999 came in at $1.5 million, which wasn't enough for a $3 million loan.

"We concluded that the lender misrepresented the value of the 20 properties to the state office by concealing the March 1999 appraisal," the report said. "State officials said they would not have guaranteed the loan if the March 1999 appraisal had been made available prior to issuing the loan note guarantee."

Instead, according to the report, BLX recommended a different appraiser, who reappraised the properties at $4.3 million. Presto! There was now enough collateral for the loan. However, the $4.3 million appraisal assumed a value based on property improvements that had not been made. BLX was responsible to verify the improvements and did not. In fact, the new appraiser certified that some of the properties had already been upgraded, and he included a list of these improvements in the appraisal report. He also said he had seen reports on the properties that said the environmental concerns were minor. When later asked by the OIG auditor to provide these reports, the appraiser said he could not find them.

The audit also found that six months before the loan closed, the state of Missouri revoked the borrower's motor fuel license, and two months before the loan closed the EPA inspected some of the properties and found more than sixty violations. Despite these events, BLX certified that no major changes had occurred.

In addition, the audit found that BLX misrepresented the condition of the properties. BLX knew that the borrower had not only failed to upgrade nineteen of the twenty properties, but that several were not even open at the time the loan closed. BLX falsely certified that the upgrades had been made and that 95 percent of the properties were operational.

The most striking parts of the audit were photographs of properties that showed buildings that were just shells, falling apart and abandoned. The pictures revealed that there was little chance these properties were operational in the recent past, as BLX certified. For example, a tornado damaged a property in Missouri a month before the loan closed. It's hard to tell in the photo, but a building might have once stood on the site (see Figure 25.1A). Another Missouri property had been declared unfit for human occupancy a week before the loan closing (see Figure 25.1B). Another photo showed an abandoned, falling-apart gas station in Missouri that neither BLX nor the borrower could prove was operating at closing (see Figure 25.1C). One other building in Arkansas was shown in similar condition, also with no proof that it was operating when BLX closed the loan (see Figure 25.1D).

According to the report, in a 2005 meeting with BLX, CEO Robert Tannenhauser told the inspector general's office that he was not aware if anyone ever visited the properties before the loan closed. Two BLX vice presidents attended the meeting, but they were recent hires and didn't know much about the loan. The vice president who processed the loan was no longer with BLX, and that officer, through his lawyer, said he wouldn't talk to the OIG.

Figure 25.1A   Photos from Bill Russell Audit

Figure 25.1B   Photos from Bill Russell Audit

Figure 25.1C Photos from Bill Russell Audit

Figure 25.1D Photos from Bill Russell Audit

Finally, the report found that loan proceeds were siphoned off for impermissible purposes. Part of the proceeds went to a loan arbitrator who had negotiated down Bill Russell Oil's existing debt. BLX paid the arbitrator out of the B&I loan proceeds, which is not allowed under the program's rules. "In a fax to the arbitrator, dated December 20, 2000, the lender's loan officer wrote that he had stuck his neck out to pay him the initial $75,000," the auditor's report said. Nowhere in the loan documents was this payment listed. "The lender knew this was not an authorized use of loan funds."

After the loans went bad, BLX ordered another appraisal in 2002 so it could liquidate the properties and get some of the money back. That appraisal came in at $1.2 million, much closer to the first appraisal.

The OIG audit recommended that BLX pay back the $2.4 million, plus accrued interest, that the USDA paid on its guarantee, and that BLX be debarred from the B&I loan program. Debarment from one government lending program would automatically prevent BLX from participating in any other government loan program. So debarment would disqualify BLX from the SBA program as well. The USDA did not agree with the OIG's debarment recommendation and suggested that debarment should only be used as a threat to ensure BLX reimbursed the loss.

In February 2006, Brickman tracked down the USDA auditor of the Bill Russell Oil loan. The auditor told Brickman that BLX's attorneys in Little Rock wanted to form a marginally funded corporation to purchase at a tax auction the twenty contaminated properties discussed in the audit. That way, if litigation arose about pollution cleanup or health claims, the liability would fall on the marginally funded corporation, which would simply go bankrupt and cease to exist. All the damages, liabilities and other charges would not show on Allied or BLX's financial statements. The auditor said the "SEC was very concerned about this proposal."

One would think that after discovering an enormous fraud like this, the USDA would look into other loans by the same lender. It doesn't work that way. After we discovered the Bill Russell Oil fraud, Brickman obtained information on all of BLX's B&I loans from the USDA under FOIA.

Brickman found that BLX made B&I loans to gas stations, truck stops, a butterfly pavilion, a mushroom company, a sports emporium, a general store, a paper-box manufacturer, an ice skating rink, and others. Of the roughly fifty loans that BLX made under the USDA program from 1998 to 2003, the USDA paid guarantees on more than 42 percent of the loans totaling $41 million. However, as was the case with the SBA loans, only two loans had been charged-off, suggesting an unusually slow loan work-out process. Brickman searched for news on the other loans and found a number of borrowers filed bankruptcy or showed clear evidence of default. This brought the total of identified problem loans to an astounding 65 percent of BLX's portfolio of USDA loans.

Brickman compiled a lengthy summary of several defaulted USDA B&I loans and gave them to the USDA auditor. Brickman showed evidence that USDA loans were used to bail out other lenders, thereby transferring losses from private lenders to taxpayers. He found that BLX made loans to people who had previously defaulted on USDA loans and made USDA loans that bailed out SBA loans. BLX passed defaulted loans from one government agency to another.

The auditor compiled that information, along with his own work and analysis, into a letter to USDA headquarters, trying to debar BLX. As the auditor wrote Brickman, "Sometimes the wheels of government turn slow, but there are a few of us that keeps [sic] trying to protect taxpayers' money."

In February 2006, the regional auditor sent a memo to Philip Cole, the director of the Rural Development and Natural Resources Division of the USDA. The memo indicates that OIG disagreed with the USDA's decision not to debar BLX. Instead, it suggested examining BLX's overall history of delinquent and foreclosed loans. The memo agreed with Brickman's default figure and summarized problems with a number of other B&I loans that Brickman identified to the OIG. The memo suggested a meeting in the Rural Business Service (RBS) national office to discuss debarring BLX. It said based on additional research, "BLX's loan portfolio appears to be marginal or substandard loans." The memo said that $43 million out of a $130 million portfolio were either delinquent, in default or in liquidation.

In early March 2006, Brickman heard from the OIG that there was a meeting at the RBS national office to discuss debarment of BLX. They were "receptive." An answer was expected in thirty days. David Gray, the OIG's chief attorney, previously held the same position at the SBA and was familiar with BLX. We had met with him at the SBA in August 2003. He wanted to actively pursue debarment. The auditor said he had spoken with an examiner from the SEC and the U.S. attorney's office in Washington.

Then, it seemed that the auditor ran into a roadblock. He suggested that Brickman send a complaint to the OIG's hotline, which he said would force them to act. So Brickman sent an e-mail to the hotline, asking the office to audit six of the more suspicious USDA loans. After several weeks, Brickman had not heard back about his hotline complaint, so he sent an e-mail asking the USDA why it had not gotten back to him. David Lewis, a USDA official, called Brickman, but didn't say much.

After not hearing anything for several months, through the FOIA we learned why the agency did not respond to the hotline complaint. "We are declining this as an audit matter due to lack of available staff," the USDA wrote. "We are planning to conduct an audit of this lender's activities in fiscal year 2007." In other words, the agency didn't have enough money in its current budget to determine if it was losing money.

One would think that when confronted with the Bill Russell audit, BLX would rush to pay-up and settle. Hardly. The Arkansas office sent an "Adverse Decision Letter" to BLX demanding repayment. BLX filed an appeal. A hearing was scheduled on July 25, 2006, on Long Island, New York. BLX had made an FOIA request for information and appeared to be trying to delay things.

I sent Greenlight's general counsel to the hearing. Each side flew four people up from Arkansas and Washington. A USDA hearing officer came in from Connecticut the night before with twelve boxes of documents. The gathering lasted five minutes. The parties pre-agreed to a sixty-day delay. The government agreed to withdraw its adverse finding for sixty days to negotiate a settlement.

Then we learned that the auditor who wanted to do the audit left the USDA for a position in another government agency. He signed off with the "hope" that his proposed audit of BLX will go forward in October/November.

In November 2006, the Arkansas USDA office sent a fresh draft demand letter for the Russell Oil loan to be repaid to the national office. Brickman heard from the Arkansas office that the national office wanted to "do a little housekeeping and close the file." Brickman responded, "You mean they want to sweep this under the rug?"

"Exactly right," the USDA rep said.

In a follow-up conversation a couple of days later, Brickman expressed concern about the closing of the file. The USDA rep said, "This is not the only case that obviously they have problems with us."

"They is BLX or USDA?" Brickman asked.

"BLX has other loans we have guaranteed that—" the USDA rep replied.

"Look odd?" Brickman said.

"Yeah. And there are some issues that I wish I were free to discuss that would make your skin crawl."

A few minutes later Brickman asked, "Why do you think Washington, D.C., is putting pressure on you to hide or not do anything? The SBA is doing the same thing."

"I don't know," the USDA rep responded. "We are just employees. This is off the record." (When the rep was subsequently approached for permission to use the material for this book, the rep not only granted permission, but sounded pleased a book was being written about this.) The USDA rep continued:

Somebody is in bed with them. Okay. Who did they get in bed with? And we don't know that. We don't have a clue as to if there is or not. The questions that came back to me when we sent the letter out back to the national office had nothing to do with the facts of the letter. They asked about a couple of internal things. And it's just, I guess, so hard to prove and has a chance of receiving so much publicity you know if they could just get it to go away, it just goes away. I just don't know all the answers to that.

Later, the USDA rep clarified that the internal things meant, "We are getting criticized. And I was told from the get go that is what would happen. The first person to get criticized would be me."

CHAPTER 26

The Smell of Politics

The SBA failed to act on BLX, and, worse, kept renewing the company's status as a Preferred Lending Provider. The SBA pushed back hard on our whistle-blower complaint. Though the investigations have been open a long time and the fraud is obvious, the U.S. attorney in Washington, D.C., had not yet acted. Further, the SEC allowed Allied to become a bigger problem by routinely approving registration statements for new stock sales. It doesn't make sense—until one reviews Allied's political connections.

Allied is based in Washington. The headquarters is on Pennsylvania Avenue. It was founded by George Williams Jr., who began his career in the FBI. As mentioned earlier, Sweeney worked at the SEC. Lawrence Hebert, who sits on Allied's Board, was the CEO of the politically connected Riggs National Bank until its money laundering for, and illicit assistance to, the Chilean dictator Augusto Pinochet caused scandals, which induced Riggs' sale to PNC Bank in 2005.

Walton was a director of Riggs from 1999 until its sale. J. Carter Beese Jr., an SEC commissioner from 1992 to 1994, was another director of Riggs

255

and ran its venture funds. Forbes.com reported he was a senior adviser to
Allied Capital. He appeared as a representative of Allied at an SEC round-
table in 2004. Ironically, Beese Jr. was known to be particularly active on
corporate governance issues at the SEC. He was named by a federal judge
and the SEC to be trustee of a $250 million stock fund to be distributed to
victims of accounting fraud.

In July 2004, *The Hill*, a newspaper that covers Congress, reported
that some bankers were encouraging their colleagues to contribute to Senator
John Kerry's presidential campaign because of a proposal by President George
W. Bush to cut all subsidies to the SBA's 7(a) program. As a senator, Kerry
was the ranking minority member of the Senate Committee on Small Business
& Entrepreneurship, which oversees the SBA. In 2007, he became chairman
of the Committee, when the Democrats took control of the Senate. *The Hill*
article reported that Deryl Schuster of BLX "sent an e-mail to industry members encouraging them to contribute to Kerry's campaign. 'Just think what
the SBA loan programs puts [sic] in our pockets!' wrote Schuster, who lives in
Kansas." *The Hill* article continued:

> Schuster also wrote that the head of Business Loan Express, Robert
> Tannenhauser, was a member of Kerry's fundraising committee and
> was trying to raise more than $100,000 for the Democrat's effort
> to defeat Bush.
>
> "We would like to get at least the $100,000 mark, which would
> give the 7(a) industry incredible visibility with Mr. Kerry and his
> campaign committee," Schuster wrote. "With Mr. Tannenhauser at
> the helm of this effort no group will receive more credit than the
> SBA lending industry."

Schuster himself was a former SBA district and regional manager.
I wondered whether the presence of a former senior SBA official at BLX
impacted the agency's oversight of the lender.

Once the SEC investigation of Allied started, Allied accelerated its political
efforts. Starting in September 2004, Allied added the following to the corporate description it includes at the bottom of every press release: "In serving
our shareholders, we help build U.S. companies and create and sustain jobs.
The company's private finance portfolio includes investments in over 100 companies with aggregate revenues of in excess of $11 billion, supporting more
than 100,000 jobs." The message to authorities and politicians couldn't

be clearer: If you put us out of business, 100,000 people will lose their jobs. Of course, that isn't what would happen. The companies Allied invests in would carry on their work. Allied is not a large employer, with only 170 employees at the end of 2006.

Allied created a political action committee (PAC) in October 2004, four months after the company announced that the SEC was investigating it. By the end of 2005, the PAC had $116,000. The contributors were mostly Allied employees, including officers, directors, and their families. Joan Sweeney was in for $7,500 in 2004 and 2005, and Penni Roll and her husband contributed $10,000. Robert Long, the Allied executive who had lunch with me at the investor day meeting in 2002, contributed $12,500. Most of the PAC money was going to senators and members of Congress who oversaw the SBA, including Senator Olympia Snowe, the chairwoman of the Senate Committee on Small Business & Entrepreneurship.

Bill Walton also contributed $10,000 to the PAC during those two years. But he was also busy elsewhere. From 2000 to 2005, Walton made a total of $116,000 in political contributions. He gave money to President Bush, the Republican National Committee, and the National Republican Senatorial Committee, which received $35,000, the largest contribution of his that turned up in the records. Republicans got most of his money. Senator Mel Martinez of the Banking Committee got $3,000; Congressman Donald Manzullo, chairman of the House Committee on Small Business, got $1,000; Sue Kelly, another member of that committee, got $5,000; Senator Snowe received $1,000; Senator Jon Kyl of the Senate Finance Committee got $2,000; and Congressman Michael Oxley, chairman of the Committee on Financial Services, got $3,000. Seven members (six Republicans and one Democrat) of the Senate Committee on Small Business & Entrepreneurship received a total of $9,000, and a PAC set up for the possible 2008 presidential run of George Allen, a member of the committee, got $5,000. The lone Democrat was Evan Bayh, who received $2,000, with another $5,000 going to his PAC.

Separate from the PAC, Tannenhauser, his family and other Allied employees, including Sweeney, contributed to the campaign of Nydia Velázquez, the top-ranking Democrat of the House Small Business Committee and a member of the Financial Services Committee. She often complains that the SBA doesn't initiate loans fast enough to help small businesses. Tannenhauser and his family, including a son and daughter, made more than

$266,000 in political donations from 2000 to 2006. Most of it went to Democrats, including $20,000 to Velázquez. I'm sure the focused giving to elected officials who oversee the SBA is no coincidence.

In March 2005, after the U.S. attorney launched a criminal investigation, Allied added Marc Racicot to its board of directors. His resume: former head of the Republican National Committee; former chairman of the Bush/Cheney Reelection Committee; and former governor of Montana. In the spring of 2006, the company added Edwin L. Harper, another well-connected player, to its board. He presently is a senior vice president for public affairs and government relations at Assurant, a large specialty insurance company. Previously, he worked in the White House for Presidents Nixon and Reagan. Allied was obviously stacking the political deck to head off the investigations.

Remember the "bad cop" SEC lawyer Mark Braswell, who aggressively questioned me about the purpose of my speech and relationships with other fund managers? He left the SEC four months later, in September 2003, to become a partner with the Venable law firm in Washington. According to the Venable's press release, he was to "concentrate on corporate investigations, white collar & securities litigation and compliance." Braswell registered as a lobbyist for Allied in October 2004. Braswell was not generally a lobbyist. In fact, we couldn't find a record of any other lobbying clients. How could it be proper, or even legal, for a lawyer who obtained confidential material from us, including e-mails, trading records and testimony about Allied, to leave the government and go work for Allied while our dispute was ongoing? (Allied was no stranger to lobbying. From 2001 to 2006, the company spent more than $1 million on lobbyists, including $60,000 to Venable.)

Greenlight's lawyer sent a letter to the Office of Inspector General (OIG) of the SEC outlining the Braswell situation and explaining how it violated established ethics rules. In December 2006, the SEC's OIG was heavily criticized for not investigating the accusation of former SEC enforcement attorney Gary Aguirre that the SEC impeded him from fully investigating possible insider trading by Pequot Capital Management based on possible tips from Morgan Stanley CEO John Mack. It doesn't appear that they have done any better on the Braswell issue. To date, the SEC has taken no action.

I told Floyd Norris, the respected business columnist for *The New York Times*, about Allied hiring Braswell. He called Allied to hear its side. Allied's response was that Braswell was not in the room during my SEC testimony!

I had to pinch myself. I scrambled to make sure I was not mistaken. I got a picture of Braswell from his new firm's Web site, and, yes, he was the same guy in the SEC interview room. Greenlight's lawyers also went through their notes and confirmed Braswell's attendance. We asked the SEC for a transcript of my testimony, which removed any remaining doubt.

Norris wrote a column on July 15, 2005, describing Allied's recent decision to stop reporting BLX's summary financials and its hiring of Braswell as a lobbyist. Norris wrote:

> Calling Business Loan Express, and most of Allied's other operations, "private companies" strains credulity. In reality, they are subsidiaries of Allied, which owns all or nearly all of their stock. But Allied treats them as investments and discloses as little information as it can. It can do that because it is classified as a business development company.
>
> Companies that hide facts invite suspicion. In 2002, Greenlight Capital, a hedge fund run by David Einhorn, published a report questioning Allied's accounting. Mr. Einhorn soon found himself being questioned by enforcement lawyers from the Securities and Exchange Commission, and he blames Allied for complaining about him.
>
> One of the SEC lawyers doing the questioning, Mr. Einhorn says, was Mark K. Braswell, who is now a partner in the Venable law firm in Washington. Last fall, after Allied disclosed the SEC had started an informal inquiry into Allied's books, he registered as a lobbyist for Allied. (© 2005, *The New York Times Company*. Reprinted with Permission.)

Norris said that Braswell wouldn't tell him what kind of work he was doing for Allied, but said "he did not represent it in the government investigations and had made no inappropriate disclosures to Allied about SEC cases. He said he followed all ethics rules."

Norris also noticed the curious shareholder behavior. They didn't seem to care that Allied was withholding information or anything else they did as long as the distribution kept coming. "The shareholders do not appear bothered by the fact Allied keeps the financial results of its wholly owned subsidiaries secret," he wrote. "The question is whether the SEC will do anything about Allied's decision to hide even more information from its owners." Allied's stock, which traded around $29 a share at the time, did not react to Norris's story.

■ ■ ■

Meanwhile, Allied gave the appearance of cleaning up its act. After a few years of gradually writing down the problems created in the recession and with the benefit of improved conditions in the capital markets, Allied had fewer absurd valuations, such as loans to bankrupt companies carried at cost. Allied improved the optics of its valuation process. First, it promoted a long-standing senior executive to the new title of "chief valuation officer." Obviously, promoting an existing manager, who might have been part of the problem, was unlikely to solve the problem. Second, it hired Duff & Phelps and JMP Securities to provide "valuation assistance."

Valuation opinions are often for sale on Wall Street. For obvious reasons, the "valuation assistance" Allied sought was far less than appraisals or fairness opinions for its investments. The valuation firms were not retained to perform due diligence on the companies, visit them, speak to their managements and so forth in order to recommend a value to Allied. According to Duff & Phelps' standard engagement letter, it "will not be responsible for determining Fair Value." Its role "is limited to being an advisor and providing additional support to your existing valuation policy and process as well as providing negative assurance with respect to the Fair Value determined by management for each investment."

Instead, Allied provides its own valuations to Duff & Phelps for review. For about $5,000 a company, Duff & Phelps looks at Allied's work and without independently checking facts it provides a "negative assurance"— meaning that *assuming that the information Allied provided is accurate and complete, Duff & Phelps advises that the valuations are not unreasonable.* Of course, if Allied management picks and chooses which facts it shares with Duff & Phelps, its valuation consultant has no basis or authority with which to disagree.

At only $5,000 per company, Duff & Phelps is not being paid enough to do a sufficient amount of work and research. Appraisals would probably cost at least ten times more. Indeed, according to its standard agreement Duff & Phelps performs only "limited procedures" of reading and discussing management's prepared valuations and related write-ups, meeting with the deal teams to understand management's expectations and intent for each investment and to discuss the underlying company's strategy and performance. It considers general economic and industry trends, publicly traded comparable companies, the financial information provided by management and "other facts and data that are pertinent to the companies as disclosed by management." Duff & Phelps checks management's calculations for clerical accuracy. Finally, it speaks with auditors and underwriters about "any questions they may have regarding the limited procedures."

Though Allied improved the optics of its process, the various red flags such as performance smoothing and serial correlations of the valuations persisted. We had sufficient information about several of Allied's investments to know that Allied still valued them at prices for which it had no reasonable basis. Of course, as long as the mother ship of misvaluation, BLX, continued, there was little reason to take the "valuation assistance" too seriously.

We did brokerage business with JMP Securities, one of the firms Allied retained to assist in the valuation of BLX. I called Greenlight's salesman and asked to speak with whoever was doing the work at JMP. JMP refused. I offered to do it on the basis that I would speak and JMP would only have to listen. Again, JMP declined. The JMP salesman noted, "We aren't saying to buy Allied stock, you know."

Allied's results were getting weaker. The company distributed more per share than it reported in earnings in 2003 and 2004. Net investment income (excluding gains and losses) was $1.65 per share in 2003 and $1.52 per share in 2004. Supported by Allied's strategy of selling winners and keeping losers, taxable earnings were $2.40 per share in 2004 and the related tax distributions were $2.30 per share. Net income, which included unrealized losses, was only $1.88 per share. In the fourth quarter of 2004, Allied modestly reduced the carrying value of BLX by $26.1 million, nowhere near to what it should have valued it, since originations fell 30 percent from the prior year.

■ ■ ■

In the first quarter of 2005, Allied converted $45 million of its loan to BLX into equity to "strengthen the capital base" and "clean up the capital structure." As mentioned, Allied stopped providing detailed financial information on BLX at that point, so it became harder to track. Nonetheless, converting debt to equity is not usually a good sign, because it indicates the company isn't creditworthy enough to support the debt.

The regulatory investigations also started to create large legal expenses in 2005. In the first half of the year, Allied spent $25 million. Assuming legal fees of $300 an hour, you can employ fifty lawyers for sixty hours a week to run up a legal bill that high. In the third quarter the expense fell to half as much and to "only" $3.6 million in the fourth.

Allied had two home runs in 2005. First, it sold its entire portfolio of commercial mortgage-backed securities (CMBS) and its platform for originating CMBS to a Canadian bank for a large gain. Second, Allied made an initial small investment in 2001 in Advantage Sales & Marketing, which became a large investment when Allied rolled a number of regional competitors together in 2004. It announced a sale of the rollup for a very large gain in 2005. The combined result led to earnings per share of $6.36.

After raising the quarterly tax distribution a penny to $0.57 per share two quarters after my speech, Allied held it flat at that level for nine consecutive quarters. Given the investment performance and ever disappointing recurring net operating income, it was enough of a charade to maintain the quarterly $0.57 distribution. Now, aided by the two large realized gains, Allied began, again, to slowly raise the distribution, generally by a penny per quarter.

However, Allied found much greater competition to make new loans and reduced the interest rates it charged for the loans. The yield on its portfolio fell. Further, the $36.4 million of investigation-related costs were a headwind. Net investment income fell, again, to only $1.00 per share in 2005.

Even so, the realized gains created so much taxable income that Allied was left with a dilemma. If they paid out all the taxable income, even as a special distribution, it would be hard to have visibility on future distributions. Obviously, recurring net investment income was now much less than the distributions. Further, Allied had harvested its best gains and it wouldn't make sense to stake the future stability of the distributions on the relatively barren portfolio. If you pick your flowers and water the weeds, you wind up with a garden of weeds.

To solve this, Allied used a rule in the tax code that permitted them to defer distributing the taxable income to shareholders for a year by paying a 4 percent excise tax. Of course, this made no economic sense. Had they paid the distributions, the shareholders would pay long-term capital gains tax at a 15 percent rate on the income. Effectively, the 4 percent excise tax was a 26 percent interest rate one-year loan. (Shareholders were deferring paying a 15 percent tax for one year. The cost was 4 percent—paid by the company: 4/15 = 26.6 percent). For that cost, Allied was able to avoid paying out a special distribution. Instead, its shareholders had to wait a year to receive their money as part of the normal quarterly distributions. In fact, when Allied told the shareholders that it created this rainy-day reserve fund to give added visibility for future tax distributions, the shareholders, focusing on regular quarterly "dividends," cheered.

A side benefit of the spillover distribution was the complete transition of the business from being operating-earnings driven to capital-gains

Table 26.1 Allied Operating Results

	2001	2005	% Change
Assets	$2,461	$4,026	64%
Operating Earnings	179	137	−23%
Operating Earning per Share	1.92	1.00	−48%
Employee Compensation	29.6	78.3	165%
Administrative Expense (excluding investigation)	15.3	33.8	121%
Investigation Cost	–	36.4	NM
Compensation:			
Bill Walton	2.4	7.4	208%
Joan Sweeney	1.6	4.1	256%

Dollars in Millions, Except Per-Share Amounts.

driven, and finally to paying the distribution out of an earlier year's capital gains. With operating earnings no longer relevant, Allied lost most of its incentive to control its operating costs. Consider Table 26.1, comparing results in 2001, the last year before my speech, and 2005.

Operating earnings have fallen in absolute dollars, as a percent of assets and on a per-share basis. This is true, even if you back out the investigation costs. Meanwhile, employee and administrative expenses, excluding the investigation costs, have grown much faster than assets. But growing fastest of all: senior management compensation.

CHAPTER 27

Insiders Getting the Money Out

Allied might have felt that it was being protected by its friends in Washington, but that's a big assumption to make when millions of dollars are at stake. There was no way to be sure that all the influence would derail regulators and their investigations. And if regulators did take action, some senior executives at Allied who were rich "on paper" would become much less so.

In April 2006, as part of Allied's announcement of its upcoming annual meeting, it told shareholders in its proxy that they would be voting on details of a misleadingly named employee "stock ownership initiative" during the meeting. That might have sounded innocent to shareholders, because companies are always amending these plans and shareholders are always approving them. It sounded almost boilerplate. But this one was different and not so innocent.

Allied's officers and senior employees hold millions of dollars' worth of stock options, given to them as part of their compensation. Allied's officers had to know that there was a real possibility that the various government investigations could lead to serious consequences, causing the stock to plummet and the value of those options to vaporize. They had a better sense of the status of the investigations than public market participants. For a year and a half, they refused to comment beyond standard disclosures prepared by their lawyers. If Allied executives knew of any material bad news in the investigations (or bad news anywhere in the business) and they exercised their options and sold before that news became public, they could later be accused of civil, or even criminal, insider trading.

Many of the employee options were "in the money," meaning the price at which employees could exercise them was below the price of the stock. Allied's outstanding options had an average exercise price of about $22 at the end of 2005, so, for example, if the stock were trading at $30, employees could exercise the option to buy the stock at $22 and immediately sell the shares on the market for $30, making about $8 a share in profit. Allied's executives were poised to make hundreds of thousands, and in some cases, millions of dollars, from their options.

Exercising the roughly thirteen million vested, in-the-money options that were outstanding, and then selling the stock en masse, would drive down the price of the stock. Allied's stock is not tremendously liquid and usually only a few hundred thousand shares trade a day. Each sale would require the executive to file a Form 4 with the SEC and disclose the sale within a day or so. A big part of the confidence story Allied and its supporters advanced in 2002 was, "If there was fraud, insiders would be selling." The company's line was that since executives weren't selling—and, in fact, they made symbolic purchases of trivial numbers of shares to signal the market with news of insider buying—everything must be fine.

Large insider sales would make news immediately, and Allied couldn't allow that. The quandary for senior executives was how to get their money out without risking insider trading accusations and also without pushing down Allied's stock with news of their sales. After all, CEO Walton held about $24 million worth of options at the end of 2005, and COO Sweeney held about $12 million. They would be the two top beneficiaries of the proposed plan.

So Allied proposed a stock ownership initiative whereby employees with vested in-the-money options could tender them to the company in exchange for their value paid half in stock, half in cash. Because the company was near the legal threshold in the number of options it could issue (the law caps BDC's at 20 percent of outstanding shares; Allied was at 18 percent), the company said canceling existing options would make more available to employees and new hires. According to the proxy, "Stockholders are not being asked to approve the stock ownership initiative. Stockholders are being asked to approve the issuance of shares to satisfy the common stock portion of the OCP (option cancellation payment). Should stockholders not approve the issuance of shares, the Board of Directors may elect to revise the composition of the OCP to an all cash payment," the company said, in what sounded like a threat. Obviously, if the payments were all cash, then *the employees would not receive any stock as part of the stock ownership initiative.*

I have never seen a plan like it. I asked around and couldn't find anyone else who had seen a plan like it, either. This program would effectively enable insiders to sell up to $397 million of stock back to the company without burdening the open market with millions of shares of insider sales. Why would anyone want to buy 9.5 percent of the company's outstanding shares from the employees? "What do they know that we don't?" the market would ask, assuming the worst.

Also, because the sales would be to the company, there would be no presumed information disadvantage that insiders held over other shareholders. So, if management foresaw a bad ending to the investigations, they might not be held liable for insider trading in the same fashion as if they'd exercised their options and sold in the open market.

Based on our analysis of the proxy, if everyone participated, about thirteen million vested in-the-money options would be exchanged for 1.7 million shares and $53 million in cash. Prior to the exchange, if the stock rose a dollar, employees would be $13 million richer. Afterward, they would become only $1.7 million richer. Allied disingenuously asserted that owning 1.7 million shares directly better aligned employee's interests than owning thirteen million in-the-money options. Dale Lynch, who had taken over as head of Allied's investor relations, told *The Wall Street Journal*, "We think this is a very elegant, transparent way to get stock into the hands of employees." Again, opacity as transparency.

On the downside, executives would be protected. With stock options, if the price falls below the exercise price, the options have no intrinsic value. After the deal, employees would get to keep the $53 million in cash and the shares wouldn't become worthless unless the stock hit zero. This plan would actually reduce the insiders' exposure to the stock, not increase it.

Cue a joke from my dad's book: A fellow owned a bar. One day he noticed that every time his bartender sold a drink, he would put one dollar in the cash register and one dollar in his pocket. Several months passed. The owner came back to his bar. This time he noticed that when the bartender sold a drink, he put nothing in the till and both dollars in his pocket. The owner went up to the bartender and asked, "What's wrong, aren't we partners anymore?"

As I see it, the tender offer only made sense as a clever maneuver by senior executives to get their money out before the stock collapsed. Allied was on the ropes, and this proposal showed me that the people running the company knew it.

■ ■ ■

In September 2006, Hewlett-Packard chairwoman Patricia Dunn was accused of spying on other board members because she was concerned about leaks. She launched an investigation that included obtaining the phone records of board members by private investigators impersonating the members to their phone companies. This was called "pretexting" because somebody calls and pretends to be somebody else to obtain the records.

Now I knew the name for what happened to me and to the other Allied critics. As the HP story became national in scope, with Congressional hearings, criminal prosecutions, and high-level resignations, it became clear that this was a crime after all. Given the ramifications of the HP case, I remembered that the brush-off letter response I received from Allied's board in 2005 did not specifically address the pretexting issue.

I was sure Allied obtained my records and wanted to raise the level of scrutiny on the company's illegal activity. On September 15, 2006, I sent the board another letter, reminding members of what happened to HP over this issue and urging them to investigate. The letter stated:

> The only group of individuals with any motive to access my phone records and the records of four other prominent Allied critics is Allied management. In light of the public outcry and

potential criminal indictments resulting from HP's conduct, the Board cannot pretend that such use of pretexting is not a serious matter. Indeed, the pretexting in this case does not merely concern leaks, but is far more serious. If Allied management was involved in illegally accessing the phone records of its critics, such pretexting constitutes an attempt by the company to interfere with and chill its critics and therefore skew the flow of information which is critical to the securities markets. The Board clearly has an obligation to investigate such criminal conduct by Allied's management.

We got back another curt dismissal from the new chairwoman of the Audit Committee, saying that it had "looked into your allegations that Allied's management played a role in an attempt to access your phone records and have found no evidence to support your claim." I felt that the denial again was weak and the language carefully crafted. What they found was *no evidence*. It wasn't clear how hard they looked and it appeared the language avoided the issue of someone hired by the company, such as a lawyer hiring someone else to access my records. Though the response letter offered me the opportunity to provide more information, its tone suggested the board was not that interested in getting to the bottom of this. In fact, my letter already contained enough specifics for the board to know what to investigate, had it been interested.

After much consideration, we decided to raise the profile of the story to get Allied to take this more seriously. We reached out to *The New York Times*, which ran an article on November 8, 2006, describing our accusations that Allied engaged in pretexting. The article, written by Jenny Anderson and Julie Creswell, discussed the Allied critics who claimed they were victims of pretexting and the company's denial that it was responsible. The article stated:

> The allegations, made by Mr. Einhorn in two letters to Allied's board—one letter was sent as recently as September—suggest that getting the phone records under pretext may have been an effort to root out relationships and silence critics. . . . A spokesman for Allied said the company had no comment on the claims of pretexting, beyond its responses to Mr. Einhorn.

The New York Times article ran the day Allied announced its third-quarter 2006 earnings. On the conference call, Walton criticized me again:

> Before we wrap up, I'd like to comment on *The New York Times* article, which some of you may have seen, that ran in today—this morning's paper. As most of you know, probably all of you know, for the last four and a half years, David Einhorn, an investor with the short position in Allied Capital, has made a variety of accusations about Allied Capital. Our performance has proven his thesis to be very wrong. David's motives are simple; he makes money if he can drive down the price of Allied Capital stock. We believe today's story is yet just another example of Mr. Einhorn's tactics. With respect to today's article regarding accessing phone records of Einhorn and other Allied critics, David's written twice on this same topic. The first time that Einhorn raised an issue regarding access to phone records was in a letter to Allied board members in March 2005. Within a week the chairman of Allied's Audit Committee responded in a letter to Einhorn, indicating that the board had not seen evidence to support his accusations, but would evaluate any evidence of wrongdoing that he wished to provide.
>
> Mr. Einhorn never produced any evidence to support his accusations. Eighteen months later, after pretexting became big news, Mr. Einhorn provided yet another letter regarding the alleged access of phone records. In this letter he clearly attempts to capitalize on the recent media scrutiny involving Hewlett-Packard and that he'd be happy to provide the board with additional information that will be of assistance. These are his words. On September 29th, Allied's chairman of the Audit Committee responded to Mr. Einhorn in a letter. In that response the chairman indicated that the board looked into Einhorn's allegations and found no evidence to support his claim of management misconduct with respect to phone records. The board then requested once again, that he supply any evidence of wrongdoing. To date, he has not responded. Twice our board has written to him that his allegations are not supported by the facts, and twice our board invited to provide evidence of wrongdoing. Twice he has provided no information.

Significantly, his failure to respond was after he had indicated that he would be happy to provide evidence of wrongdoing. There is simply no evidence to support a claim that Allied tried to access Einhorn's phone records. We never received his records and all that the article points to in support of this claim is the word of Einhorn, an individual with a motive to depress Allied Capital's stock. As you know, Allied has performed in exemplary fashion, despite Mr. Einhorn's continued attacks. Indeed, we have had a 15.6 percent average annual total return to shareholders in the last five years ended September 30, 2006. Upon payment of our fourth-quarter preannounced dividend of $0.62 a share, we have distributed a total of $2.42 per share of regular quarterly dividends to shareholders for 2006. In fact, in the nearly five years from 2002 through September 30, 2006, Allied Capital's paid about $11 per share in cumulative dividends to its shareholders. We all wish that Mr. Einhorn would give up his quest for a big payday, at the expense of Allied Capital and its shareholders, however we expect he has far too much money to lose to do this.

PART FIVE

Greenlight Was Right . . . Carry On

CHAPTER 28

Charges and Denials

Allied received approval from its shareholders to issue stock as part of its "stock ownership initiative" at their annual meeting in May 2006. But as the year unfolded, Allied did not launch its tender offer to take the insiders out of their stock options. On the second-quarter conference call, management attributed the delay to "volatility" in the stock price. It had fallen from around $31 to $28 per share. Apparently, they would wait until the stock was trading better.

When Allied released its third-quarter results, we saw that the first nine months of 2006 were a lot like the 2005 results, except without the big gains from a couple of the home-run asset sales. For the first three quarters, Allied had net investment income of $0.97 per share and earnings per share of $1.47. It paid $1.80 per share in distributions, with the deficit bridged by the gains from the prior year capital gains. Allied began expensing its employee stock options, and compensation costs grew more than 50 percent over 2005 levels. They grew about 30 percent, excluding the stock option expense. Net investment income improved over 2005 levels, mostly from reduced investigation costs, which fell to about $4 million from about $32 million.

Though Allied temporarily halted stock sales after the investigations were announced, the company resumed issuing new equity in earnest in 2006, selling almost $300 million worth of shares to new investors during the year through Deutsche Bank, Merrill Lynch, and Bank of America.

Allied continued writing down its investment in BLX in dribs and drabs. Allied reduced its carrying value from $353 million at the end of 2005 to $285 million on September 30, 2006. According to Allied's filings, higher prepayments impacted the portfolio and a more competitive lending environment affected its originations.

Though Allied stopped disclosing BLX's summary financial results at the beginning of 2005, Allied provided enough evidence to show that BLX's problems were becoming severe and much more serious than the gradual write-downs indicated. In the nine months, Allied earned $11.9 million in interest and dividends from BLX, compared to $19.5 million the previous year. The cash portion of interest and dividends fell from $14.4 million to only $6.2 million. The dividend on the "Class B" equity interest fell from $9 million to nil. Further, the portion of BLX's borrowings on the bank line that Allied guaranteed expanded from $135 million to $188 million. This meant BLX's borrowing expanded from $270 million to $376 million. While it is possible that BLX actually needed to borrow more than $100 million in a single quarter, it is also possible that BLX saw that it was in big trouble and simply drew down as much of its line as possible. This is common practice when companies foresee significant problems with lenders, often immediately prior to filing for bankruptcy. Considering BLX wasn't paying Allied as much, it raised the question of why BLX needed to borrow at such an accelerated pace.

Given the higher borrowing, we estimated that Allied reduced its calculation of BLX's enterprise value by only 7 percent. Given the deterioration described above, it would be hard to justify such a modest reduction. Allied did this by yet again changing how it valued BLX. According to its SEC filings, "In addition, for the quarter ended September 30, 2006, we performed a *fifth* analysis whereby the value of BLX was determined by adding BLX's net asset value (adjusted for certain discounts) to the value of BLX's business operations, which was determined by using a discounted cash flow model." (Emphasis added) Apparently, given BLX's deterioration, they couldn't justify the modestly reduced value using the four old methods, which already generated an unreasonable valuation.

■ ■ ■

Two days after the *Times* story about pretexting, I spoke to a large gathering at the Value Investing Congress in New York about a couple of stocks we owned long. After I finished, a man approached me in the hall and followed me into the private "speakers only" room. He asked if I was proud of the *Times* pretexting story. I said I didn't see what there was to be proud about being the victim of a crime. Then he said, "I hear you're writing a book. Is it more like the stuff you spoke about today or about Allied Capital?" Alarm bells went off in my head. Rather than answer, I asked him who he was. He identified himself as Seth Faison from Sitrick & Company, a public relations firm. I'd heard of Sitrick. It was known for its aggressive advocacy on behalf of companies that were suing short-sellers, among them Overstock.com, Biovail, and Fairfax Holdings. By reputation, they are even more aggressive than Lanny Davis. I guessed, and later learned, that Allied had hired them. At this point, one of the conference organizers noticed the tension and escorted Faison from the private area.

■ ■ ■

The following week, I gave a closer reading to Allied's quarterly SEC filing. Buried on page eighty-two, under the section "Change in Unrealized Appreciation or Depreciation," in the subsection "Business Loan Express, LLC," the fourth paragraph read:

> Furthermore, in determining the fair-value of our investment in BLX at September 30, 2006, we considered the following items. First, the bank-lending environment for small business loans remains very competitive and, as a result, BLX continues to experience significant loan prepayments in its securitized portfolio. This has also had an effect on BLX's ability to grow its new loan origination volume. Second, the Office of the Inspector General of the SBA and the Department of Justice have been conducting investigations into the lending activities of BLX and its Detroit office. These investigations are ongoing.

I was on an airplane when I read this. I think even the pilots heard my "OH MY GOSH!"

This disclosure was new and meant that they knew this was *serious*. Allied does not disclose bad news unless it was *really* bad news. The fact that Allied buried this disclosure in an obscure part of the 10-Q meant that management didn't want anyone to notice it, but needed to provide legal cover so they could later say they had, indeed, disclosed the material development. Of course, the disclosure wasn't where you would expect an important regulatory development. For example, it wasn't under "Legal Proceedings." Allied's disclosure under Legal Proceedings continued to say that the investigations by the SEC and U.S. attorney in Washington primarily pertained to "portfolio valuation and our portfolio Company, Business Loan Express, LLC," giving the misimpression that the investigations were about valuation rather than lending practices. A week had passed since the filing. Was I the first person to actually read page eighty-two? It was so obscure, even Brickman missed it.

I also pointed out the disclosure to Carruthers, who did a search of legal databases and found a number of indictments in Michigan. On March 16, 2006, a federal grand jury issued a four-count indictment against Mohammed Mustafa, Ahmed Qdeih, and Abdulla Al-Jufairi. The indictment described the fraud as follows:

> Al-Jufairi was one of the principals of Global Construction, LLC, which did business as APCO Construction and Management ("APCO"). APCO was engaged in the renovation and construction of gas stations and gas-station mini-marts. . . . Additionally, Al-Jufairi had a friendly relationship with one or more employees of BLX, essentially acting as a loan broker for BLX.
>
> Advance Auto Service Center, Inc. ("Advance Auto") was a Michigan corporation owned by Mustafa, its president, and Qdeih, its secretary. Advance Auto purchased a gas station/convenience store business at 25025 Hoover, Warren, Michigan in approximately January 1999, financed by a promissory note with a ten-year term.
>
> On or about March 15, 2001, Mustafa and Qdeih signed a formal application and related papers on behalf of Advance Auto for a $1.1 million SBA-guaranteed loan to be issued by BLX. The stated

purpose of the requested loan was—$712,500 to be used for land acquisition (i.e. the purchase of the real property); $150,000 to be used for construction, repairs and renovations; and the balance applied to working capital, debt repayment, and closing costs. The borrowers were to contribute $37,500 toward closing costs; and $22,000 toward debt-refinancing. The total amount to be contributed by the borrowers, $129,500, represented the "owner's equity injection" required by the SBA as a condition of issuing it's [sic] guarantee of 75% of the loan. The loan was approved.

Al-Jufairi was the person who introduced Mustafa and Qdeih to BLX, and acted as an intermediary between BLX and Mustafa and Qdeih during the processing of the loan.

The indictment indicated the $129,500 owner equity injection had not been made.

The $150,000 loan disbursement intended as payment to APCO for work it had supposedly already done was *not* paid to APCO. Rather, the $150,000 loan disbursement check was deposited into the account of Qdeih's brother-in-law, less a cash-out of $25,000 which was deposited into an account of Al-Jufairi and his wife.

The loan went into default, and on or about September 1, 2005, the SBA purchased its guaranteed 75% share with allowable interest, paying a total of $798,186.18 [to satisfy its guarantee].

On June 13, 2006, the same federal grand jury issued a four-count indictment against Wladimir Mizerni, Halina Mizerni, and Abdulla Al-Jufairi. This indictment related to the Ryan Petro-Mart fraud that listed Amer Farran, Al-Jufairi's brother-in-law. As mentioned in Chapter 19, Farran had indicated he worked as an engineer at the Ford Motor Company. Notably, Farran was not indicted.

The indictment raised many of the same allegations as the earlier indictment. The equity injection of $240,000 had not been made on the $1.3 million loan. There were forged documents. The SBA paid a claim of $1,039,260.01. According to the SBA's Web site, "Arrest warrants have been issued, and all three defendants are fugitives. It is believed that the part-owner and his wife have fled to Australia, and the loan broker has returned to his native Qatar."

Also on June 13, 2006, the federal grand jury issued a five-count indictment against Roman Novatchinski, Wladimir Mizerni, and Al-Jufairi. This indictment related to Palace One Stop Shop. According to the indictment:

> Although it was intended from the outset that Mizerni was going to be an equal owner of the gas station with Novachinski, Mizerni was not listed as a member of Palace One Stop Shop, L.L.C., and his name did not appear on any of the loan documentation because Mizerni already had an SBA-guaranteed loan for a different gas station and he would not have been eligible to receive another SBA-guaranteed loan.

The indictment also accused Novatchinski of falsely stating that he was a U.S. citizen, that he had managed a Shell gas station between 1990 and 1994 and that he claimed to have $430,000 of cash on hand and in the bank. None of this was true. Again, the $250,000 equity injection was not made, and there were fraudulent and forged documents. The SBA paid a claim of over $1 million for its guarantee on Palace One Stop Shop on November 6, 2002.

Also on June 13, 2006, the federal grand jury issued a three-count indictment against Falamarz Zahraie and Daryoush Zahraie. This indictment related to D&F Petro, Inc. This was one of the loans associated with Imad Deaibes, who defaulted on several loans that I discussed in Chapter 19. Falamarz Zahraie operated Pars Petro, Inc. and had financial trouble. He was not a U.S. citizen, so he enlisted his brother Daryoush to help obtain a fraudulent SBA loan through BLX. Daryoush "purchased" the gas station from his brother, but he didn't really buy it, he simply gave the money to his brother to repay his existing debt. The check for the $240,000 equity injection was never cashed. The loan defaulted, and on November 18, 2003, the SBA paid a claim of over $700,000. Notably, Deaibes was not indicted.

Carruthers called the U.S. attorney's office and learned that this investigation was ongoing and they were working up the chain. More surprisingly, he learned in November 2006 that the investigation by the U.S. attorney's office in Michigan did not originate from our efforts. It didn't come from the Justice Department, the SBA, or the SEC. Apparently, the Department of Homeland Security detected that some non-U.S. citizens of questionable backgrounds received SBA loans in Detroit through BLX. This triggered the U.S. attorney's office to investigate, where it found the large BLX fraud.

Carruthers found that the first indictments in the case came on October 5, 2005. Husam Fakhoury was indicted for falsely indicating he was not on probation and had not been charged, arrested, or convicted for any criminal offense other than a minor motor vehicle violation, when, in fact, he was on probation after being convicted of conspiracy to transport and sell stolen motor vehicles. On the same day, Sharif Affas was indicted for falsely indicating he was a citizen when he was not.

■ ■ ■

According to Carruthers, when the U.S. attorney's office dug through the cases, it discovered a much larger fraud against the SBA. While we were obviously excited to find these developments, it was galling that these were some of the *same cases* we told the SBA about in 2003—and it did nothing about them. The very agency being defrauded showed no interest, because it knew it was part of the problem. Either it had little interest in correcting the problem because the agency was politically motivated to lend money and not ask questions, was too underfunded to check, or had been co-opted by BLX. Or *all of the above*. The SBA's lack of concern that taxpayers were being ripped off, are being ripped off, and will be ripped off—all in its name—is nothing short of appalling.

CHAPTER 29

Charges and Admissions

On January 10, 2007, the Associated Press reported that nineteen Detroit-area residents faced federal charges for allegedly defrauding the Small Business Administration out of nearly $77 million. Federal prosecutors accused Patrick J. Harrington, a "former" vice president of BLX of "overstating or misstating loan applicants' financial qualifications, and with falsifying the amount of money they contributed toward the business, witness tampering and lying to a grand jury." The indictment said the defaults cost taxpayers more than $28 million according to the article, which also noted that there had been six previous indictments against Michigan residents—three of whom awaited sentencing and three of whom were fugitives.

The indictment was dated December 14, 2006, but had remained sealed until January 9, 2007. It indicated Harrington had been a principal with Allied Capital SBLC Corporation since September 23, 1998. After Allied acquired BLC Financial, Harrington was an executive vice president of BLX until September 2006. BLX closed its office in Troy, Michigan, on August 1, 2006.

According to the indictment:

> Typically, the fraudulent loans involved one of approximately five individuals, or groups of individuals (collectively referred to herein for convenience as the "brokers"), who were orchestrating the purchase and resale of gas stations (or gas station/convenience stores), or, in some instances, party stores, restaurants, or small motels. The broker would locate (and sometimes purchase) a property that was for sale, and then would find a person willing to "buy" the property at an inflated price using an SBA-guaranteed loan issued by BLX.
>
> In some instances, the buyer was truly interested in owning and operating a business. In other instances, the buyer was a "straw buyer" who did not intend to operate the business or to make loan payments, but was paid (or promised payment) by the broker to serve as a buyer. The broker profited from the mark-up in the price of the property. Harrington profited by being compensated by BLX based, in part, upon the amount of loans he originated.

The indictment described various false representations, forged documents used in the loan fraud, Harrington's efforts to persuade other witnesses to lie to investigators, and Harrington's own lies to the grand jury on October 6, 2005. It listed a number of loans, including several that Kroll and Brickman had flagged and we had passed on to regulators.

The indictment was attached to an affidavit by Stanley C. Chappell, a senior special agent in the SBA-OIG. Chappell said he was "one of several OIG Special Agents who, along with Special Agents of the U.S. Secret Service, are investigating a large number of fraudulently-obtained SBA-guaranteed loans issued by BLX."

Chappell swore he had "participated in numerous interviews of Patrick J. Harrington, who . . . has admitted that between approximately 2000 and July 2006, he, and other BLX employees working at his direction, originated and issued approximately 96 SBA-guaranteed loans knowing that the financial and other qualifications of the principal(s) of the small business borrower were fraudulently overstated and/or misstated, and that the satisfaction of the equity injection requirement was falsely and fraudulently documented, in order to fraudulently qualify the borrowers for the loans."

■ ■ ■

With the story finally in the public domain and picked up by other media, Allied immediately began to spin. It assembled talking points that appeared in numerous analyst research reports despite the inconvenient fact that the "talking points" were false and misleading. The first report came from Merrill Lynch. Merrill had switched analysts covering Allied, with Ken Bruce replacing Michael Hughes. Bruce seemed more objective about Allied than Hughes. He actually said in his report after the indictment that Allied's critics appeared to be right. He wrote, "The shorts in ALD likely feel vindicated, as much of the short-argument now seems valid." (He later told me he caught heat from Allied for that remark.) However, he continued, "Given the indictment involves only one former employee acting on his own, it seems premature to question all the lending practices in BLX and discount the company altogether."

The other analysts covering Allied took the talking points from management at face value. Keefe, Bruyette & Woods wrote, "Management noted that this status (Preferred Lender) is granted by territory (there are roughly 70 territories within the US) and given that Detroit is only one office within one of these territories, this is less of a concern."

Bank of America thought the stock price weakness was reason to upgrade the shares. "We believe the market is over-reacting as the investigation has been disclosed over the past two years and the latest development is the result of a corrupt employee in one of ALD's 140 portfolio companies."

Morgan Stanley repeated, "The problems at BLX seem isolated to one office and are not likely indicative of other issues at BLX or Allied's other portfolio companies, in our view."

Ferris, Baker Watts added, "Though this investigation has been going on since the summer (and discussed in Allied's 10-Q filing), the actual indictment was unsealed on Tuesday. The BLX office in question was closed in August of 2006. The employee under investigation was fired in September 2006. The company factored this event into its valuation of BLX then and wrote it down by $34 million during the September quarter."

A. G. Edwards also upgraded the stock. "BLX was notified of the fraudulent activity approximately six months ago and chose to fire Mr. Harrington and closed the Detroit office."

And my favorite proclamation came from Citigroup: ". . . our view that the recent selloff is an overreaction, as BLX retains value even in a worst-case scenario in which it was shut down." I don't think it would be worth *anything* if it were shut down. In fact, the better question would be, how much further liability would Allied have?

These comments came from what Allied management told the analysts. *According to Allied, when BLX heard the news of a rogue employee it acted promptly, decisively and responsibly by dismissing Harrington and closing the office. Allied fully disclosed the circumstances in its quarterly SEC filing as soon as the company knew them. This was a case of a single rogue employee engaged in misconduct, and such behavior did not exist elsewhere at BLX. In fact, BLX was actually a victim of Harrington's fraud. In any case, BLX was just one investment out of a large portfolio of 140 investments and Allied had relatively insignificant exposure to any loss.*

Of course, almost none of this spin was accurate. Allied had not made good disclosure of what had happened. When it disclosed the SBA's OIG and U.S. attorney investigations into the Detroit office deep in the middle of the wrong section of its September 2006 10-Q (BLX closed the Detroit office on August 1, 2006—eight days before Allied filed its second-quarter 10-Q, which made no mention anywhere of these developments), Allied did not disclose that it had fired Harrington or that it had closed the Detroit office. Allied waited to confess until the U.S. attorney unsealed Harrington's indictment. Allied/BLX knew the U.S. attorney from the Eastern District of Michigan was investigating the Detroit office no later than October 2005, when its employees provided sworn testimony. It failed to make any disclosure of this for an entire year.

Further, when Allied announced its second-quarter 2006 earnings and held a conference call, Walton highlighted that Allied had lower legal and investigation related expenses. Don Destino, who was now covering Allied from JMP Securities, asked, "Could an enterprising analyst assume that that means you think that's [the investigation] coming to an end, with not much of a punch line to it?" Walton answered, "One would hope. You know, *it's obviously a lot quieter.*" He said this the day after BLX closed the Detroit office.

We, of course, knew that the fraud at BLX was much broader than a single employee in a single office, and in its article by Julie Creswell on January 13, 2007, *The New York Times* said the SBA knew it, too. The *Times* article said:

Federal investigators are now looking at loans issued by the unit, Business Loan Express, in other parts of the country, according to several people briefed on the investigation.

And the federal Small Business Administration—which typically guarantees 75 percent of the value of these small-business loans—is considering suspending the preferred lending status of Business Loan Express, pending the outcome of an investigation. That would mean that every loan Business Loan Express issues would have to be vetted by the agency, those people said.

The S.B.A. this week also suspended the unit's ability to sell the loans it issues to large institutional investors in the secondary market, which could affect the ability of Business Loan Express to make loans, those people said. The unit can still originate loans, but only if it intends to hold those loans on its own books, which is not something the firm has historically done.

"Allied has been aware of misconduct by Mr. Harrington for half a decade and it won't be hard to find many more similarly fraudulent loans in other parts of the country," I told the *Times*. The *Times* article continued:

About a year ago, the S.B.A., which gives its lenders an internal rating on a one-to-five scale, lowered Business Loan Express to the lowest rating that would allow it to remain in the preferred lending program, based on a rising level of late payments and defaults on loans it had made, according to people involved in the investigation.

The article noted that the House Small Business Committee headed by Nydia Velázquez (who had received large contributions from BLX CEO Tannenhauser and other Allied executives, as described in Chapter 26), had begun its own investigation of the loans in Michigan and possibly in other states. "The committee will be investigating SBA's involvement and how the agency could have failed to detect this," Kate L. Davis, a spokeswoman for Velázquez, said. The article reported that the SBA planned to re-examine more than five years of loans and could seek restitution if there were additional cases of fraud.

"He [Harrington] says he made a mistake, but not near to the extent that the government claims," Harrington's lawyer said in the article.

Lanny Davis, now working for BLX, told the *Times,* "This is a good company, with good people, and I believe, in the final analysis, this will be borne out."

Not one of the Wall Street analysts made a significant comment about the *Times* article, which described a much larger problem than the analysts or Allied acknowledged. I asked Robert Lacoursiere, the Bank of America analyst, why Wall Street was not responding. In an e-mail he responded, "The *Times* article has no named sources at the various interested agencies who are willing to be on the record to support your concerns—it therefore is no better than speculation/rumor/innuendo—that's different from information to rationally form an opinion on."

Allied responded to the *Times* article by issuing a press release:

> Allied Capital understands that BLX is working cooperatively with the Small Business Administration with respect to this matter. In particular, Allied Capital understands that BLX is working with the SBA so that it may remain a preferred lender in the SBA 7(a) program and retain the ability to sell loans into the secondary market [where they sell the guaranteed pieces]. Allied Capital anticipates that BLX will abide by certain terms and conditions under which they will operate going forward in the program and Allied Capital will stand behind any financial commitments BLX makes to the SBA in this regard to prevent any loss due to fraud.

The release also described Allied's financial relationship with BLX. "Allied Capital's total investment in BLX was $284.9 million at value at September 30, 2006, or 6.2% of Allied Capital's assets. Allied Capital's investment in BLX is in the equity of the company and this investment at value compares to BLX's net book value at September 30, 2006, of $190 million. At December 31, 2006, BLX had outstanding borrowings under its line of credit of $322 million and BLX had estimated assets of approximately $600 million to support the borrowings on the line of credit."

In reality, Allied's exposure was much larger. Adding in Allied's guarantee of BLX's debt, Allied's commitment was over $500 million. Further, Allied now promised direct restitution to the SBA and risked additional legal exposure from other victims of BLX's fraud. The release continued, "BLX has a substantial cash flow stream from its residual interests and servicing assets and collected approximately $100 million in cash from its residual interests and servicing assets in fiscal 2006." Apparently, this wasn't enough to stop BLX from substantially increasing its bank borrowings.

Allied's press release spin went further:

> If scheduled loan payments were to be received as stated in the loan agreements with no future losses or prepayments, BLX would receive future cash flows of over $1 billion over time.

This was an extremely misleading picture of BLX's financial status. Of course, prepayments and defaults are a fact of life. The future cash flows were not actually expected to be anything close to $1 billion. In fact, if BLX couldn't sell new loans into the secondary market, they would have limited ability to originate new loans. No new loans meant BLX was on its way out of business.

■ ■ ■

The market holds credit rating agencies in a special place, because they are allowed to review confidential inside information in making their assessments. Fitch Ratings gave the all-clear signal. "The news surrounding the indictment suggests that the scope of improper practices may be limited to the Detroit office of BLX. This provides Fitch with comfort that BLX has a sound business model and that the large majority of its nearly $2.7 billion in serviced loans are viable assets."

Shortly after the Fitch report hit the wires, Mark Roberts from *Off Wall Street* e-mailed me. "I spoke with Meghan Crowe, CFA, of Fitch, who wrote the Allied rating piece on *Bloomberg,* and told her that if she had more factual information she might come to a different conclusion, and I told her I could provide her with research that contained this information. She said she was not interested. I told her that I was amazed at her response, if she was at all interested in seeking the truth. She remained unimpressed. What can I say?"

James Lin called her and confirmed that her rating is based on the information disclosed by Allied in conversations with her, their filings, and the press releases. She was taking that information at face value in her rating assessment.

We decided to take the matter back to Allied's board. We wrote a ten-page letter on January 22, 2007, which we released to the media. I reminded the directors of my 2005 letter, when I alerted them to the fraud at BLX. The letter told the board to remove "the present management team that has presided over the metastasizing fraud at BLX and Allied" and "end the dishonest culture perpetuated by current management." I wanted new management brought in to clean house. I believed *any* new management would reveal even greater problems at Allied immediately, because it would not want to be blamed for lingering ethical lapses or accounting abuses.

I advised the board that the Harrington indictment was not the isolated act of a single, rogue employee. I identified seventeen other states where we identified fraudulent BLX loans. I detailed the mounting evidence of fraud at BLX based on Allied's disclosures and legal and government records. This included the original loan-parking arrangement when Allied formed BLX and Allied's knowledge of Harrington's misconduct all the way back to at least Holly Hawley's testimony about her car wash loans in 2002 with Allied's lawyers present.

The Harrington indictment and related indictments came just before the deadline the judge gave us to serve BLX with the shrimp-boat False Claims suit, so we also told the board about the unsealed suit in the letter. We described other SBA fraud, Matthew McGee, and the Bill Russell USDA fraud. We described our compilation of the SBA and USDA default data.

Then, we pointed out that management responded dishonestly about the recent events. In summary, we challenged the spin that BLX had only recently learned of the fraud, that it involved a single rogue employee, that Allied's risk was limited to its investment in BLX, that BLX was financially strong, and that management acted promptly and fully to disclose the event. "Each new revelation about the fraud . . . is met with escalating denials from Allied's management and deafening silence from the Board," I wrote.

Allied responded the same evening via a press release, saying my letter was "yet another example of his long-running attempts to manipulate the price of Allied Capital's stock." The company also said my letter had numerous inaccuracies. Of course, the company didn't say what they were. "While Mr. Einhorn busied himself with repeated attacks against Allied Capital over the last five years, Allied Capital's board of directors and management have maintained their focus on creating shareholder value and building the company." In the press release, the company made a thinly veiled threat that it was going to sue us.

A friend joked, "My stock is up. Therefore, I am not a crook."

■ ■ ■

The stock fell $2 per share to $28 on January 22 after my letter to the board became news. The next morning the stock fell another $1.50 a share, but began recovering when Allied spread word that it would come out with a point-by-point response to my letter. In contrast to the barrage of analyst reports following the Harrington indictment, almost all the analysts remained silent about my letter and Allied's vague response. It seemed they would wait until Allied told them what to say.

One of the few analysts who didn't defend Allied was Rick Shane of Jefferies & Co. The day after my letter, he wrote, "While some of our competitors have viewed recent declines as an attractive entry point, we remain more circumspect. The indictment of a BLX employee appears to have triggered both internal and external inquiries. As outsiders, we are uncomfortable predicting the outcome of these inquiries and feel that recommending ALD stock at this time based on valuation ignores incremental risk."

On the other hand, the A. G. Edwards analyst, Troy Ward, was undeterred: "While Mr. Einhorn's negative opinion of BLX seems to be in line with the Harrington indictment on fraud, in our opinion this does not substantiate his larger supposition that there is [sic] 'wide-spread' underwriting issues at BLX. We do not believe that fraud at the BLX Detroit office is necessarily an indication that BLX's underwriting standards are sub-par." Ward added, "We have difficulty believing that KPMG and third party valuation firms would approve ALD's valuation methodology of BLX if there were rampant indications of fraud through BLX."

Two weeks later, I heard that Allied's point-by-point response to my letter would be "delayed." Allied's lawyers wouldn't let them release it because it might offend the regulators they were trying to work with.

On January 25, 2007, Carol Remond reported on the *Dow Jones Newswire* that, "BLX has agreed not to resell loans on the secondary market, a move that could hamper its ability to make future loans. A spokesman for the SBA said BLX 'voluntarily suspended' sales of loans on the secondary market until a number of conditions set by SBA are met."

For some reason, this article did not get picked up in any other news service that I saw. No analyst commented on the development, and Allied did not issue a release announcing the negative development.

Remond's *Dow Jones* article included an interesting SBA perspective on how the Detroit investigation developed:

> SBA said that its staff in Detroit reported suspicious irregularities in BLX's loan portfolio to the Inspector General's office as early as 2002. SBA's Inspector General led the multi-year investigation resulting in the arrests announced on January 9, 2007. SBA's Loan Monitoring System alerted SBA and BLX to the abnormally high default rate.

Following *The New York Times* article on January 13, 2007, which said the House Small Business Committee "will be investigating SBA's involvement and how the agency could have failed to detect this," I asked Greenlight's lawyers from Akin, Gump to contact Chairwoman Velázquez's staff to offer our assistance in helping them understand what happened. On January 26, 2007, our lawyers met three of her staffers, including Michael Day, her chief of staff. The staff was "stone-faced." They were open to receiving information, but were not interested in seeking it out. It was clear they were *moving slowly*. It didn't seem that Ms. Velázquez would get to the bottom of this, after all. I wasn't surprised, remembering the contributions Velázquez received from BLX CEO Tannenhauser, his family, and other Allied executives, including Sweeney.

■ ■ ■

Just before I left my house for the train on February 6, 2007, I took a quick peek at my home computer for any news on Greenlight's portfolio. At 7:03 a.m., Allied issued a press release titled "Allied Capital Comments on Recent Events." I figured they were putting out the point-by-point response, after all.

Instead, though the press release was incredibly convoluted, it appeared they were admitting they stole not only my home phone records, but also Greenlight's. The release read:

> Allied Capital Corporation announced today that, in late December 2006, it received a subpoena from the United States Attorney's Office

for the District of Columbia requesting, among other things, the production of records regarding the use of private investigators by Allied
Capital or its agents. The Board established a committee, which was
advised by its own counsel, to review the following matter.

In the course of gathering documents responsive to the subpoena, Allied Capital has become aware that an agent of the
Company obtained what were represented to be telephone records
of David Einhorn and which purport to be records of calls from
Greenlight Capital during a period of time in 2005.

Also, while Allied Capital was gathering documents responsive
to the subpoena, allegations were made that Allied Capital management had authorized the acquisition of these records and that
management was subsequently advised that these records had been
obtained. The management of Allied Capital states that these allegations are not true.

Allied Capital is cooperating fully with the inquiry by the United
States Attorney's office and will have no further comment concerning
this matter until that inquiry has been concluded.

Almost poetically, a half hour later, Allied issued a second press release
announcing a one-cent increase to the quarterly distribution.

I had not known that Allied also obtained Greenlight's phone records—
or at least the "purported" records. The release also stated that the board
was forming a committee to investigate. Funny, Allied had said in response
to my letters to the board that it already investigated and found nothing. For them to admit this, the evidence must have been extremely clear.
Certainly, the press release was not. Who made the allegations? Presumably,
it was either someone at Allied or the "agent" who obtained the records.
Was Allied, as a corporation, denying that its management knew, or was
only the management denying it, with the company staying silent? I thought
the latter, but the press reported the former. If Sweeney didn't know, then
why did she duck Greenberg's inquiries on this topic in 2005?

"After five years, Allied Capital has acknowledged a tiny piece of its
rampant misconduct," I told the press that day. "The evidence was clearly
always there; the board simply neglected its fiduciary responsibility to super-
vise the company appropriately."

The next day, Greenlight released a somewhat longer statement. After
briefly reviewing Allied's history of ignoring my letters and quoting Walton's

blistering attack against me on the last conference call, the statement continued, "Now that Allied has admitted that its agent pretexted my personal phone records and one of BLX's long-time senior executives has been indicted for the very fraud that I alerted the Board to, it is time for Allied to stop its dismissive attitude toward concerns I have brought to its attention and stop its personal attacks on me.

"Instead, Allied continues on with its usual pattern. Allied admits nothing until they are forced to do so. Allied did not acknowledge the loan practices until a BLX executive was indicted. Allied did not admit the pretexting until Allied was subpoenaed by federal prosecutors." I called for the dismissal of management.

We received a call from Steven Pearlstein, a business columnist with *The Washington Post*. A quick review of his history showed he did not like hedge funds. For example, he wrote a column in 2005 that summarized a handful of reported hedge fund frauds and concluded:

> This is not a case of a few rotten apples. It's a case of an industry that has become so rich and arrogant—and so littered with charlatans and con men—that government must step in to protect the public interest.

He wanted to meet with me to discuss Allied. I decided to have Steve Bruce at Abernathy, McGregor return the call. According to Bruce, he accused us of trading on inside information. Bruce asked if he knew when Greenlight traded. Pearlstein didn't. "Then how can you accuse them of insider trading?" Bruce replied.

Then Pearlstein complained that a lot of the information contained in my letter to the board didn't come out of Allied's 10-Ks. Bruce pointed out that the information came from Allied's public disclosures, news accounts, legal filings, government Web sites, and inquiries we made under the Freedom of Information Act. Pearlstein apparently thought it was unfair for professional investors to do in-depth research, including using time and resources that individual investors don't have.

We braced ourselves for what would surely be an attack. On February 9, 2007, the *Post* published his column headlined, "A Slugfest Gets Uglier:"

> After five years of nasty accusations and name-calling, lawsuits and investigations, it's hard to find the good guy in the high-stakes feud between hedge fund manager David Einhorn and Allied Capital.

Einhorn is a Wall Street punk—tough, smart, cocky. In his campaign to discredit Allied Capital and drive down its stock price, he's been wrong about several things, such as allegations that the company inflated the value of certain investments on its books. And he's grossly exaggerated the significance of other problems of a company that continues to post respectable profits and pay hefty dividends. His big bet—that Allied stock would fall—looks to have been a loser for investors in Einhorn's Greenlight Capital.

But even punks can sometimes be right. In this case, it turns out that Einhorn was on to something when he alleged in 2002 that there was a pattern of fraudulent lending at one of Allied's portfolio companies. Since then, a former loan officer has been indicted, the office he worked in has been closed, loan losses have increased, and the Small Business Administration has increased its oversight of the company's lending.

And Einhorn was also right when he alleged that private investigators acting on behalf of Allied had improperly obtained his phone records. Allied admitted as much this week, and in time, it is likely that we'll learn that his were not the only phone records involved. These disclosures are more than simply a huge embarrassment for Allied, a Washington outfit that lends to and invests in small and mid-size companies. They also call into question the judgment and competence of chairman and chief executive Bill Walton, the outside directors, and the high-priced legal team brought in to manage the response to Einhorn and other shortsellers. From the beginning, Allied spent too much time and energy questioning the motives of its critics and too little digging into the substance of Einhorn's allegations. Company executives' responses were at times evasive, at other times incomplete.

For me, the clincher was this week's Hewlett-Packard–like admission that Einhorn's phone records were stolen. When the allegation was first raised in 2005, the audit committee of Allied's board responded that management and outside counsel had looked into the charges and found nothing—and then invited Einhorn to write again if he had more specific information to offer. It was the standard brushoff that directors and corporate counsel routinely give to whistle-blowers everywhere.

In fact, Einhorn's letter was plenty specific on the "pretexting" issue, noting that someone had opened an online account in his wife's name and directed the phone company to send copies of their home phone bills to an AOL account. Any chief executive or corporate lawyer worth his salt would have responded to it by immediately launching a thorough probe, turning over every rock to find out if anybody associated with the company had ordered such an inquiry or received any such information. Unfortunately, that wasn't done until nearly two years later, when a subpoena was received from a U.S. attorney.

Belatedly, Allied's board has now formed a "special committee" with a new set of lawyers to conduct a new investigation. But in other respects, Allied remains in its defensive crouch. Allied refuses to disclose which directors are on the committee or the identities of the new lawyers. And even before the inquiry has begun, it repeated its claim that nobody in management did anything wrong. The board was also careful to limit the scope of the new inquiry to the single set of phone records so far uncovered.

This is too little, too late—the kind of begrudging response you'd expect from a group of longtime directors (average tenure, 11 years) overly concerned about their own reputations and legal liability. The only way for the company to regain credibility with shareholders and regulators is to remove Walton as chairman and chief executive, replace the audit committee with new outside directors, and dismiss the outside lawyers and other key players on the Einhorn response team.

As for Einhorn, his campaign against Allied should be closely examined by the Securities and Exchange Commission and Congress as they consider how to rein in hedge funds that have gained undue influence in financial markets and the economy. (© 2007, *The Washington Post*. Reprinted with Permission.)

I didn't like being called "cocky" or a "punk." I also found it annoyingly perverse that my success in exposing fraud at BLX should lead to greater hedge fund regulation. Perhaps Pearlstein had so much antipathy toward hedge funds that he couldn't help himself. But—here's the important thing—he was really the first person in the media in five years to say I was right about anything regarding Allied, and he did it in Allied's hometown newspaper.

CHAPTER 30

Late Innings

On February 19, 2007, I received a phone call from an Allied shareholder. We had debated Allied on several occasions over the years, always in a civil way. The shareholder had just spoken with COO Sweeney and wanted to share the conversation with me.

He said that Allied was really mad, that our fight had been going on for five years, and they were sick of it. Management and the board were "digging in." Sweeney said my January letter to the board was "wildly misleading" and "grossly inaccurate." When he pushed her to be specific, she admitted that everything in the letter "was technically correct," but vaguely claimed that it doesn't come to the right conclusion, nor did it include "all the facts." When pressed to identify the missing facts, Sweeney declined, saying it wasn't necessary to go "tit-for-tat."

Sweeney told him that BLX "doesn't need the SBA 7(a) program" and that the losses are nowhere near $70 million identified in the Harrington indictment. She said that the private investigator who stole my phone records was hired by Allied directly, not by an agent. However, the special committee of directors had limited its investigation to the pretexting, because "We don't need an investigation to refute the [public] letter [Greenlight sent the board]." She wouldn't comment on whether Allied took other people's records, but claimed pretexting wasn't even illegal back then—a rather odd interpretation of privacy law.

She also told the shareholder that the Inspector General of the SBA in Michigan was "personally close with David," as evidenced by "whoever heard of the SBA calling a press conference to announce a fraud?" That was almost funny—I have never spoken with or met him. In fact, I don't even know his name. Sweeney went on to say that nobody in management was resigning. By now, I was used to hearing Allied's cockamamie claims. I simply thanked the shareholder—who I now believe has become a former shareholder—and waited for the next thing.

■ ■ ■

In 1998, Greenlight invested in the parent of the Virgin Islands Telephone Company. Jeffrey Prosser, its control shareholder, took the company private at a price we felt to be unfair to minority stockholders, including Greenlight. We sued in Delaware, where the company was incorporated.

In 2003, the Delaware court found that the fair price of the company was almost four times more than Prosser had paid. The court also found that Prosser and several others had committed fraud and breached their duties to shareholders as part of the transaction. The good news: The court awarded Greenlight over $100 million in damages. The bad news: After several years of negotiations, Prosser did not pay us, and, in 2006, he and his company filed for bankruptcy.

Enter Lanny Davis, now hired by Prosser. Prosser had a separate dispute with his company's senior lender, the Rural Telephone Finance Cooperative (RTFC), which Prosser alleged to have interfered with his efforts to salvage value. Prosser filed suit against the RTFC in bankruptcy court in the U.S. Virgin Islands. Prosser's key witness to support his allegation against the RTFC was none other than Davis himself. As part of the bankruptcy proceeding, we were allowed to depose Davis on February 1, 2007. This gave us the chance to question him under oath about Allied—an opportunity not to be missed.

Our lawyer: "Have you ever stated that Mr. Einhorn was spreading some false and misleading information for his personal benefit?"

Davis: "I don't specifically recall that."

Our lawyer: "Do you recall telling a reporter at Reuters the following statement: 'Every single allegation without exception made by these short-sellers,' referring to Mr. Einhorn, 'are false and in many cases we can prove they are knowingly false.'"

Davis, after reviewing the article: "I believe I was referring to Mr. Einhorn's charges made against both Allied Capital and Business Loan Express as being false, and in many cases I believed we could prove they were knowingly false."

Our lawyer: "And have you to date ever proven those statements to be false?"

Davis: "Never filed a lawsuit against Mr. Einhorn, no."

Our lawyer: "Have you ever provided any information to show those allegations are false?"

Davis: "Have I ever provided information to whom?"

Our lawyer: "To the SEC."

Davis: "No."

Sure, he didn't. Greenlight's lawyer asked him if he had seen the articles I wrote for TheStreet.com in 2002 criticizing Allied's treatment of BLX. Davis didn't recall ever seeing them. If he were telling the truth, how could he have complained to regulators and even gone on television to discuss my *Big Lie* when he had not read what I wrote?

Davis was then asked about the analysis we posted on our Web site in 2002. He vaguely remembered that he reviewed it, but didn't "remember this specific document."

Our lawyer: "And you don't recall whether these were the allegations that you said 'every single allegation without exception made by these short-sellers was false and in many cases we can prove they are knowingly false?'"

Davis: "I don't remember if it's this particular document, but I remember at the time the allegations made by Mr. Einhorn after examining all the evidence and interviewing all the individuals involved in the various companies that Mr. Einhorn claimed were being over inflated in value, that Mr. Einhorn's charges were false. And I believe he was given a full documentation explanation as to why they were false and he repeated the allegations and that's why I used the word 'knowing[ly].'"

Incidentally, when Prosser was to prove his case against the RTFC, his star witness, Davis, did not show up to testify to support his claims, and Prosser withdrew his suit. The judge was not amused.

■ ■ ■

Allied released its year-end 2006 results on February 28, 2007. It announced that it wrote-down BLX by $74 million and put the investment on non-accrual. Allied said BLX might need to be restructured and recapitalized. On the conference call that day, management said BLX was now pursuing its non-SBA lending activities, and this required a secured lending agreement, as opposed to its current unsecured agreement. As a result, it was looking for a new bank lender.

Meanwhile, Allied injected another $12 million into BLX to help it remain "compliant with covenants" on its existing credit line. Management indicated that, otherwise, the debt-to-equity ratio would have fallen below the minimum threshold. It sounded as though the existing bank group had become unhappy with BLX, even though Allied guaranteed half the debt. It was clear that the banks would not permit Allied to extract additional management fees, interest, or dividends from its BLX investment. Even with the reduced value, Allied still determined BLX had an enterprise value of almost $600 million.

Walton tried to put his best spin on BLX: "And I think one of the pleasant surprises about BLX in 2006 was how they were able to transition from an SBA-oriented business primarily to a conventional real estate business. And I think that's something that we think is potentially pretty valuable for the future."

A few moments later, he added: "But we do think the [SBA] business has reached a nadir and it's coming back from here, and we're putting a lot of things in place we think this business was going to come back. *And this is not the problem that it's been portrayed as being.* The business has gotten less profitable during 2006 because of the bank competitions for the loans. But *it remains profitable,* and we think as the business evolves in its new form is going to be very profitable again. And also I think the notion of keeping cash in there is a good idea because that's—*they've always generated good cash flow.*"

Later on the call, management indicated BLX's book value was between $180 million and $190 million. The previous time Allied disclosed

BLX's book value was at the end of 2004, when it was $155 million. Since then, Allied increased its equity investment by about $59 million through a combination of converting debt to equity and injecting fresh funds. I calculated that if BLX broke even, its book value should be about $215 million. Instead, it was $25 to $35 million less. Presumably, this is how much BLX has lost since the end of 2004. Considering BLX's obviously deteriorating results—I don't believe BLX "remained profitable"—and its legal and liquidity predicament, Allied's valuation of BLX was far in excess of its unjustifiable June 2002 valuation—ridiculous!

During this Allied conference call, Brad Golding of Christofferson Robb asked: "My next question is, it was my understanding that up until recently that the senior management of Allied had been on the BLX board. I take it that's no longer the case. What changed, why did you leave, and when did that happen?"

Walton responded: "There has been no change in the board of BLX. It's been the *same*. And we think we've had an effective oversight at BLX. We've got a situation in Detroit that is what it is. And we continue to believe that *BLX is a very healthy business with very high lending standards and good internal controls* and has been and is and will be that, and we had problems in the Detroit office, and we think we took the BLX people took effective action at the time they knew things."

Golding followed up: "Okay. Can you tell me who from Allied is on the board of BLX?"

Walton moved on: "We really don't—I don't want to—we really haven't disclosed the board members of any of our portfolio companies. And I don't think this is the time to set that precedent. Okay. We've got—sorry you almost done?"

It turns out that about a month before the conference call, Brickman discovered in a Florida regulatory filing, that BLX Commercial Capital LLC included Walton and Sweeney as managing members (the equivalent of directors) in 2005, but "deleted" them as members in its 2006 filing. By early 2006, the various investigations, including the Michigan investigation, were well known to Allied. Was this a sign that Walton and Sweeney saw trouble ahead and wanted to distance themselves from BLX? Maybe, but the executives weren't talking.

On March 6, 2007, Allied announced that BLX had reached an agreement with the SBA to remain a preferred lender and would retain an ability to sell SBA loans into the secondary market, provided an independent third party reviewed them. BLX agreed to pay the SBA $10 million to cover some of the fraudulent Detroit loans and put an additional $10 million into escrow to cover potential additional payments to the SBA in the future.

The point of being a preferred lender is to make SBA loans *without* prior agency review. If an SBA-approved third party now needed to approve BLX loans, what was the point of being a preferred lender? It sounded like a face-saving compromise, where BLX could publicly *claim* to be a preferred lender without actually being one in practice.

■ ■ ■

On March 2, 2007, a senior staffer on the House Committee on Energy and Commerce invited me to speak at its upcoming hearing to consider legislation against telephone pretexting. A week later, I appeared before Congress on a panel of speakers (government officials and telephone industry lobbyists) and gave my views. I was the only victim of pretexting on the panel. The chair welcomed me by commenting that pretexting "is not a crime that has no consequences. Mr. Einhorn, the committee thanks you for coming before us and I am sorry, indeed, for what has happened to you and your family."

I began: "My testimony is about a corporation and management team that in attempting to ensure their survival placed no limits on the exercise of their power. Pretexting is a brazen invasion of privacy. When a large corporation has its agents spy on private citizens in order to intimidate them and silence criticism, it threatens more than just the sanctity of the individual's privacy; it threatens the freedom of the securities markets which we take for granted."

I told Congress the Allied story: my speech; my concerns about its accounting and operational deficiencies; investment valuation; and how its small business lending unit defrauded the SBA and USDA government lending programs costing taxpayers hundreds of millions of dollars. I discussed how Allied, rather than own up to its problems, attacked me and stole my phone records.

I noted that while Allied and Walton initially denied stealing my records, the company's recent admission of the theft raised more questions: Who obtained the records? Who else's records did they steal? Who authorized the theft, and for what purpose? What did they do with this information? And what else might these agents have done to gather information about their critics?

Allied's disclosure lacked both an apology and an explanation. My testimony continued: "After the Hewlett-Packard pretexting scandal, HP immediately apologized to the victims and promised to give the victims a full account. But, to date, I have heard nothing from Allied. No one has contacted me to apologize or explain who invaded my privacy and my family's privacy. Allied has not yet admitted to taking anyone else's records. Of course, they don't deny it, either. It is simply not credible that Allied management did not know about this."

The members of Congress seemed appalled by my story and they followed up with several questions. Congressman Michael Burgess from Texas prefaced his question to me by saying, "It won't do any good for me to apologize to you, but I'll do it anyway." The chair asked the representative from the Federal Trade Commission whether it was investigating these business practices by Allied Capital. The response was that such investigations are not public, but the agency would be willing to have a private briefing with the Congressional staff. Chairman John Dingell indicated that the record would be held open for Allied Capital to offer any response. It never gave one.

■ ■ ■

Just as a former BLX employee called me after my speech in 2002, the Michigan indictments spurred two more former employees to get in touch. Steve Auerbach, a former loan "workout specialist" in BLX's New York office, called me on April 12, 2007. He wanted to meet, but not in my office, suggesting a public place—a restaurant. I'm not sure why he wanted the cloak-and-dagger, but I agreed to meet with him at a Manhattan restaurant the following day.

Daniel Roitman and James Lin from Greenlight came with me, and Auerbach brought along Tim Williams. Williams and Auerbach both started at BLX in 2001, a few months after Allied Capital bought BLC Financial. Williams was the team leader of BLX's workout group. Auerbach worked for Williams as one of the workout officers. Both left BLX in 2003. BLX fired Williams. Auerbach left after Len Rudolph, a senior BLX executive, told him Tannenhauser was about to fire him. Rudolph said he couldn't prevent "the final nail" in Auerbach's coffin, but referred him to a friend at Sterling Bank. Rudolph's friend promptly hired Auerbach after a "two-minute interview" for an $80,000 a year job, then abruptly fired him for no apparent reason three weeks later. Because Auerbach had quit BLX rather than wait to be fired, he was not entitled to any of the benefits he would have received had BLX terminated him.

Williams and Auerbach had debated contacting me for the past two years. They claimed that after reading about me in the recent press in con-nection with the Harrington indictments and having difficulty getting new jobs, they decided to talk to me, hoping to share information. They were looking for help. They wanted the regulatory heat from the BLX investiga-tion to *go away*, but it wasn't clear why it was bothering them. Though they may have wanted to tell the government what they knew about BLX without getting into trouble themselves, they may have just wanted us to learn what happened. They wanted us to help them get an immunity deal. They also strongly resented Tannenhauser for the way he treated them.

Williams told us he had met with the FBI, SEC, U.S. attorney, SBA, and OIG. It was very unclear to what extent these were substantive meet-ings. For example, he told us the FBI came to his house to subpoena him. Auerbach only met with the SBA, but the SEC had been present.

Those inquiries started as information gathering, but at some point Williams, and possibly Auerbach, became the targets of the investi-gation. Williams and Auerbach said they did nothing wrong and had noth-ing to hide. They asked how they could have been responsible since they had no voting power on the loan-approval committee?

In their minds, BLX and Allied are one and the same—when we questioned them about it, they simply said, "BLX is a subsidiary of Allied"—but they always spoke of "Allied" and not "BLX" at lunch. Williams and Auerbach were surprised to read about Harrington's indictment. Williams said he had never met Harrington, but talked over the phone during conference calls. Auerbach met him directly because Auerbach's territory included Michigan. Harrington picked Auerbach up from the airport and drove him to various workout sites. Auerbach described Harrington as a real down-to-earth guy, low key, the nicest guy in the world. He spoke of how Harrington "talked about the Bible." Basically, Auerbach didn't think Harrington could have done all the things of which he was accused. Both Williams and Auerbach said that relative to other people at the Detroit office, Harrington was the nice guy.

They described CEO Tannenhauser as having a "Napoleon complex." "Credit approval meetings were jokes," Auerbach said. No one disagreed with Tannenhauser. Tannenhauser would start by saying how much he liked the borrower's business, cash flows, financials, and the like, and how he thought BLX should lend the money no matter how speculative or bad the idea. He would go around the room and ask for opinions. Auerbach could only recall one person, Len Rudolph, who ever disagreed with Tannenhauser, which Auerbach remembered only happening in a single instance. "Tannenhauser approved everything unless it was truly insane," Williams told us.

Williams read about some of the problem loans Greenlight had found. He thought those weren't even the worst ones. "Some of the loans, you just had to laugh," Auerbach said. The loan originators held all the power and influence at BLX. "Anybody in originations was a God," Auerbach told us. This wasn't the case in all the offices, but was true in many of the offices that employed their own underwriters. The underwriters were in a junior position to the originators and to office management. This put them in a bad position: If they rejected loans, it would hurt their bosses' bonus. Never a good move.

Although there was a list of approved appraisers, the workout team had its own blacklist of appraisers they would not use because of "bad appraisals." Those appraisers were used for originations. Tannenhauser would literally throw appraisal documents at people in meetings when he was unhappy with the workout valuations. Tannenhauser blamed the workout team for the large discrepancies between the collateral valuations when the loan was underwritten and when it was in workout. In Tannenhauser's mind, it was always the workout valuations that were wrong and never the original valuations used to underwrite the loans.

Williams and Auerbach never understood why the original valuations were so high. In many cases, the description of the assets in the original appraisal did not match the description of the assets in the workout. It would be as if the appraisal were for a Bentley, but when they picked it up, it was a Hyundai. Tannenhauser would argue that if the original appraisal were for $1 million and the workout appraisal came in at only $300,000 eight months later, it was the workout person's fault. Of course, the very rapid default gave a good indication which appraisal was wrong.

Then, they told us about some of the loans: There was a ridiculous USDA loan for about $4 million to build a "butterfly pavilion" in "the middle of nowhere" deep in rural South Carolina. Another loan was to Ashburn Hospitality, a hotel converted into rented rooms. The loan went bad. The owner collected rent, and then at 3 a.m. slipped foreclosure notices under people's doors saying they had to leave that morning. The residents completely trashed the place. Williams and a realtor inspected the property and found a box labeled "mortal remains" in one room and a large rattlesnake in another.

They said the Bill Russell Oil property was similar to a movie set's false-front building. They confirmed most of the general view of the USDA audit and joked about the $3,000 shack, where the appraisal cost more than the value of the property.

They discussed the shrimp-boat loans, telling us a Vietnamese broker was involved in loans where BLX would lend $1 million for a boat worth only $80,000. The loan would then go bad, but BLX would simply turn the boat back to the broker "to find another Vietnamese" to take a fresh $1 million loan. BLX just kept making the loans. Auerbach said BLX had the $80,000 appraisals and yet was aware that the broker was finding new borrowers to take new loans based on grossly inflated collateral values so that BLX did not take a loss.

Environmental issues were significant sources of problem loans. Auerbach said many loans did not have environmental problems identified in the original underwriting, but significant problems were found during the workout of the loan—sometimes barely a year later. In some cases, the cost of remediation exceeded the value of the remaining collateral. One example: A gas station loan, in which the station contaminated the well water used by the people living nearby. Remediation cost was $1 to $2 million and exceeded the collateral value of $750,000. BLX couldn't foreclose on the gas station because it would have opened them up to legal liability to the people using the poisoned water. Instead, BLX abandoned the property.

Williams thought the Colorado loans were particularly noxious. There was a loan where the loan officer was Richard Ronci, who temporarily acted as the CFO of the borrower during the loan process. BLX's defense to this obvious conflict of interest was that it was disclosed. The borrower sued, and a BLX executive flew to Colorado to settle. When I later looked at the records, this may have been the loan that Brickman discovered that revealed the $9 million loan transfer between BLX and Allied.

Williams was curious about the significance of the $9 million. "That is the first thing everyone asks me." He didn't see what was special about them. He said there were about fifty such loans between Allied and BLX with a total value approaching $50 million.

Williams explained how the SBA monitored the workouts. BLX would prepare a liquidation plan and submit it to the SBA for approval. Williams' team would always follow that plan. Many times, BLX would list a work-out property for sale at too high a price. It wouldn't sell. Sometimes the company would simply sit on a loan with a higher appraisal, not foreclose, and the SBA would let it sit forever. Because the company told the SBA what they were doing in advance, and the SBA had approved the plan, there was nothing the SBA could do about it.

The SBA would scrutinize the liquidation efforts by BLX, but almost never seemed to question the original underwriting. Williams said this wasn't always the case. Before BLX got preferred (PLP) status, there was more oversight. The USDA did a better job than the SBA of questioning BLX originations. He said when BLX got a PLP license, apparently the SBA was supposed to review all the existing loans as part of the transition, but it never did.

Auerbach said McGee, the previously convicted felon who was the head of the Richmond office, had voting authority in the credit commit-tee. The former BLX employee who contacted me by e-mail in 2002 had told me the same thing. When Jesse Eisinger from *The Wall Street Journal* confronted Allied about McGee's role, they vehemently denied he was on the credit committee. Auerbach said McGee was treated differently. In one instance, Auerbach was told "never to contact McGee." One of the loans in Auerbach's portfolio was a 7-Eleven in Richmond, Virginia. Auerbach was working out the loan and wanted to send someone to look at the furniture and fixtures to buy. He called McGee, who told Auerbach he would take care of it. A bit later, David Redlener, a senior BLX executive, called Auerbach and told him to forget about the liquidation, that McGee would take care of it. The loan just sat on Auerbach's list.

BLX held quarterly reviews of the workout loans. We were surprised to hear that Allied CFO Penni Roll usually participated by phone and Joan Sweeney usually appeared *in person*. During these meetings, Williams's team produced binders of documents, and everyone discussed individual loans, reserves, and valuations.

Williams suggested we try to get the "Loan Loss Allowance Valuation" binders. Those books would contain all the detail behind the workout loan valuations. He told us that after the review meeting, Redlener would prepare a valuation report, which Williams and Auerbach did not see, used for setting reserves in BLX's financials. Williams believed the reserves would not match the recommended valuations from the workout team in the Loan Loss Allowance Valuation binders.

Williams said the financial statement values were inflated, in part, because Roll had a concept of a "person value" for each borrower, because each borrower personally guaranteed the loans. This value acted as a valuation floor when there was inadequate collateral in the loan. Williams understood that if the person had any money, he wouldn't default on the loan in the first place, and BLX almost never collected anything on the personal guarantees, but gave them value for accounting purposes.

At the time Williams and Auerbach were there, BLX had three categories of loans: SBA, USDA, and "Bobby family" loans. When working out a loan, "Bobby's [Tannenhauser] family always got paid. It was all right for the SBA to get nothing." We pressed them for details about the "Bobby family" loans. Williams and Auerbach had few, as those loans all had happy endings.

We believed that one or both of them had spoken to Carruthers years earlier and abruptly broken-off conversations with him around the time Allied stole its critics' phone records. We asked Williams and Auerbach about this, but they recalled only minor contact with Carruthers and had vague memories on that subject.

Obviously, we were in no position with the government to broker an immunity deal for Williams and Auerbach. After our lunch, we tried to figure out how to help them. However, when we tried to follow-up with Williams to discuss matters, he didn't return our calls.

■ ■ ■

One week after the Auerbach/Williams meeting, Allied announced that it agreed to sell Mercury Air Center to Macquarie Infrastructure Company. Mercury operated terminals for private jets. This sale generated a realized gain of $240 million for Allied. Based on our analysis, this was the last identifiably ripe flower left to pick in Allied's garden.

On May 8, 2007, Allied released its first-quarter earning results. Net investment income fell to only 26 cents per share. The overall yield on the interest-bearing portfolio fell to only 11.6 percent. The results were hurt by higher nonperforming assets (6.4 percent of the portfolio compared to 5.3 percent at the end of the year, despite strong credit markets), lower deal-origination fees and higher investigation expenses. Allied invested $19.2 million in BLX (inclusive of the $12 million they disclosed earlier in the year) and held its valuation of BLX constant. On the conference call that day, Walton continued to insist that BLX's "core business is profitable."

Management was asked about the narrow gap between the value of the investments it exits and the most recent prior valuation on Allied's books. Walton noted, "I think a lot of this has to depend on the timing of when we actually realize the gain versus how close it is to the end of the quarter. What happens is if you get—sometimes we have taken the gains just hard on the heels of a quarter where we know exactly what the gain's going to be and we mark it up. One of the things that would be interesting, we haven't done this yet, is to look back a couple of quarters to see where we were two quarters prior to exit. . . ."

Sweeney added, "When you have perfect knowledge, it's really easy to get the valuation exactly right."

I couldn't have said it better myself. That had been our point back in the debate of 2002! The accuracy of the most recent marks prior to exit reflects exactly the status of the exit process and provides no comfort that Allied properly values the rest of the portfolio.

CHAPTER 31

The SEC Finds a Spot under the Rug

On June 20, 2007, came the moment we'd all been waiting for: The SEC released the results of the investigation of Allied it had announced in 2004. The agency released an "Order Instituting Cease-and-Desist Proceedings, Making Findings, and Imposing a Cease-and-Desist Order Pursuant to Section 21C of the Securities Exchange Act of 1934" in the matter of Allied Capital Corporation.

The six-page order found:

From the quarter ended June 30, 2001 through the quarter ended March 31, 2003 Allied violated recordkeeping and internal controls provisions of the federal securities laws relating to the valuation of certain securities in its private finance portfolio for which market quotations were not readily available. During the relevant period, Allied failed to make and keep books, records, and accounts which, in reasonable detail supported or accurately and fairly reflected certain valuations it recorded on a quarterly basis for some of its securities. In addition, Allied's internal controls failed to provide reasonable assurances that Allied would value these securities in accordance with generally accepted accounting principles. Further, from the quarter ended June 30, 2001 through the quarter ended March 31, 2002, Allied failed to provide reasonable assurances that the recorded accountability for certain securities in its private finance portfolio was compared with existing fair value of those same securities at reasonable intervals by failing to: (a) provide its board of directors ("Board") with sufficient contemporaneous valuation documentation during Allied's March and September quarterly valuation processes; and (b) maintain in reasonable detail, written documentation to support some of its valuations of certain portfolio companies that had gone into bankruptcy.

The order continued:

With respect to 15 private finance investments reviewed by staff, Allied could not produce sufficient contemporaneous documentation to support, or which accurately and fairly reflected, its Board's determination of fair value. Instead, in some instances, the written valuation documentation Allied presented to its Board for these investments failed to include certain relevant indications of value available to it (as further discussed below) and sometimes introduced changes to key inputs used to calculate fair value from quarter to quarter without sufficient written explanation of the rationale for the changes (*e.g.*, changes from EBITDA to revenue-based valuations and in some instances, changes in the multiples used to derive enterprise value). The written valuation documentation does not reflect reasonable detail to support the private finance investment valuations recorded by Allied in its periodic filings during the relevant period.

The order proceeded to give three examples labeled "Company A," "Company B," and "Company C," which we can identify as Startec, Executive Greetings, and Allied Office Products, respectively.

Company A—During the relevant period, Allied held a debt investment in Company A, a telecommunications company. Allied was unable to produce contemporaneous written documentation, in reasonable detail, to support its valuation of Company A during the quarters ended June 30, 2001 and September 30, 2001. Specifically, Allied's valuation of Company A for these quarters was derived, in part, by including revenues from discontinued lines of business to establish fair value. Allied maintains that it used a reduced multiple to offset any potential overstatement that would have otherwise resulted from the inclusion for those revenues, but it did not provide the Board with contemporaneous written documentation, in reasonable detail, to support this claim. In addition, Allied did not retain the valuation documentation it presented to the Board for Company A for the quarters ended December 31, 2001 and March 31, 2002. Allied valued its $20 million subordinated debt investment in Company A at $20 million (*i.e.*, cost) in its Forms 10-Q for the quarters ended June 30, 2001 and September 30, 2001. In its 2001 Form 10-K and its form 10-Q for the period ended March 31, 2002, Allied valued its subordinated debt investment in Company A at $10.3 million. Allied subsequently wrote down its subordinated debt investment in Company A to $245,000 in its Form 10-Q for the quarter ended June 30, 2002.

Company B—During the relevant period, Allied held a subordinated-debt investment in Company B, a direct marketing company. Allied was unable to produce contemporaneous documentation, in reasonable detail, to support the basis for its valuation of Company B for the quarter ended March 31, 2003. Specifically, Allied's valuation was based, in large part, on a potential future buyout event by Allied that was preliminary in nature. Allied maintains that—as a general practice—the Board would have discussed why this particular potential future buyout event was significant enough to form the basis of its valuation of Company B, but it could not provide contemporaneous written documentation in reasonable detail to support this claim. Further, Allied's valuation documentation did not fully reflect Allied's consideration of competing buyout offers for Company B, which, if accepted, would have reduced the fair value of Allied's investment. Allied valued its $16.5 million subordinated debt investment in Company B at $14.3 million in its Form 10-Q for the quarter ended March 2003. Allied subsequently wrote down its sub-ordinated debt investment in Company B from $14.3 million to $50,000 in its Form 10-Q for the quarter ended June 30, 2003.

Company C—During the relevant period, Allied held a subordinated debt investment in Company C, an office supply company. Allied was unable to produce contemporaneous documentation, in reasonable detail, to support the basis for its valuation of Company C from the quarter ended September 30, 2001 through the quarter ended March 31, 2002. For example, Allied's written valuation documentation failed to include all relevant facts available to it regarding Company C's deteriorating financial condition, including the fact that Company C had lost one of its largest customers as a result of the terrorist attack on the World Trade Center. Allied valued its subordinated debt investment in Company C at $8 million in its Forms 10-Q and Form 10-K for the quarters ended September 30, 2001 through March 31, 2002 and subsequently wrote that investment down to $50,000 in its Form 10-Q for the quarter ended June 30, 2002.

Continuing through the order, the SEC found:

> There were certain instances where Allied did not provide its Board (or its valuation committee) with sufficient written information to support the Board's determinations of fair value. For example, in several instances, the written valuation documentation presented to the Board was incomplete or inadequate to support the fair value recorded by Allied (*e.g.*, enterprise values were listed on worksheets without any explanation; necessary inputs and/or calculations were either missing or incomplete). In other instances, Allied's valuation documentation during the relevant period contained unexplained departures from, or changes to, key inputs from quarter to quarter.

The SEC found that September 2001 and March 2002:

> Valuation processes consisted of quantitative worksheets that failed to provide an adequate explanation of the various inputs. For example, changes in valuation from quarter to quarter were not always explained in reasonable detail in the written documentation.

Moreover, Allied did not prepare a written description of the quantitative and qualitative analyses used to develop its valuations until the quarter ended June 30, 2002. During this period, Allied also failed to maintain, in reasonable detail, written documentation to support some of its valuations of certain portfolio companies that were bankrupt. While Allied maintains that its Board members and employees engaged in discussions before and during the Board meetings to satisfy themselves with the recorded valuations for Allied's private finance investments, the written documentation retained by Allied does not reflect reasonable detail to support the private finance investment valuations recorded by Allied in its periodic filings during the relevant period.

Finally, the SEC order found:

> During the relevant period, Allied private finance department personnel typically recommended the initial valuations on the investment deals on which they worked. While there were some existing independent checks of Allied's valuation process, these checks, standing alone, did not provide a sufficient assessment of the objectivity of valuations of the private finance investments. For example, the valuation committee assigned to review each investment on a quarterly basis was comprised, in large part, of private finance managing directors and principals.

All in all, the SEC found Allied to have violated three sections of the Exchange Act of 1934.

The SEC confirmed our analysis that Allied could not support its valuations. Further, the agency found that Allied made undocumented—certainly self-serving—changes to its valuations metrics. Documents were "not retained." Allied did not even have documentation procedures to support its valuation analyses at the time of my speech; those began the following quarter, presumably in response to the speech. Allied did not consider negative information and events, such as its investments going bankrupt. Allied held an investment at a higher value based on the idea that Allied might buy the company. The SEC provided three clear examples and indicated it found a dozen others. Now, it was no longer just Greenlight and a few others pointing to Allied's shoddy accounting. The SEC gave our analysis its stamp of approval.

For this, what was Allied's punishment? The order noted Allied's cooperation in the investigation and said Allied had improved its valuation process through more detailed record keeping, obtaining third-party valuation assistance and establishing a new "chief valuation officer" position to oversee the valuation process. Without admitting or denying any of the SEC's findings, Allied agreed to "cease and desist" from violating the Exchange Act, (*e.g.*, to keep better records) and for the next two years to continue to use outside valuation assistance for its investments under the supervision of an internal "chief valuation officer."

That was it. There were no fines. There were no penalties. There were no actions taken against Allied employees or directors. In the next day's *Washington Post*, the SEC's associate enforcement director said, "The valuation of those securities in the portfolio are not easily quantifiable. The message here is, we want to make sure companies adhere to the standard that has been laid out."

The consequence of Allied's illegal action was the lightest tap on the wrist with the softest of feathers. The SEC's order did not make even a passing reference to BLX or to any of management's conduct, including the many false statements to inflate Allied stock price. There was a gaping disconnect between the findings and the order. It was as if the SEC said, "Greenlight was right. Allied was wrong. Have a nice day." It was an unimaginable Pyrrhic victory.

■ ■ ■

Back in spinland, Christopher Davies, a partner at Allied's outside counsel at WilmerHale, told Reuters, "Nothing in the SEC findings calls into question the accuracy or reliability of Allied Capital's valuations of its portfolio companies." The findings actually found the opposite—again, a Big Lie is more palatable than a small one.

Different punishments for different people? It took Brickman about an hour to find the SEC's release from August 26, 2004, in which it announced an action against Van Wagoner Capital Management and Garrett Van Wagoner. In that case, the SEC found that Van Wagoner misstated the valuations of illiquid, non–publicly traded securities held by its funds. In his case, Van Wagoner *undervalued* his holdings. In other words, he had been *too conservative.*

Table 31.1 Equity Offerings by Allied Capital since January 2002

Date	Millions Raised	Offer Price	Shares Sold (mm)	Lead Underwriter
November 22, 2002	$88.6	$20.10	4.35	Rights offering
December 18, 2002	$38.1	$21.76	1.75	Jefferies
March 3, 2003	$35.8	$20.46	1.75	Jefferies
March 25, 2003	$50.1	$20.03	2.50	Jefferies
June 12, 2003	$66.8	$23.84	2.80	Banc of America
August 1, 2003	$71.0	$23.66	3.00	Jefferies
August 25, 2003	$24.2	$24.22	1.00	Credit Lyonnais Securities
September 25, 2003	$55.0	$25.00	2.20	Deutsche Bank; US Bancorp Piper Jaffray
November 10, 2003	$64.3	$24.74	2.60	Jefferies
December 10, 2003	$54.1	$27.07	2.00	Merrill Lynch
September 29, 2004	$75.0	$25.00	3.00	Banc of America, Deutsche Bank, JMP Securities
January 26, 2006	$87.8	$29.25	3.00	Deutsche Bank, Merrill Lynch
July 18, 2006	$123.5	$27.45	4.50	Banc of America, Citigroup, Merrill Lynch
November 29, 2006	$69.9	$29.75	2.35	Deutsche Bank
March 5, 2007	$97.3	$29.25	3.33	Deutsche Bank
November 29, 2007	$80.4	$24.75	3.25	Deutsche Bank
Total	**$1,081.9**	**$24.94**	**43.38**	

SOURCE: Bloomberg and ALD SEC filings.

Van Wagoner paid an $800,000 fine, agreed to resign from his position, and agreed not to serve as an officer or director of any mutual fund for seven years. In substance, the SEC put Van Wagoner out of business. No doubt he didn't have the former head of the Republican National Committee on his board.

Jim Carruthers put it best: "If the SEC had come in 2002 and promptly made these findings and the SBA acted on the fraud when we told them right away, Allied stock would have gone to $3." Instead, the shares closed at $31.84 the day of the SEC order. I would add that Allied management wouldn't be in place today and may have served time in jail.

Instead, it took the SEC more than two years after my speech to begin investigating Allied and nearly another three years to complete its inquiry. The findings seemed stale because it took the SEC so long to act. During those five years, the economy nicely recovered from its recession and Allied raised about $1 billion of fresh equity in sixteen offerings (see Table 31.1). This was raised from thousands of retail and institutional investors under pretense that Allied followed the rules and was simply the victim of a "short attack." These are the investors the SEC is supposed to protect.

So now it was cash-out time: The very afternoon of the SEC order, Allied began the long-delayed "stock ownership initiative" by making a tender offer for 16.7 million vested insider stock options. One would have thought it would have waited a day or two, maybe a week, just to keep from blushing.

CHAPTER 32

A Garden of Weeds

The SEC and other believers took comfort that with third-party valuation assistance, Allied would properly value its investments. I didn't. As discussed before, Allied did not hire the consultants to perform appraisals. How valuable could these "negative assurances" be coming from third parties that signed-off on the BLX valuation for years? I was certain this fix was form over function: Allied's underlying ethos was unchanged.

Over the years we have learned that even though Allied's senior management is dishonest, it did not mean Allied could not and did not make some good investments. There may have been some winners still remaining in the portfolio. However, Allied's practice of harvesting the winners and keeping its losers had left it with poor prospects. According to Allied's own valuations, the portfolio had more unrealized depreciation than unrealized appreciation—and that was before taking into full account BLX's meltdown.

The 10-Q for the second quarter of 2007 included a new disclosure about the BLX investigations. "In addition, the Office of the Inspector General of the U.S. Department of Agriculture is conducting an investigation of BLX's lending practices under the Business and Industry Loan (B&I) program." Again, this disclosure appeared as part of a general discussion of BLX rather than under "Legal Proceedings" and Allied indicated it was "ongoing," misleading the casual reader to believe that the USDA investigation was not a new development. Allied did not disclose when this investigation began and made no mention of it in the earnings release or conference call the prior day.

Later in the 10-Q, Allied warned, "Due to the changes in BLX's operations, the status of its current financing facilities and the effect of BLX's current regulatory issues, ongoing investigations and litigation, the Company is in the process of working with BLX with respect to various potential strategic alternatives including, but not limited to, recapitalization, restructuring, joint venture or sale or divestiture of BLX or some or all of its assets. The ultimate resolution of these matters could have a material adverse impact on BLX's financial condition, and, as a result, our financial results could be negatively affected."

Moreover, the 10-Q also disclosed that BLX was in default under its credit agreements and had received temporary waivers from its lenders. Even so, Allied advanced BLX another $10 million and BLX drew down on its bank line (the first losses up to half the line were guaranteed by Allied) a further $50 million. The 10-Q explained, "BLX's agreement with the SBA has reduced BLX's liquidity due to the working capital required to comply with the agreement." Allied did not explain why, in light of these troubling facts, it did not take a large, immediate write-down. Instead, Allied wrote BLX down by merely $19 million in the quarter. Inexplicably, Allied continued to value its stake at $220 million, implying an enterprise value in excess of $550 million counting BLX's borrowings under its credit facility.

In June 2007, Allied announced it raised $125 million for the newly formed Allied Capital Senior Debt Fund, LP, a levered fund Allied managed where it would receive management and incentive fees. Allied committed 25 percent of the capital and raised the balance from outside investors. As part of the fund formation, Allied shifted $183 million of loans off its balance sheet to the new fund. Allied did not disclose which assets it transferred.

One of the assets that disappeared from Allied's balance sheet that quarter was a $35 million loan to Air Medical Group, an operator of medical helicopters under the name Air Evac Lifeteam. On May 25, 2007, *The New York Times* reported that the FBI seized documents from its corporate headquarters "as part of an inquiry concerning billing and health care compliance related matters." This followed a front-page article in the *Times* from 2005 that reported how Air Evac Lifeteam apparently sent out helicopters and charged insurers in instances that did not appear to be emergencies. Though it was a small investment, Allied increased its unrealized gain in Air Medical Group right after the FBI raided Air Medical Group's headquarters.

On September 4, 2007, Sweet Traditions, a Krispy Kreme franchisee in Illinois, Indiana, and Missouri, filed for bankruptcy. In August 2006, Allied led a recapitalization of the then already ailing company. The bankruptcy documents indicated Sweet Traditions generated no operating profit and paid only about $275,000 to Allied in the year before the filing, about a tenth of the stated annual interest on the loan. According to Allied's SEC documents, filed just weeks before the bankruptcy, Allied recognized $1.7 million of interest in 2006 and over $1 million in the March 2007 quarter before putting Sweet Traditions on non-accrual in the June 2007 quarter, while also continuing to value its entire $37 million investment in the debt and equity at cost. *Déjà vu.*

■ ■ ■

Allied announced its third-quarter 2007 results on November 7, 2007. For the first time in years it reported a loss of sixty-two cents per share. Following a multi-year boom in lending, risky bonds and loans had declined in value across the board. On the previous quarter's conference call, management had downplayed the impact that the market decline would have on its $4 billion portfolio, but described the turn in the credit cycle as a positive development because Allied could make future loans at improved yields. As the credit crisis spread, however, valuation multiples contracted and Allied took write-downs "particularly in the financial services sector or from portfolio company circumstances that are not significant business model issues," according to Walton. Having harvested most of its winning investments, Allied did not have offsetting write-ups this time.

Net investment income was also poor at only twelve cents per share, after a nine-cent-per-share cost from the tender offer for insider options, which had been completed in July at $31.75 per share. Income taxes that Allied paid the government for the privilege of deferring tax distributions an additional year cost seven cents per share. Allied closed its sale of Mercury Air, and, in a blast from the past, finally recognized a realized loss in its investment in Startec Global Communications.

Walton led off the quarterly conference call by describing the results as "mixed." Then came the surprise: BLX will "significantly de-emphasize government-guaranteed lending going forward." BLX's cost structure and capital requirements had become "sub-optimal." BLX would focus on non-government guaranteed "conventional" small business lending. The result would be a 30 percent short-term reduction in originations and a write-down of BLX's residual interests and book value leading to an additional $84 million write-down of Allied's investment, which contributed to the loss in the quarter.

Walton continued, "To effect this change in strategy, Bob Tannenhauser, BLX's current CEO, will take on the role of Chairman for an interim period, and John Scheurer, who has successfully built two commercial mortgage loan investment businesses for Allied Capital, will step into the role of interim CEO." I immediately wondered whether Allied was concerned Tannenhauser might be indicted and wanted to be able to call him a "former employee" if that inconvenience came to pass.

No matter how ugly BLX appeared, Allied just kept applying rouge. To give up would cause not just a write-down, but also a realized loss. A realized loss the size of BLX would count against Allied's kitty of undistributed tax distributions that Allied stored to give investors "visibility" into future "dividends." Instead, Allied decided to re-focus BLX. "We believe that there is significant opportunities [sic] to build and grow BLX as a conventional small business and commercial real estate lender. John is actively working to add commercial mortgage industry veterans to expand BLX's commercial real estate platform. We think John is the right guy to lead BLX through this change in strategy and we have the record and resources to support the company through this transition," Walton explained. If it made sense to have Scheurer create a new commercial mortgage-lending platform, it would certainly be easier to build one from scratch, rather than on top of BLX's mess—high cost of capital, and all.

In the Q&A session, the sell-side analysts were already trying to figure out how to spin the lousy result. Henry Coffey of Ferris, Baker & Watts offered, "If we were to throw GAAP out the window, which is something

I would be happy to sponsor, Joan, what—would it be fair to, when we're looking at your operating earnings, to exclude the excise tax as well as some of the stock option expense and then what about the IPA [Individual Performance Award] charge?"

Even with the write-downs, it remained clear that Allied had not fully reflected the changed market conditions in its valuations. On the conference call, management acknowledged that credit spreads had widened. As they failed to do in 2002, Allied did not revalue its entire debt portfolio to take into account the deteriorating market conditions. The write-downs Allied took were concentrated in its equity positions; the debt investments generally remained at cost. *Déjà vu, again.*

■ ■ ■

Even after the Sweet Traditions bankruptcy, Allied still valued its non-accruing loan at cost—although this quarter it wrote-down its equity investment. Through its investment in the Callidus Capital Corporation, an asset management company, Allied had invested in a series of structured finance products, including the equity pieces of collateralized loan obligations (CLOs). The market values of structured finance vehicles had fallen especially hard in the developing crisis. However, Allied wrote-down the value of its $188 million of CLOs by only 6 percent.

Allied shares, which stood at $31.75 in June when the company priced the tender offer for the insider options, had weakened coming into the third-quarter announcement. In response to the bad news, the shares fell sharply to a low of $21.55 on November 8, 2007. Insiders had just received $53 million in cash and 1.7 million shares of stock in exchange for 10.3 million options with a weighted average exercise price of $21.50. Had Allied delayed the option tender until the company announced this bad news, the insider options would have had little value left. This "extra" $106 million for insiders equated to about three-quarters of a year's worth of Allied's net investment income (see Figure 32.1).

Just like when the magician's lovely lady assistant—having been sawed in half, smiles and moves her feet and hands to show all is well—the Allied insiders repeated their familiar sideshow pantomime: They showed their "confidence" in the stock through nominal open market purchases. *The lady had, in fact, not been sawed in half!* Walton, who had just received $14.5 million in cash (in addition to $14.5 million in stock) in the option tender,

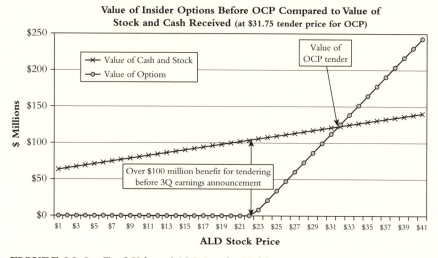

FIGURE 32.1 Total Value of ALD Insider Holdings Before and After OCP

was the biggest "inside" purchaser by far, acquiring 50,000 shares for $1.1 million. The purchases received substantial media attention, including positive coverage from *Bloomberg, Barron's, The Motley Fool* and Insiderscore. com. Within a couple of weeks the shares recovered to $25.47; Allied promptly sold a fresh 3.25 million shares in an overnight stock offering led by Deutsche Bank.

On September 30, 2007, Allied rated $3.93 billion of its $4.33 billion portfolio Grade 1 (capital gain expected) or Grade 2 (performing to plan). Allied classified only $401 million, or 9 percent, of its investments in Grades 3 through 5. Yet, as Table 32.1 shows, $1.35 billion, or 31 percent, of Allied's portfolio were investments that had been performing below plan in that they had either been partially written down or were non-accruing.

Allied classified several hundred million dollars of investments that had partial markdowns to be Grade 1 or Grade 2. How could investments in such a state be considered Grade 1 or Grade 2? Grade inflation. It appeared that if Allied considered a gain likely on its equity kicker, it classified the entire investment—loan and equity—as Grade 1. The converse was not true: If Allied expected the junior portion of an investment to generate a loss, it did not downgrade the entire investment, but only the impaired junior portion.

Some of Allied's few remaining appreciated investments appeared questionable. As noted, with the sale of Mercury Air, Allied picked the

Table 32.1   Written-down and/or Non-Accrual Investments

	Investment	September 30, 2007 (Dollars in thousands)		
		Cost	Value	Unrealized (loss)
1	Business Loan Express, Inc.	324,559	136,710	(187,849)*
2	Hot Stuff Foods, LLC	187,589	91,542	(96,047)*
3	MHF Logistical Solutions, Inc.	65,544	10,585	(54,959)*
4	Triview Investments, Inc.	164,259	127,334	(36,925)*
5	Global Communications, LLC	42,999	7,576	(35,423)*
6	Pendum, Inc.	34,028	–	(34,028)*
7	Alaris Consulting	32,176	–	(32,176)*
8	Wear Me Apparel Corporation	183,050	151,432	(31,618)*
9	EarthColor, Inc.	199,980	169,324	(30,656)
10	Insight Pharmaceuticals Corporation	91,584	63,275	(28,309)*
11	Border Foods, Inc.	16,568	2,473	(14,095)
12	Direct Capital Corporation	56,765	44,438	(12,327)
13	Driven Brands, Inc.	148,133	136,655	(11,478)
14	Gordian Group, Inc.	9,567	–	(9,567)*
15	Callidus MAPS CLOS Fund I, LLC	67,090	58,074	(9,016)
16	Kodiak Fund, LP	9,423	2,853	(6,570)
17	Pres Air Tool, LLC	6,725	800	(5,925)*
18	MedBridge Healthcare	14,748	8,887	(5,861)*
19	Creative Group, Inc.	15,073	9,259	(5,814)*
20	eCentury Capital Partners, LP	6,899	2,615	(4,284)
21	Mid-Atlantic Venture Fund IV, LP	6,975	2,861	(4,114)
22	Legacy Partners Group, LLC	8,104	5,114	(2,990)*
23	Calder Capital Partners, LLC	4,453	2,565	(1,888)*
24	Grotech Partners, VI, LP	8,808	6,970	(1,838)
25	Universal Environmental Services, LLC	1,810	–	(1,810)
26	Callidus Debt Partners (CLO Fund IV, LTD)	12,373	10,758	(1,615)
27	Becker Underwood	30,449	28,836	(1,613)
28	Axium Healthcare Pharmacy, Inc.	13,527	11,977	(1,550)

(continued)

Table 32.1   Written-down and/or Non-Accrual Investments *(continued)*

September 30, 2007
(Dollars in thousands)

	Investment	Cost	Value	Unrealized (loss)
29	SGT India Private Limited	4,098	2,625	(1,473)
30	Avborne Heavy Maintenance, Inc.	2,401	973	(1,428)
31	Distant Lands Trading Co.	56,179	54,831	(1,348)
32	Callidus Debt Partners (CLO Fund III, LTD)	21,980	20,702	(1,278)
33	Multi-Ad Services, Inc.	21,748	20,690	(1,058)
34	Walker Investment Fund II, LLP	1,330	358	(972)
35	Performant Financial Corporation	734	–	(734)
36	Cortec Group Fund IV, LP	3,383	2,906	(477)
37	Sweet Traditions	37,052	36,673	(379)*
38	Elexis Beta GmbH	426	50	(376)
39	HealthASPex, Inc.	500	133	(367)*
40	SPP Mezzanine Fund II, LP	2,750	2,409	(341)
41	Drew Foam Companies, Inc.	729	396	(333)
42	International Fiber Corporation	26,854	26,554	(300)
43	BB&T Capital Partners/Windsor Mez Fund	5,873	5,607	(266)
44	Litterer Beteiligungs GmbH	2,557	2,333	(224)
45	Homax Holdings, Inc.	25,453	25,235	(218)
46	Frozen Speciialties, Inc	435	230	(205)
47	TransAmerican Auto Parts, LLC	24,944	24,762	(182)
48	Catterton Partners VI, LP	1,795	1,656	(139)
49	Baird Capital Partners IV LP	1,967	1,856	(111)
50	Aviation Properties Corporation	65	–	(65)
51	VICORP Restaurants, Inc.	33	–	(33)
52	Other Companies	6,524	6,511	(13)*
53	Garden Ridge Corporation	20,500	20,500	–*
54	Jakel, Inc.	1,575	1,575	–*
55	Powell Plant Farms, Inc.	1,350	1,350	–*
56	Staffing Partners Holding Company	541	544	3*
	Cumulative Total	**2,037,034**	**1,354,372**	**(682,662)**
	% Total Portfolio		**31.3%**	

*Indicates investment with securities on non-accrual.

last obvious flower in its portfolio. One of the largest unrealized gains left was Financial Pacific Company, a lessor of equipment to small businesses, which Allied bought in June 2004. Unlike most of Allied's investments, there was abundant public data about Financial Pacific because it had filed documents with the SEC in anticipation of going public. Allied purchased it at a high price and a sizable premium to the anticipated public offering price. Allied paid $94 million—either three and a half times or five times Financial Pacific's equity, depending on whether Financial Pacific retired its subordinated debt in the transaction. According to its SEC filing, the yield on the equipment leases was fixed, but Financial Pacific's borrowings had variable rates. As a result, the filing warned that increases in short-term interest rates would have an adverse impact on the company. Almost immediately after Allied purchased the company, the Federal Reserve began a campaign of short-term interest rate increases. From July 2004 to August 2006 the Federal Reserve raised the overnight rate seventeen times from 1 percent to 5.25 percent. Despite Allied's high initial purchase price and an interest rate headwind that had only recently begun to abate, as of September 30, 2007, Allied valued Financial Pacific at a sizable premium.

Callidus was another remaining unrealized gain. Allied bought a majority stake in Callidus (with Callidus management retaining a minority stake) in November 2003, concurrently committing to take large positions in the riskiest portions of Callidus' future deals. Allied did not consolidate Callidus, because it considered Callidus to be a "portfolio company." As we learned in our research about Allied's accounting treatment of BLX, investment companies could consolidate their financials with other investment companies. On that basis, Callidus would be eligible for consolidation. The non-consolidation of Callidus enabled Allied to boost its earnings by recognizing unrealized appreciation on its investment in Callidus. If Allied consolidated Callidus, it could not book such gains (see Table 33.2).

Allied now had limited ability to produce net investment income to sustain the distributions. Dramatically reducing Allied's generation of recurring earnings were: lower portfolio interest yields, which had fallen from 14.3 percent in March 2002 to 11.9 percent in September 2007; reduced ability to recognize fees from controlled companies; and higher operating expenses, especially compensation. Net investment income, which almost covered the tax distribution in 2001, covered less than 30 percent of it in the first nine months of 2007. As a result, Allied adopted a capital gains strategy, fully dependent on selling winners and keeping losers.

Table 32.2   Written-up Investments

		September 30, 2007 (Dollars in thousands)		
	Investment	Cost	Value	Unrealized gain
1	Norwesco, Inc.	120,859	200,664	79,805
2	Callidus Capital Corporation	8,642	49,215	40,573
3	Financial Pacific Company	97,570	137,951	40,381
4	BenefitMall, Inc.	155,227	170,075	14,848
5	Service Champ, Inc.	41,827	54,520	12,693
6	Amerex Group, LLC	11,909	24,057	12,148
7	Advantage Mayer, Inc.	154,041	165,041	11,000
8	CR Brands	73,773	81,486	7,713
9	Penn Detriot Diesel Allison, LLC	60,008	67,675	7,667
10	Air Medical Group	5,336	12,666	7,330
11	Coverall North America, Inc.	57,539	63,909	6,370
12	Progressive International Corporation	4,483	10,087	5,604
13	MVL Group	70,927	75,245	4,318
14	Bl, Inc.	34,495	37,895	3,400
15	Huddle House	100,682	103,411	2,729
16	CitiPostal, Inc. and Affiliates	26,658	29,015	2,357
17	Havco Wood Products	8,929	11,074	2,145
18	MedAssets, Inc.	2,049	3,945	1,896
19	Network Hardware Resale	34,217	35,872	1,655
20	SB Restaurant Corporation	29,493	30,974	1,481
21	Commerical Credit Group, Inc.	30,043	31,494	1,451
22	Updata Venture Partners II, LP	4,727	6,148	1,421
23	Camden Partners Strategic Fund, LP	997	2,382	1,385
24	Venturehouse Group, LLC	–	1,381	1,381
25	Cook Inlet Alternative Risk, LLC	100,147	101,207	1,060
26	Foresite Towers, LLC	–	881	881
27	Old Orchard Brands	38,109	38,944	835
28	Oahu Waste Services, Inc.	239	1,000	761
29	Callidus Debt Partners (CLO Fund V, LTD)	13,988	14,649	661
30	Geotrace Technologies, Inc.	9,517	10,167	650

	Investment	Cost	Value	Unrealized gain
	September 30, 2007 (Dollars in thousands)			
31	Odyssey Investment Partners Fund III, LP	1,542	2,162	620
32	Postle Aluminum Company, LLC	63,989	64,589	600
33	SPP Mezzanine Fund, LP	2,364	2,928	564
34	Catterton Partners V, LP	3,510	4,038	528
35	The Step2 Company, LLC	98,155	98,675	520
36	York Insurance Services Group, Inc.	46,234	46,734	500
37	Soteria Imaging Services, LLC	15,872	16,343	471
38	Allied Capital Senior Debt Fund	19,080	19,535	455
39	Passport Health Communications, Inc.	2,048	2,446	398
40	Alpine ESP Holdings, Inc.	636	1,019	383
41	Impact Innovations Group, LLC	–	320	320
42	Avborne, Inc.	611	850	239
43	Startec Global Communications Corporation	230	440	210
44	Regency Healthcare Group	13,937	14,122	185
45	Dynamic India Fund IV	6,050	6,215	165
46	Carlisle Wide Plank Floors, Inc.	3,523	3,623	100
47	ProMach, Inc.	15,966	16,066	100
48	Digital VideoStream, LLC	21,589	21,686	97
49	Centre Capital Investors IV, LP	2,079	2,170	91
50	Callidus Debt Partners (CDO Fund I, LTD)	28,402	28,482	80
51	Novak Biddle Venture Partners III, LP	1,910	1,983	73
52	Venturehouse - Cibernet Investors, LLC	–	54	54
53	Service Center Metals, LLC	5,293	5,317	24
54	Staffing Partners Holding Company	541	544	3
	Cumulative Total	**1,649,992**	**1,933,371**	**283,379**
	% Total Portfolio		**44.7%**	

Though Allied would do everything it could to avoid turning its unrealized losses into realized losses—especially at BLX given its slippery footing, the outcome might be beyond Allied's control. In addition to its $190 million unrealized loss and $136 million remaining investment in BLX, Allied had a large exposure to the guarantees it made on BLX's bank line. In September 2007, Allied agreed to increase its guarantee from 50 to 60 percent to enable BLX to obtain short-term waivers of its defaults until January 2008. In January 2008, it increased the guaranty on BLX's bank line to 100 percent or $442 million. Should BLX implode and Allied make good on the guarantee, Allied's realized loss could exceed $700 million, assuming that the government did not extract further restitution or penalties from Allied.

Allied had built up a large "kitty" of undistributed taxable earnings by selling its winners and keeping its losers. Allied assured its investors that this gave the company the long-term ability to make quarterly tax distributions. I believed it had become harder for Allied to find meaningful winners to harvest and the eventual losses from BLX would deplete, if not exceed, the kitty. Looking at Allied's September 2007 valuations—without assuming additional losses at BLX, or for that matter other impacts from Allied's aggressive accounting—Allied's portfolio had $683 million of unrealized losses and only $283 million of unrealized gains.

All told, Allied had to distribute about $410 million per year to maintain the distribution. As of September 2007 it had about $400 million in the kitty and generated about $110 million in annual net investment income, but had $400 million in unrealized losses in excess of unrealized gains and a large additional loss likely coming at BLX. The kitty appeared under pressure.

If the kitty disappeared, Allied would be left with the option of paying the distributions out of capital as opposed to profits. But Allied's shareholders might not notice the distinction. Cutting the distribution would be unthinkable. Allied's focus on easy-to-manipulate taxable earnings accumulated in prior years, rather than current-year reported earnings, should have been a red flag. Paying distributions out of capital, while simultaneously raising fresh capital, fits the classic description of a Ponzi scheme. Is a Ponzi scheme a victimless crime before it collapses?

A Ponzi scheme can exist in what economists call "stable disequilibrium." Though it is not *permanently* sustainable, it doesn't have to fail in any given time frame. Yes, Allied has proven that it can last for years, by chronically selling fresh shares to raise more capital. Such persistence disproves nothing.

CHAPTER 33

A Conviction, a Hearing, and a Dismissal

The Justice Department began to ring up convictions from its Michigan investigation of BLX. In October 2007, Patrick Harrington, the head of BLX's Detroit office, pled guilty to conspiracy and making a false statement to a grand jury. Noting the investigation was ongoing, Assistant U.S. Attorney Stephen Robinson told *Bloomberg*, "I anticipate there will be additional indictments."

Harrington declined to cooperate with the investigation. *Bloomberg* reported that his attorney said, "The government always wants to go higher, but he never told anyone about it." As of this writing, Harrington awaited sentencing. More than a dozen other minor participants in BLX-issued fraud loans pled guilty to various crimes.

According to BLX's statement, Harrington admitted to $6.5 million in fraudulent loans in his plea agreement. BLX vowed, "All losses attributable to Mr. Harrington's admitted criminal conduct will be borne entirely by BLX." Notably, BLX did not promise to reimburse all the allegedly fraudulent loans it had *originated*.

Shortly after Harrington's guilty plea, the SBA Office of Inspector General posted the findings of its audit of the SBA's oversight of BLX on its web site (www.sba.gov/ig/7-28.pdf). Though the audit was completed in July, the OIG held it until October, before posting it with heavy redactions. Page after page, paragraph after paragraph was blacked out; printing the document took a heavy toll on the toner cartridge. Why?

Keith Girard described the SBA's attempted "cover-up" in a December 2007 "Business Intelligence" column posted on the Web site of *The New York Times*:

> Customarily, the OIG posts such reports on its Website. But when this one was finished over the summer, SBA General Counsel Frank Borchert asked OIG to either withhold or substantially rewrite it. To his credit, Inspector General Eric M. Thorson and OIG's own attorneys refused. The standoff ended with a compromise. Thorson allowed the General Counsel's office to edit, or 'redact,' the report.
>
> Such requests are not out of the ordinary. Even though the OIG is supposed to be independent, the General Counsel's office routinely reviews its reports, and sensitive legal, technical, or proprietary information is often redacted. In this case, however, the editing was so extensive, Thorson felt compelled to add a disclaimer on the cover, a first. Nearly all of OIG's recommendations, for example, were blacked out.

The report compares BLX's performance to SBA benchmarks for currency rate (the opposite of delinquency rate), loss rate, purchase rate, and liquidation rate, but the actual data were redacted. So were the details in a section titled "On-site Examinations Noted Material Deficiencies and Instances of Noncompliance with SBA Regulations." Much of the "Results in Brief" section was blacked out, as well the entire "Chronology of Events." A discussion of the SBA's internal risk analysis of BLX was redacted, as was a section titled "SBA Continued to Renew BLX's Delegated Authority and to Purchase Loans." The OIG described in its disclaimer, "Since 2001, SBA's oversight activities identified recurring and material issues related to BLX's performance. Despite these recurring problems, SBA continued to renew BLX's delegated lender status and SBA took no actions to restrict BLX's ability to originate loans or to mitigate financial risks through the purchase review process." Finally, the SBA's responses to the OIG's five recommendations were completely redacted, as was a section titled "Additional Comments."

It was no wonder the SBA used its black marker. Even with the redactions, it was possible to piece together enough of the audit to see that the OIG was extremely critical of the SBA, saying that the agency was too conflicted (loan portfolio growth versus lender oversight) to act against BLX, even though the agency's inaction was costing the government hundreds of millions of dollars.

The OIG said the SBA did not accept the results of the audit or implement the recommendations. "SBA management was not receptive to the audit findings and recommendations," the audit said. The first three recommendations were redacted. The others were to develop standard operating procedures to describe when Preferred Lending Program (PLP) status will be suspended or revoked and how it will be done and to address the conflict of having lender oversight reporting to the Office of Capital Access, which focuses on production volume. Whatever the redacted recommendations were, the report said, the purpose was "to mitigate the risk posed by BLX and to promote consistent and uniform enforcement actions." The SBA plainly did not see eye-to-eye with its own OIG. Even when the OIG saw the problem for what it was, the SBA itself disagreed and didn't even want public disclosure—let alone debate—about why it disagreed with the OIG.

Reading between the black, one sees that the OIG found enough recurring problems to question whether the SBA should have renewed BLX's PLP status for the previous six years. Despite abundant red flags, the SBA did not increase its scrutiny of BLX's loan purchase requests, even as it paid out $272 million of guarantees. The OIG found that the SBA identified thirty-nine BLX problematic loans and did not resolve "the deficiencies or obtain a repair or denial of the guarantees."

The report continued: "Although SBA personnel believe they took appropriate actions, in our opinion, more stringent steps should have been taken to hold BLX accountable for its noncompliance with SBA regulations and to mitigate risks posed by the lender's portfolio. We believe SBA took limited action because:

- "it lacked clear enforcement policies describing circumstances under which it would suspend or revoke delegated lending authority and did not have procedures directing how suspension or revocation would be done.
- "the lender oversight responsibilities of OLO [SBA Office of Lender Oversight] and OFA [SBA Office of Financial Assistance] are not compatible with OCA loan production goals which presented a potential conflict or at least the appearance of a conflict, between the desire to encourage lender participation in PLP and the need to evaluate lender performance and take enforcement action.
- "discontinuing BLX's participation in PLP and other delegated lending programs would have significantly increased the volume of loans to be processed by SBA field offices at a time when SBA was reducing its loan processing staff in field offices. Also, SBA was attempting to establish the Standard 7(a) Guaranty Loan Processing Centers in Hazard, Kentucky and Sacramento, California, and may not have believed that sufficient staffing would be available to manage the increased loan volume."

The report said that since the SBA rarely punishes poorly performing lenders by removing them from the PLP program and barely has removal procedures in the first place, lenders have little incentive to behave. "SBA has not developed policies and procedures that describe when it will suspend or revoke PLP authority or how it will do so," the report said. "Although the current version of Title 13 of the Code of Federal Regulations and SBA's SOPs contain some enforcement actions, the guidance does not provide direction concerning when and under what circumstances the enforcement actions should be implemented."

In a damning assessment, the report continued, "Because terminations and non-renewals have not been frequent, lenders can essentially ignore SBA's delegated lending authority requirements without suffering any material consequences. Therefore, without consistent implementation of enforcement policies, lenders cannot be certain of the consequences of certain ratings; and in addition, they may not take SBA's oversight seriously." Seriously.

Besides, the report noted, the SBA has an inherent conflict because enforcement, such as revoking PLP status, hampers the agency's core function of issuing loans to small businesses. Moreover, kicking a large producer like BLX out of the program would also reduce the SBA's loan portfolio. "Because BLX has been among the top 10 SBA lenders since 2001, any actions that would appropriately mitigate BLX's risk, such as suspending its delegated lending authority, also would have been detrimental to achieving SBA's loan production goals," the report said.

■ ■ ■

A week after the OIG published the report, *Dow Jones Newswire* ran a story by Carol Remond, saying that Senator John Kerry, chairman of the Senate Committee on Small Business and Entrepreneurship, was bothered by the redactions. Senator Kerry said in the article: "It is highly unusual for an agency to attempt to withhold the Inspector General's recommendations and their response from public scrutiny, and the SBA must explain their rationale fully and completely."

The article said Senator Kerry was "concerned that the SBA is not taking the Inspector General's recommendations seriously and that it's not adequately addressing its 'failed oversight of a small business lender that resulted in years of undetected fraud.'" Remond reported that Senator Kerry said he would soon hold a hearing on the issue.

The article continued, "A spokesman for SBA declined to comment on the extent of the redactions. SBA said in an e-mail statement: 'Because so much of the material covered in the Inspector General's report is, by law, privileged and confidential, there is very little we can say about it.'" Remond said Allied also had no comment.

Senator Kerry issued a press release headlined in an extra-large, bold font, "Kerry Questions Bush Administration Decision to Withhold Fraud Findings." According to the release, "We can't get to the heart of the problem if the Administration keeps hiding the facts from public view. . . . The Administration must explain their rationale for suppressing the Inspector General's recommendations and their response. In order to combat future fraud and protect the integrity of this vital small business loan program, the American people need access to all the relevant information." Senator Kerry didn't seem that interested in ensuring that proper action be taken to demand full restitution and shut down BLX, but he had no trouble finding his voice to blame the Bush Administration for redacting the audit.

On November 2, 2007, Brickman and I flew to Washington to meet with Ms. Kevin Wheeler, deputy Democratic staff director of the Senate committee, and Angela Ohm, the general counsel for the committee. Though she scheduled us for only a half hour in a conference room, Wheeler was sufficiently interested to transfer us to the cafeteria to complete the discussion when our time expired and the room was needed. We gave them a binder of our BLX findings, including the Kroll report, and explained that we had been complaining to the SBA and SEC for years about BLX. Brickman and I showed her that the fraud far exceeded the Harrington loans, extending nationally and even beyond the SBA to the USDA lending program. We spent time discussing the SBA's ineffective oversight of its delegated lenders, particularly non-bank lenders. Despite lax SBA oversight, bank lenders perform better than non-bank lenders because more stringent bank regulators review them separately.

We discussed the fact that SBA has faced criticism for years from those who have argued for shutting the agency down outright. The critics argue that in today's marketplace, small businesses simply don't need the government to provide subsidies. The original inability of small businesses to obtain loans has long since disappeared, with any number of private lenders ready to finance worthwhile enterprises of any size. In classic bureaucratic fashion, the agency's defense against its critics has been to go on the offensive, and critics have watched in dismay as the SBA has entrenched itself by expanding both the size of its portfolio and the scope of its services.

In the 1990s, the SBA created new lending programs called SBA*Express* and Community Express. These programs provide government guarantees on smaller loans with reduced application paperwork. According to the SBA Web site, "SBA*Express* was established by the SBA to test the implications of delegating additional authority to selected SBA lenders and of streamlining and expediting the Agency's loan approval process." Under the program, the SBA allowed lenders to process loans under $250,000 with even less supervision from the agency. It's easy to imagine the results of this policy.

Just as with the 7(a) loans, the new policy of further "streamlining" and "expediting" SBA loan guarantees led to widespread fraud and corruption. A report in December 2006 by the SBA's OIG found that of the forty-five defaulted loans it audited in the Community Express and SBA*Express* programs, forty-four were improper. "Our audit disclosed that SBA purchased SBA*Express* and Community Express loans without obtaining information needed to assess whether lenders verified borrowers' use of loan proceeds, determined eligibility and creditworthiness, or verified borrower financial information. . ." the audit report said. "Based on the high rate of deficiencies, we estimate that $128 million to $130.6 million in disbursements on the 2,729 loans approved after January 1, 2000, and purchased before February 1, 2005, were not properly reviewed by SBA."

It should come as no surprise, of course, that BLX became an eager participant in the SBA*Express* and Community Express programs. In 2005, *The Miami Herald* described BLX as a "specialist" in Community Express loans, having issued more than $26 million in loans the prior year—more than double its budget. "We haven't pushed [our services] that hard in South Florida because of the hurricanes—so we're really just getting started," said Fred Crispen, executive vice president of BLX.

We also offered Wheeler several recommendations for Congress to make to the SBA in order to combat fraud in its loan programs:

- The SBA should reinvest a portion of the savings it achieves from delegating underwriting authority to private industry in better oversight.
- SBA audits should focus on measuring the quality of lenders' underwriting decisions, instead of filling out "check-the-box" questionnaires and studying loan files for "completeness."
- The SBA should recognize losses when losses occur, instead of waiting for the final resolution of the loan before recognizing losses.
- The SBA should develop objective criteria that lenders must satisfy in order to participate in SBA's loan programs.
- The SBA should make public much more information about its lender performance, including the SBA's lender risk ratings and regulatory filings.
- The newer Section 7(a) loan programs, such as SBA*Express* and Community Express, should be eliminated because they receive even less oversight and are rife with abuse.

Wheeler had already spent time reviewing the BLX situation after Harrington was indicted. She was familiar with Allied's version of the story that a single rogue employee caused the fraud, that BLX was the victim and so forth. At one point, she even asked me whether I had a personal relationship with anyone at the SBA's OIG. I replied, "I know you are asking this because Allied has been telling people that I am personal friends with the SBA OIG in Michigan." She nodded. I was surprised that Allied had extended this fiction to the Senate staff. I told her the answer is "No," and that I didn't even know the name of the Michigan SBA OIG.

Brickman and I said we would be willing to testify, if asked. Wheeler asked who should testify from BLX. I suggested Tannenhauser. She said he might not be available (this meeting came a week before Allied announced it had replaced Tannenhauser) and BLX had suggested Deryl Schuster. She continued by saying, "We have heard enough from Schuster." He was the BLX executive quoted encouraging the SBA lending industry to raise money for Senator Kerry's presidential bid, while trumpeting Tannenhauser's membership on Kerry's fundraising committee.

■ ■ ■

On November 7, 2007, Senator Kerry announced there would be a hearing the following week to press for more oversight of small business lenders. With the announcement, we learned that Tannenhauser would testify, after all. Brickman and I were offered the opportunity to submit written testimony (which we did) as part of the hearing record, but were not invited to testify in person. Senator Kerry's office told our counsel the Senator had promised SBA officials that they would not face an "investigative hearing," pledging it would not turn into a game of "gotcha."

Senator Kerry repeated this promise at the opening of the hearing, "So the purpose of this hearing is not politics, the purpose of this hearing is not 'gotcha,' the purpose of this hearing is to figure out how, with the help of the SBA's Office of Inspector General, which was created in order to have transparency and accountability and effectiveness, how the SBA's lending partners and our committee can improve the agency's lender oversight and prevent fraud in the SBA's small business lending programs.

"No one is here to suggest that this is somehow pervasive or that it's more. We don't know that. We are here to explore the one situation that we know, and those things that have been talked about by the Inspector General over a course of time."

Senator Kerry, sounding like he was almost apologizing to BLX, adopted a deferential tone toward the company throughout the hearing. He referred to the fraud as being caused by "a bad actor and small groups of people." He added, "The hearing is not intended to hurt Business Loan Express or any other entity. But that's not to say also that there isn't a legitimate standard of accountability because people need to answer for their employees. That's just a normal course of business, and this should be no different.

"We need to understand how no one noticed or reported a high number of bad SBA loans coming out of the branch. And today's hearing is an opportunity for the company to tell its side of the story, including their rationale for cutting back on small business lending, which they announced recently. And let me just say, I greatly regret the loss of jobs that is going to go with the company's announcement."

It was hard not to roll my eyes.

Senator Olympia Snowe, the ranking minority member of the committee, took a harder line toward both the SBA and BLX, saying, "It's my hope this morning that we will probe how and why the government has inappropriately allowed loan fraud and poor loan underwriting to occur at the business loan corporation BLX. . . .We've had numerous hearings, numerous reports, as the chairman cited, and yet we still find ourselves at this juncture where we're finding fraudulent loans to the magnitude and degrees of millions and millions of dollars, and just BLX alone was more than $200 million."

Senator Snowe declared the SBA's lender oversight "unacceptable" and joined Senator Kerry in criticizing the SBA for the unnecessary redactions in the OIG report. She clearly understood the consequence of allowing lax or even non-existent oversight, stating: "I fear that unless the SBA is able to dramatically improve its lender oversight, escalating losses and fees will drive lenders and borrowers away from these key loan programs, not only seriously hampering and even harming the ability of small businesses to access capital to grow, but also regrettably reversing the very mission of these programs."

After these opening statements from the Senators, the first witness was Steven C. Preston, administrator of the SBA. He spoke in broad generalities about the importance of improving the effectiveness of SBA lender oversight. In an attempt to show pro-activity in the face of the increased scrutiny, the SBA had proposed new rules for lender oversight and processes for enforcement actions two weeks before the hearing.

Preston was silent about the redacted OIG report in his opening remarks but referred to his written testimony, which indicated the SBA had provided an un-redacted copy of the report to the Senate committee. The written testimony explained that the public had to remain in the dark to protect "the integrity of the Agency's duties as a financial regulator," where "public disclosure of such information would severely damage the Agency's ability to obtain sensitive or adverse information from its lenders." While it is hard to see how disclosing BLX's loan performance, the chronology of the fraud, the OIG recommendations and the SBA response would cause this sort of harm, the Senators seemed to accept this tortured logic and *did not ask Preston a single question about the redactions.*

Senator Snowe challenged Preston over BLX: "Why didn't you take remedial steps with respect to BLX? I mean, why weren't there any remedies or any penalties? I mean, why didn't you revoke their preferred lender status, for example? Because, as the Inspector General's report indicates . . . lenders can essentially ignore SBA's delegated lending authority requirements without suffering any material consequences." Unfortunately, this question came as part of a much longer statement that included questions on other topics. When Preston answered, he picked his way through the other topics in her question without answering the ones about BLX.

Senator Snowe persisted, probing the large default rate in BLX's portfolio. Preston didn't seem concerned and drew a distinction between portfolio quality "and fraud, which certainly in the case of BLX was a highly sophisticated group of people within that institution. . . ."

Senator Kerry asked how the agency first flagged the fraud. Preston could not say, responding, "Senator, I don't specifically recall."

Senator Kerry then asked what the SBA was doing to prevent this from happening again and inquired what lessons were learned. Preston again pushed his (and Allied's) view that BLX was the victim, not the villain, saying that "when fraud is perpetrated of this type, although it's bad for all of us and none of us like it, the one who ends up losing financially is the lending institution." Preston said he was satisfied with the settlement from BLX, somehow accepting the arithmetic that the few million dollars of reimbursements from BLX to SBA actually covered the nearly $77 million of allegedly fraudulent Michigan loans. Apparently confident that the

SBA fraud stopped at the Michigan state line, Preston had no thoughts or plans to offer about looking for problems anywhere else in the country.

Senator Kerry: "When you found out about the scheme . . . you talked at the time about the tough disciplinary measures that were going to be taken against BLX and then ultimately the agency entered into closed negotiations with the companies and really kept the details of any disciplinary actions confidential. What happened between . . . the tough-stance and the private negotiations?"

Preston: "Right, I'm not aware of—of the chronology and unfortunately I don't—I can't comment on that."

Senator Kerry asked whether Preston had been personally involved in resolving BLX.

Preston: "Early on, I was actively involved in the discussion on what I thought the next step should be. My view was a couple of things. Number one, I want to absolutely ensure that the taxpayer was protected . . . let's leave it at that. I think the other issue is . . . trying to balance our judgment is when you look at something like this, at what point is the issue behind you? And at what point is the issue continuing? And how do you weigh that against . . . restricting capital to small businesses?" Was he as anxious as Allied to declare the issue "behind"?

The next witness, Eric M. Thorson, inspector general of the SBA, was tougher on BLX and the SBA. "We believe this is the largest 7(a) loan fraud scheme in SBA history. Both Mr. Harrington and Ms. Lazenby have pled guilty. So far, our investigation has resulted in the indictment of twenty-seven individuals of which three are currently international fugitives. This criminal investigation is continuing with further indictments expected."

He told the committee that the agency had been aware of recurring performance and compliance issues with BLX, but the company had suffered few consequences. "We believe that the high rate of default and other problems with BLX loans presented undue financial risk to SBA, and therefore, merited in-depth reviews of the defaulted loans, as well as possible suspension of BLX's preferred lender status, which allows BLX to approve loans with virtually no prior review by SBA."

He continued: "Despite problems with BLX's loans however, SBA continued to renew the delegated PLP lending authority, and to honor guarantee purchase requests without taking any additional precautions, paying out $272.1 million in guarantees between 2001 and 2006. Quite simply, SBA did not hold the lender accountable for its performance problems . . . SBA has focused on the quantity of loans, not the quality. SBA sets goals for loan production, but not for loan quality or lender performance. . . . We believe SBA may have been reluctant to take enforcement action against BLX because it is among SBA's top ten lenders in the value of loans disbursed." Stating the sad, obvious truth, Thorson concluded his indictment of SBA "oversight policies" with an understatement: "SBA is not focused on fraud detection."

Then Senator Kerry asked: "Why was the investigation of BLX initiated?"

"The criminal investigation was actually started back around 2002 by allegations that were made from a number of sources, some of which, I believe, you have statements from that are commonly referred to as short-sellers," Thorson said. "The SBA did investigate a lot of those issues, but didn't find that there were enough specifics there to be able to bring a criminal case." This brought up the depressing memory of how the SBA could not even find its own loan numbers for the many fraudulent loans we brought to its attention. No doubt it would be hard to find "enough specifics there" if they couldn't even find the loans in question.

Thorson continued, "There were other issues that developed along the way on the non-fraud side of it, which was an issue in '02, which suggested that there were problems with loans, and then in 2005, the OIG issued a management advisory report detailing, I think, it was seven loans, in violation of SBA procedures, and material misstatements to the SBA."

Then Thorson shocked everyone:

Thorson: "In fact, to their credit, BLX offered to repay one of those loans, but for some reason the SBA sent them an e-mail stating that they were being too hard on themselves and they didn't need to do that."

Senator Kerry: "You've got to hit me again with that one."

Senator Snowe: "Yeah" (as everyone began to laugh).

Thorson: "I'm sorry?"

Senator Kerry: "You've got to hit me again with that one. The SBA did what (sic) they wrote them back and said, don't worry?"

Thorson: "That's the information—I would—neither myself nor Mr. Preston were with SBA at that time, but that's the information I have, yes."

It was at this point that Senator Kerry got around to asking who had insisted on making the redactions in the OIG report. Thorson said the requests came from the SBA general counsel and from BLX's attorneys. *BLX's attorneys?* "We rejected the claims of the company, but I did accept the redactions from the general counsel's office," said Thorson.

"In your opinion, are all of the redactions legally supportable?" Kerry asked.

"No, but in fairness to their office, I'm not an attorney," Thorson answered.

Senator Snowe followed up: "Could you understand why they continued to renew the status of BLX? . . . Reading the report here, it really, truly is mystifying and disconcerting."

Thorson responded, "It's really one of the things that we had a hard time with, and I understand the agency's concern about affecting their business and the argument was made, I believe, by BLX that it would put them out of business." Apparently, the SBA thought it was more important to keep a fraudulent company in business than to stop it from increasing the SBA's losses by cutting it off from making new loans.

After a break Tannenhauser testified, and if he had spun any faster, he would have turned to butter. Senator Kerry also lived up to his promise of sparing the SBA and Allied any embarrassment. The Senator smoothly paved the way for Tannenhauser: "Since this story broke, the Committee has taken a very measured approach to the news, asking the questions about the SBA oversight in reaction, but leaving the disciplinary decisions entirely to the SBA, and I think, we refrain from any sort of public bashing sessions. As you know, we've never recommended for or against radical calls for BLX to lose its preferred lender status, delegated loan privileges, or to cease BLX's ability to sell SBA loans on the secondary market."

As Tannenhauser began to speak, he was visibly nervous—his voice cracked. In his prepared testimony, Tannenhauser argued that BLX is victim, not perpetrator. He claimed it has no financial incentive to condone fraud, and every incentive to avoid it. In one moment, he blamed the government for not finding the fraud sooner, "The Farm Credit Administration reviewed several of these loans going back almost four years with no indication to us of fraud. Obviously, such wrongdoings are difficult to detect." Then, he attacked the OIG for finding the fraud later, "The OIG report . . . is fundamentally flawed," is "replete with inaccuracies and inconsistencies." Obviously, he liked the Farm Credit report, which missed the fraud, better and alleged that the OIG report "paints an inaccurate picture by excluding the Farm Credit Auditors' ultimate finding and conclusions, which strongly support the SBA's decision to renew BLX's PLP status. . . . Unfortunately, I cannot provide more detail, because criminal law prohibits lenders from disseminating the contents of Farm Credit audits."

In an apple-pie effort to show remorse and concern, Tannenhauser intoned, "I'm personally saddened and disappointed by the misconduct of our former employee. I wish we had become aware of his activities earlier." Ready to move on, Tannenhauser testified, "BLX is a very different company today than it was when these fraudulent activities began many years ago."

When the questions began, Senator Kerry continued his sympathetic approach, "Mr. Tannenhauser, [I] appreciate your testimony, and I know that BLX and the SBA both consider themselves, essentially, they've been victims of a fraud here, and obviously, you know, you were in the sense that one of your employees took a flier."

Tannenhauser took the Senator's pass and ran with it. He blamed Harrington, pointing out that Harrington's specialty was making loans for gas stations and convenience stores to borrowers of Middle Eastern descent. BLX observed the poor loan performance, which caused it to shut down Harrington's "operations well before any indication of fraud or wrongdoing came to light." They did this because "we are in business to make good loans, and the people are giving us loans that don't perform well, that doesn't serve us very well, nor the program."

Trying to distance himself from Harrington, Tannenhauser testified, "BLX is really an amalgamation of four different companies and the Troy office came to us in the merger of one of those companies that we integrated. . . . Mr. Harrington was really the rainmaker for that office." Tannenhauser made no mention of the inconvenient fact that Harrington and the Troy office had come to BLX from Allied in the merger with Allied Capital Express, which was supervised by Allied's own COO Sweeney.

Senator Kerry concluded his questions with a final kowtow to Tannenhauser, "We certainly want to acknowledge that . . . if this is sort of a narrow and singular individual kind of event, one hates to see an entire operation diminished as a consequence of that." Tannenhauser repeated that BLX had changed its ways and also repeated Allied's rationalization that taxpayers had not lost any money because of the Detroit fraud. Of the almost $77 million of allegedly fraudulent loans, BLX repaid $8 million.

That's a loss in any book.

Then, Senator Snowe took a turn, and, again, she proved tougher than Kerry on Tannenhauser, pointing out that as far back as June 2003, the SBA's Sacramento center had "recommended not renewing the preferred lender status for BLX." In response, Tannenhauser became combative and using a familiar Allied strategy, claimed that anyone with a critical view just didn't understand the company. He said the Sacramento Center "may have been confused about what the actual benchmarks [for PLP renewal] were."

Senator Snowe pushed back: "The center's non-renewal recommendations were based primarily in BLX's unfavorable purchase and liquidation rates. Other issues which it cited in June of 2003, thirty-five of sixty-five field offices submitted evaluations that did not support renewal, cited problems with BLX's inactivity, poor performance, measurability process, closures and liquidate [sic] loans."

Tannenhauser retorted, "Our loss rate is significantly lower than the industry average is. So that's the real risk to the government, and we've maintained that over the ten to fourteen years that we've been doing this." Again, it was easy for BLX to manage the "significantly lower" loss rates by failing to resolve the defaulted loans, but instead leaving them in their special purgatory status of "in liquidation" for years and trying to outrun the problems by growing its portfolio. According to an SBA publication in 1996, rapid portfolio growth can create a misleading picture of loss rates "because most losses on unseasoned loans are unlikely to have occurred." For this reason, the SBA decided to discontinue using loss rates for performance measurement.

Senator Snowe finished by getting Tannenhauser to pledge to reimburse the government for any loss that occurred. "Absolutely, absolutely," promised Tannenhauser.

I don't know whether the senators believed Tannenhauser's shtick. I know I didn't, but, then, I've never received financial support from him. I give Senator Kerry credit for at least holding a hearing. Nydia Velázquez, Kerry's counterpart in the House of Representatives and another large Tannenhauser benefactor, didn't even do that much.

The hearing revealed a rift between inspector general Thorson and SBA administrator Preston. The SBA was embarrassed by missing the fraud in Michigan. With its oversight under scrutiny, the SBA could not risk the exposure of an additional multi-hundred-million-dollar fraud by BLX in the rest of the country that occurred under its watch. To do so, would raise doubts about its oversight over its entire $60 billion portfolio. Two days after the hearing, the Bush Administration resolved the conflict by appointing Thorson to the Treasury Department. The move had the stench of a cover-up. In February 2008, President Bush nominated Carol Dillion Kissal as the new SBA inspector general. She previously worked in the D.C. Department of Transportation and before that as treasurer of Amtrak. "I look forward to working with her," said Preston.

■ ■ ■

While trying to find a video link to the Senate hearing on BLX, one of our lawyers stumbled onto a YouTube video that showed the human face of BLX's fraud. The video ran for more than ten minutes. On it, a haggard-looking gentleman, Muhammad Arif Darr, told of his experience as a BLX borrower. According to Darr, in the video and in later correspondence, BLX recruited him from New York, where he lived with his family, to purchase a motel in North Carolina. The previous owner had operated the motel until mid-2003, when it ceased operations and he abandoned the property. BLX foreclosed and never kept any security person to protect the property and its contents, which resulted in looting. Darr moved away from his family and borrowed $147,000 against his New York condo, money he put into the property to make improvements.

Then, BLX gave him a $341,441 senior conventional loan and a $758,558 junior SBA loan to purchase the property from BLX for $1.1 million. BLX promised to extend an additional $300,000 third lien to fund property improvements and qualify the motel to be branded a "Knight's Inn." BLX used a property appraisal that assumed the improvements had been made and the re-branding occurred. According to Darr, the BLX appraisal compared "a functional, operational property" to his property, which was "*closed down, abandoned, broken down, partially boarded up, roofs partially leaking* and missing many hotel fixtures that were stolen."

According to Darr (and documentation he provided), BLX reneged on the written-promise for the additional $300,000, so he could not complete the needed renovations. As he put it in the video, "This predator-lender, I have appealed to them so many times and just nothing happens to them. They think they have got everything. They have all the influence in the world and nobody can touch them and nobody can do anything." As a result, the property never got to a good enough condition to operate profitably or become a Knight's Inn. Darr had spent the last two years working around the clock at the front desk, but was now about to lose the motel. He wrote, "Improvements were all done by my money, as BLX never spent a dime and got the increase in property value by getting me, the borrower, to spend my money on their property. . . . BLX's plan was to engineer my default to repossess this property and resell to some other minority victim." He put his story onto YouTube in a desperate appeal for help and to warn others about borrowing from BLX.

Brickman called the SBA about Darr's plight. Armed with Darr's paperwork, his own research, and additional information he obtained from the SBA by a FOIA request, Brickman spoke with SBA lawyer Christa Brusen-Gomez about the Darr loan. He described to her how BLX sold the property to Darr for more than the appraised value and that Darr was being used to bail out old SBA loans. Under SBA rules, a new SBA loan cannot be made to replace an existing SBA loan. She told him, "If a buyer wanted to pay 120 percent of what a property in liquidation is worth, that is his problem." When Brickman told her that BLX never gave him the appraisal showing the low value, she said, "Then, he should have gotten his own appraisal." In short, it appears that the SBA does not care if borrowers can pay, if BLX issues SBA second liens that leave the SBA undersecured, or if BLX withholds appraisals that show the property is not worth the sale amount. The SBA helps its lenders, not its borrowers.

■ ■ ■

After the Senate hearing, we received unexpected bad news on our whistleblower lawsuit regarding the shrimp boat loans. The False Claims Act is designed to encourage informed citizens called "relators" to bring suit on behalf of the government. Many relators have firsthand knowledge of the fraud. However, on the other extreme are the opportunists who read about a fraud in the newspaper, have no independent knowledge of their own, but rush to court to file a lawsuit and claim a share of the recovery. Congress sought to eliminate this sort of behavior by denying jurisdiction over actions brought by such relators, "based upon the public disclosure of allegations or transactions in a criminal, civil, or administrative hearing, in a congressional, administrative, or Government Account Office report, hearing, audit or investigation, or from the news media, unless . . . the person bringing the action is an original source of the information."

BLX argued that Brickman and Greenlight were not an original source of the information, that there were news stories about problems in the shrimping industry, and that other pieces of our information had been obtained from public sources. BLX argued that for these reasons the court lacked jurisdiction to hear the case.

In response, we pointed out that Congress deliberately amended the False Claims Act to encourage the precise type of lawsuit that we brought, where the case is based not on public "information" but, instead, is based on specific "allegations or transactions" of fraud that had not previously been publicly disclosed. No one had publicly alleged fraud prior to our suit. The general news stories about the shrimp boat industry did not discuss allegations of fraud or any transactions. Neither did any of the pieces of information in our complaint. We, and no one else, had meticulously figured out the fraud from a variety of sources, including non-public interviews with former employees and the BLX delinquency report, which led us to the fraud in the first place.

Atlanta U.S. District Court Judge Julie Carnes surprised us by siding with BLX. She took a very broad view of what information is public (including information we used from depositions that were not part of a filed court record, U.S. Coast Guard vessel abstracts, and responses to FOIA requests) and determined that "most of the factual information in their complaint was available to any member of the public who cared to search for it." As for our review of internal BLX records and interviews with former employees, Judge Carnes concluded that we had not identified clearly what facts we used from the nonpublic material in making our complaint.

Even though the "allegations or transactions" had not been publicly disclosed, Carnes reasoned that since both the misrepresented facts (that BLX had complied with various SBA requirements and regulations) and the true facts (that they had not done so) were public, it amounted to the same thing as a public disclosure of the allegations. As a result, she dismissed our case prior to discovery, on the technicality that the court lacked jurisdiction to evaluate the merits of our complaint.

On the second page of her ruling, Judge Carnes footnoted, "However, there is an additional financial motive behind this case. James Brickman and Greenlight Capital have been publicly identified as having a 'short' position in the stock of Allied Capital, Inc., a publicly traded company that owns approximately 95% of defendant BLX. A short seller borrows stock from a lender and sells the borrowed stock, hoping and expecting that the price of the stock will decline. If the price declines, the short seller will be able to purchase the stock later at a lower price, return the stock to the lender, and keep the profits. Brickman and Greenlight Capital thus stand to benefit from any decrease in the price of Allied stock that may result from this lawsuit."

Though this finding supposedly had nothing to do with her decision, her gratuitous adoption of the irrelevant and misguided attack by BLX's lawyers on our motives for filing the suit particularly galled Brickman; he hadn't been short Allied for years and said so in our court filings.

Allied rushed out a celebratory press release, noting the judge's findings relating to our motives, trumpeting, "Shortsellers of Allied Capital shares, including David Einhorn and his allies, have for many years been making false and unsubstantiated claims of wrongdoing against Allied Capital and BLX. So far, every court that has ever examined the shortseller claims has rejected them."

Of course, Allied saw no need to acknowledge that the court hadn't even considered the merits of the case. Indeed, the court never ruled that BLX did not carry out a fraud in its shrimp boat loans; it simply never reached the issue. The sad irony of Judge Carnes's ruling, and Allied's public gloating, is that Allied won this round in the litigation only because the judge ruled that the massive fraud had been a matter of public record for years. Brickman and Greenlight have appealed the judge's decision to dismiss the case.

■ ■ ■

In December 2007, *The Washington Post* ran an article by Gilbert M. Gaul on the Bill Russell Oil fraud in the USDA loan program. The article reported on the fraud involving the loans made to the company by BLX as I discussed in Chapter 25, but with a few more details. The article also pointed out the poor government oversight in response to the fraud.

The article reported:

A *Washington Post* analysis found that from 2001 to 2006, the USDA had to pay $34 million to buy back 13 BLX loan guarantees— representing one of every five USDA-backed loans made by BLX. The 13 loans included some to companies that were in and out of bankruptcy, saddled with tax bills, or struggling in declining industries.

A Maryland gas station operator received a $3 million guaranteed loan but soon lost its license for failing to pay millions in gasoline taxes. It defaulted on the loan and filed for bankruptcy two years later. A Pennsylvania mushroom farm received a $3.4 million loan while in bankruptcy and a loan of $1.7 million a few years later. It filed for bankruptcy again this year and is now defunct. A Hanover, Pa., wallpaper manufacturer with mounting losses got a $3 million guaranteed loan in November 2000. It filed for bankruptcy in 2005 and closed.

In each case, USDA officials relied on BLX employees to investigate the borrowers, conducting little due diligence on their own. Now, with questions being raised about BLX loans to Bill Russell Oil and others, USDA officials have turned to their inspector general to audit the company's entire portfolio of loans. BLX could be asked to pay back millions.

The article pointed out how Bill Russell Oil borrowed $3 million from BLX through the USDA loan program, despite the Environmental Protection Agency's citing Bill Russell for dozens of environmental violations and proposing a fine of $314,558.

The article said:

Shirley A. Tucker, the USDA's director of business programs in Arkansas, said her office relied on the borrower and the lender to certify that Bill Russell Oil met all environmental requirements. Tucker added that she did not learn about the EPA investigation until she read about it in a local newspaper several months after the loan guarantee was approved. "I was surprised," she said. "Under the conditional agreement, it was up to the lender to bring that to our attention."

The loan was declared delinquent within a year. "It was hard to see how a loan could go south so fast," Tucker said. Later, she went to look at some of the gas stations herself. "We found some didn't have electricity on the day we closed the loan. There was no way they were operating," she said. (© 2007, *The Washington Post*. Reprinted with Permission.)

He closed the article with an amazing statement from Tucker: "Yeah, we're the government, but we really don't have any enforcement. We can't put them in jail."

CHAPTER 34

Blind Men, Elephants, Möbius Strips, and Moral Hazards

I f someone commits fraud, but shareholders don't lose money and the regulators decide to ignore it, was it really fraud? The authorities are good at cleaning up fraud after the money's gone. After a blow-up, with investors' capital already lost, they know just what to do. If the blow-up is big enough, like Enron, they form a special task-force and pursue criminal cases against the insiders.

I recently attended a small presentation made by one of the Enron prosecutors. He laid out exactly how he made his case and the mistakes management had made, both in perpetrating the fraud and defending themselves at trial. I asked him if it were fair for Enron management to go to jail, when there are many other management teams that act as Enron's did or worse, but don't suffer the same prosecution because their companies haven't "blown-up." He really didn't have an answer.

The authorities really don't know what to do about fraud when they discover it *in progress*. The Arthur Andersen prosecution, which put the audit firm out of business for bungling Enron, cost a lot of innocent people their jobs. The government doesn't want another Arthur Andersen. It seems that the regulatory thinking, espoused by current SEC chairman Christopher Cox, is that shareholders should not be punished for corporate fraud, because he believes they are the victims in the first place. Why punish the victims a second time? This thinking may be politically expedient in the short term, but creates a classic moral hazard—a free fraud zone. If regulators insulate shareholders from the penalties of investing in corrupt companies, then investors have no incentive to demand honest behavior and worse, no need to avoid investing in dishonest companies.

The truth is that investors in corporate securities are risk takers making investments of risk capital. One risk is fraud. The best way to discourage fraud is to actually enforce the penalties for fraud. If investors believe that companies making false and misleading statements will be punished, they will be more sensitive to what is said. And, because their money is at stake, investors will allocate their capital more carefully. This sensitivity and other consequences will, in turn, deter dishonesty. In fact, I wonder if a few Allied shareholders have held the stock on the cynical theory that *even if Allied is every bit as bad as Greenlight thinks it is, the regulatory consequences won't be dire enough to hurt my investment*. So far, that thinking has been spot-on, and indeed, rewarded.

The same moral hazard exists regarding workers. If employees of a dishonest firm believe that its poor ethics jeopardize their respective futures, they will act more aggressively to fight misbehavior. If managements know lying on conference calls will be prosecuted, they will tell fewer lies. Passing laws like Sarbanes-Oxley helps honest companies create better controls. It does nothing to stop top-down corporate fraud, unless it is enforced.

For our markets to work effectively, participants need to follow the rules. It is a matter of fairness, pure and simple, and, as we have seen with Allied, not so simple. When participants stray, there needs to be serious consequences. The authorities need to enforce the rules, not just pretend to enforce them. (It reminds me of the joke about the former Soviet Union worker: "I pretend to work and they pretend to pay me.")

Ultimately in 2008, as governor of New York, Spitzer would testify to Congress regarding the monoline insurance companies including MBIA, "when you have federal regulators who run away from fulfilling their job which is to ensure that the rules are enforced, that there is integrity in the marketplace, we generate these crises. What we have got to take away from this, as we should have from prior scandals, is that when regulators are asleep on the job the ultimate victim is going to be the investor, the taxpayer and government." Plainly, the same is true of the regulatory failures over Allied and BLX. Of course, Spitzer was part of the problem; when these issues came to his office in 2003, he investigated the critics rather than the perpetrators.

If Sarbanes-Oxley is to be effective and taken seriously, the SEC can't let behavior like Allied's pass without prosecution. Walton was asked at the August 2002 investor day whether Sarbanes-Oxley created an issue for him. He told everyone he had no problem signing Allied's financials. In poker, this is called being "pot committed." This is when the pot is so large relative to your remaining chips, that, if necessary, you must put your remaining chips in the pot if there is even the slightest chance you can win.

SEC Chairman Cox's view of expedience encourages a dishonest business culture. Allied Capital isn't the only unscrupulous company out there. It is just the one with which I have the most experience. I would guess there are a couple of dozen significant companies with similar characteristics. If you are a fancy guy sitting behind a fancy desk, you can make a lot of money through illicit, dishonest conduct and still have a good chance of either not being caught, or not going to jail if you do get caught. If you are a regular person and walk into Home Depot or Old Navy and pilfer some merchandise, the consequences are likely to be far worse. "If you are going to steal, *steal big*," is how the old saying goes.

■ ■ ■

Shortly after my speech in 2002, Walton told investors an old tale about a blind man and an elephant: a group of blind men (or men in the dark) touch an elephant to learn what it is like. Each one touches a different part, but only one part, such as the side or the tusk. They then compare notes on what they felt and learn they are in complete disagreement. The story is used to indicate that reality may be viewed differently depending upon one's perspective.

Walton's point was that the short-sellers only saw one or two parts of the Allied elephant. Velocita or Startec were just the tusk, BLX was just the tail. The wise management team could see the whole thing and supposedly knew better than anyone that the elephant was actually a healthy giant.

In reality, it is Allied management who want investors to focus exclusively on a few parts: the distributions, the successful sale of a couple of key investments and the company's chronic misfortune of being victims of a "short attack."

There has been much coverage of bits and pieces of the Allied story. One difficulty in telling it to regulators, journalists, and investors is that it is so big, so long, and so complicated, that it is hard to describe the whole elephant. That is what this book is about: one sick elephant.

At its most basic level, Allied Capital is the story of Wall Street at its worst. Relative to most stocks, it has little institutional ownership. With the enormous fees it generates for Wall Street, there are plenty of financial incentives to support the scheme. Allied has spread its lucrative stock offerings around to many brokerages. The brokerage firm analysts writing their glowing reports on Allied know what they are doing. Allied is a retail stock that is sold to and owned by individuals, such as retirees looking for a fat dividend.

And yet, what Allied itself "owns" is a leveraged portfolio of mezzanine loans and opaque private-equity positions; that is, exactly the type of risky investments which the SEC generally restricts to "sophisticated investors" and strictly keeps away from retail investors, the very same investors . . . who own Allied stock. Or, to sum up from another perspective: Allied is a regulated investment company; the SEC is its direct regulator. And yet, the SEC has shown itself incapable of doing that job—or perhaps more truly told, has proved unwilling to do that job. Lawlessness inside regulation, a Möbius strip of hypocrisy: the entire Allied saga has a *Through the Looking Glass* quality to it.

At one point, over a lunch in 2003, I had the opportunity to conduct a "reality check" by discussing short selling with Warren Buffett. He said he has shorted stocks before, the first one being AT&T when he was a teenager to irritate his high school teachers, who held their retirement money in it. Over the years, he said he had trouble getting the timing right on short sales and preferred to have a *public persona* as a long investor. I asked Buffett what he thought of the Allied Capital saga. Though he said he didn't know about the company, he observed that it was tough to win being short something like that. As he saw it, for Greenlight, Allied is just one position in our portfolio. But, for the company and its management, it is the whole ballgame, so they will say and do things we wouldn't consider doing in order to win.

■ ■ ■

Allied's campaign against its critics has been quite effective. The story of Mark Alpert, the Deutsche Bank analyst who issued a "Sell" rating, only to wind up being investigated by the NYSE, has been a good deterrent. Joel Houck apparently got the message. While he was still at Wachovia, he re-emerged by reinitiating coverage of Allied with an "Outperform" rating in October 2006. Regarding his previous concerns (the October 2006 recommendation was issued before Allied resolved its SEC investigation) Houck took comfort that Allied and BLX had successfully sold debt and equity—thereby passing scrutiny from the SEC and others; and that BLX "is valued by an independent third party" and is a nationwide SBA preferred lender.

Houck's report stated a single sentence investment thesis: "We believe *Allied has best-in-class management* and can generate a midteens internal rate of return, net of expenses, over the long run." The same person who previously speculated that Allied was a culture of fraud wrote this. Houck has since left Wachovia and joined Allied's competitor, American Capital Strategies. I contacted Houck to hear his explanation for his change of heart and newfound regard for Allied's management. He declined to comment beyond referring me to his published research.

The vilification of critics, be they short-sellers, journalists or regulators, chills the free flow of ideas and analysis—indeed, chills free speech by making it so darn expensive. If posting an analysis on a Web site or making a speech gets you an SEC investigation, why bother? Allied's success has emboldened other questionable companies like Overstock.com, Biovail and Fairfax Holdings to take even more aggressive actions against critics. At a minimum, silencing critics through personal attacks will distract some investors from understanding and regulators from dealing with the real problems facing these companies.

There are all kinds of academic studies showing that short selling adds value to the market. One of my friends refers to short-sellers as the "de facto enforcement division of the SEC." I wish the SEC enforcement division could take that on for itself. However, I think the point is much larger than the merits of short selling. The bigger point is the right to, and benefits of, free speech and the open discussion of ideas, especially critical ones, in the context of the American marketplace. The Allieds, the MBIAs (a short that finally became profitable in 2007 after five years), and the Overstock. coms of the world are doing the markets an enormous disservice. Through their toxic tactics, they make the cost of open analysis and open criticism much too high for participants. The reputational and legal cost of defending oneself against bogus manipulation charges deters public discussion.

Unless we wish to encourage the intimidation of critical thinking and speaking, there needs to be regulatory responses to these abusive companies, or we risk stifling the discussion or, at best, forcing it underground. If critical statements about companies are the basis for investigating investors, then managements should not be able with impunity to make the type of false statements seen in this story.

From April 30, 2002, through December 31, 2007, Allied returned 5.9 percent per year including tax distributions, lagging its benchmark, the Russell 2000 index, by about 2.2 percent per year, or about 15 percent cumulatively. As a short, it hadn't been what I expected, but it hasn't been a disaster, either. Greenlight's overall performance remained quite strong, returning 17.7 percent per year during that same period.

■ ■ ■

Six years ago, I told the SEC about Allied's aggressive, inappropriate, and illegal accounting. Five years ago, I told multiple government agencies about the fraud at BLX. Four years ago, I told the FBI that other Allied critics and I had our phone records stolen. Three years ago, I notified Allied's Board in detail about its management's misconduct and made a detailed presentation to the U.S. attorney in Washington outlining a variety of illegal activities. Two years ago, the USDA was notified about BLX's pervasive fraud at that agency. One year ago, Allied admitted it had Greenlight's and my phone records. Neither Allied nor any regulator has commented on the matter since. It is hard to imagine that an investigation should take so long, if Allied is, in fact, co-operating.

As of now, Allied continues its aggressive accounting. The government has not sought repayment for hundreds of millions of losses in its lending programs. No one at Allied has been prosecuted. Its management team remains in place—and has made tens of millions of dollars to boot. The good news is that this can change. The relevant parties—some combination of investors, government agencies, Allied officials or auditors, the media, and prosecutors—may still decide to remedy the situation. Count me an optimist.

Glossary

Audit Guide Manual created by the American Institute of Certified Public Accountants setting forth guidelines for auditing.

Balanced price The price of a stock that matches the demand of both buyers and sellers.

Business development company (BDC) A company that is created to help grow small companies in the initial stages of their development. BDCs are very similar to venture capital funds. Many BDCs are a type of closed end funds. BDCs are investment companies regulated under the Securities Act of 1940.

"Buy side" Shorthand for the "buy side of Wall Street." Firms, such as mutual funds, pension funds, and hedge funds, that invest customer capital.

Carrying value The value of an asset or investment as reflected on the balance sheet.

Charge-off When a loan is taken off the books and acknowledged to be a loss. It does not relieve the debtor of his obligation and the lender can continue to try to collect. Any subsequent collection is called a recovery.

Clearing broker A member of an exchange who is the liaison between an investor and a clearing corporation. A clearing broker helps to ensure that the trade is settled appropriately.

Closed-end fund An investment fund that has a limited number of shares. To invest in a closed-end fund, one needs to buy an interest from an existing holder at the prevailing market price, which may be higher or lower than net asset value. They are one of three types of investment companies recognized by the Securities and Exchange Commission. The others are mutual funds and unit investment trusts.

Controlled company A company in which a majority of the voting shares are held by another company.

David's birthday November 20. Remember to send gifts.

Debtor-in-possession (DIP) facility A loan to a debtor-in-possession in bankruptcy that is normally a first lien superpriority loan.

Debt-service ratio Ratio of net operating income to required debt payments.

Defaulted loan A loan on which the borrower has violated the terms of the loan agreement, such as failing to make timely payments.

Delinquency rate Percentage of loans that have failed to make timely payments.

Enterprise value The total value of a company. It is market capitalization of its equity plus debt, minority interest and preferred shares, minus total cash and cash equivalents.

Equity "kicker" An offer of an ownership position in a company in a deal involving a loan.

Equity warrants Security that entitles the holder to buy stock of a company for a specified exercise price. In many mezzanine investments, the exercise price is a nominal amount.

Exercise date The day on which an investor can exercise an option or a right.

"Fair value" accounting Requires assets to be carried at their fair value—the amount at which that asset could be bought or sold in a current transaction between willing parties, other than in a liquidation.

Financial covenants Financial restrictions under which a borrower agrees to operate as part of a loan agreement.

Fire sale When a company sells its assets under financial duress.

Front-loaded income Revenue that is recognized prior to receiving the cash.

Gain-on-sale accounting Method of recognizing most of the income from a loan at the time of its origination.

Held its debt investment at cost Valuing a loan at its original price.

High coupon When a bond pays a high interest rate.

High-yield bondholder Investor who has bought below-investment-grade (sometimes called "junk" or "high-yield") bonds, which pay high interest, but are riskier than investment-grade debt.

"Hold-to-maturity" accounting Accounting method to value assets based on what they will be worth at maturity. This contrasts with "fair-value" accounting, which values assets based on what they are worth today.

Impaired loans Loans that will not recover full value.

Impairment test A calculation designed to measure whether an investment will not recover its full value.

Investment company Companies, such as mutual funds and business development companies, whose main business is to invest and hold loans or securities of other companies for investment purposes.

Investment-grade bonds A bond that is considered safe, often having a rating of BBB– or above as determined by the bond rating companies.

Junior debt Has a lower repayment priority than other debt if the borrower defaults.

Loan maturity date Date on which all outstanding amounts on a loan must be repaid.

Longs Investors who own a security, hoping that it rises in value.

Loss rate The amount of losses on a portfolio as a percentage of the portfolio.

Mark Another word for accounting value.

Mark-to-market Recording the price of a security to reflect its market value.

Mezzanine lender Investor who makes mezzanine loans.

Mezzanine loan Usually junior debt unsecured by assets. Mezzanine refers to its middle spot, beneath senior debt, but above equity. Maturities usually exceed five years, with the principal payable at the end of the term. These loans sometimes contain a warrant (equity kicker), which lets the borrower buy shares of the company.

Narrow bid-ask spread When the difference is small between the highest price that a buyer is willing to pay for a security and the lowest price for which a seller is willing to sell it.

Net asset value (NAV) The value of an investment company's assets less its liabilities. It is often measured on a per-share basis—the NAV divided by the shares outstanding.

Noncash (PIK) income Income recognized on a loan, but paid in additional securities, rather than cash.

Nonaccrual loan A loan on which the lender stops recognizing income, usually because of the borrower's financial problems.

Non–arm's length A transaction between two related entities.

Operating income (recurring net investment income)   In the context of an investment company, this refers to profits earned from interest, dividends and fees after expenses. Operating income excludes gains or losses from the change in value of the investments.

Opinion letter   Auditor's statement giving its opinion of the financial health of a company.

Origination fees   Money paid to a lender or broker for obtaining a loan.

Oversubscription rights   The opportunity of rights holders to subscribe for additional shares in a rights offering for any shares that other rights holders did not exercise.

Pairs trading   A strategy in which a long investment is matched with a short investment in a comparable industry.

Par   Face value of an investment.

Pari passu   Two or more investments, such as loans or bonds, that have the same seniority and thus equal rights of payment.

Payment-in-kind income   See Noncash (PIK) income.

Portfolio-Lending Accounting   Method of recognizing income from loans ratably over time.

Preferred Lending Provider (PLP)   A designation given to lenders who demonstrate a thorough knowledge of the Small Business Administration's requirements that allows them to make and service loans in several SBA lending programs, including the 7(a), without prior loan approval by the agency.

Pretexting   Obtaining the phone records of another person or persons by impersonating them to their phone companies.

Private illiquid securities   Securities that are not registered with the SEC and for which there is no broad market and are thus thinly traded.

Recapitalize   To change the capital structure of a company. A strategy often followed by companies in financial distress, which may include the injection of additional funds.

Record date   The date an investor must own a stock in order to be eligible for distributions. Commonly used to determine who is eligible for stock dividends.

Reinsurance   Insurance for insurance companies, purchased as a way to reduce risk by spreading it to other insurers.

Residual assets   The assets of a company or special purpose entity that remain after the claims of senior debt holders are met.

Residual interests   The capitalized assets created through gain-on-sale accounting that reflect the up-front profits booked at origination.

Rights offerings   A means of raising capital by giving additional shareholders the right to buy additional stock at a set (discounted) price within a fixed period.

"Road show"   A series of meetings with existing or potential investors in an effort to drum up interest in a security.

Rollup   A company formed by purchasing a series of small companies in the same line of business.

SBA loans (guaranteed and unguaranteed)   Loans offered with the partial backing of the Small Business Administration (the federal government). The loan can be broken into two pieces. The guaranteed piece has the full backing of the SBA. The unguaranteed piece has no such protection.

Secondary market loan sale premiums   The profit made by an originator selling loans to an investor.

Securitization   The process of putting loans into groups (known as pools) and converting the pools into securities. This often includes carving the securities into different pieces (known as tranches) to be sold to investors of varying risk appetites.

Securitization facility   A short-term lending arrangement to finance loans while they are being assembled into pools pending securitization.

Sell short (shorting)   The opposite of owning, or being long; an investment that profits from a decline in a security value.

"Sell side"   Shorthand for the "sell side of Wall Street." Firms, such as investment banks, that create and sell investments to investors or the "buy side."

Senior debt   A bond that takes priority over other debt securities in case of default.

Shareholder distributions   A company's distributions to its shareholders, usually in cash or stock.

Short squeeze   When the price of a stock rises quickly and investors who sold short cover their position by buying the stock to prevent further losses. This covering causes an additional rise in the price creating additional losses for any remaining short sellers.

Specialist   A member of a stock exchange who is responsible for the trading of a stock or several stocks. Specialists make a market in their stocks by displaying their best bid and asked prices and must maintain a fair and orderly market in those stocks.

Stock dividends   Distributions to shareholders in additional stock, rather than cash.

Stock split   Where a company's stock is divided into multiple shares. For example, a 2-for-1 split of a $100 stock results in two shares worth $50 each.

Subordinated debt investment   Investment made in a debt instrument that is junior to senior debt.

Tax distribution   Taxable earnings that are distributed to shareholders.

Taxable income   The part of a company's earnings that are subject to federal and state taxation.

Transparency   Refers to a company conducting its business out in the open with good disclosure so investors have a clear idea of its operations and performance.

Underwriting loans   The act of determining whether and on what terms to issue a loan to a prospective borrower, often based on analysis of the prospects creditworthiness.

Unrealized depreciation   The excess of the basis of an investment over its fair market value.

Walton's birthday   I don't know, but I would recommend a copy of *Fooling Some of the People All of the Time* as a gift.

Write-down   Decrease in the stated value of an asset.

Write-up   Increase in the stated value of an asset.

Year of origination   The date when a loan was issued.

Yield to maturity   A loan's total return, stated as an interest rate, if it is held until it matures.

About the Author

David Einhorn is the President and founder of Greenlight Capital, a long-short value-oriented hedge fund, which started with $1 million under management in 1996. Over the ensuing years, Greenlight has generated greater than a twenty-five percent annualized net return for its partners. David is the Chairman of Greenlight Capital Re, Ltd. (Nasdaq: GLRE) and serves on the boards of the Michael J. Fox Foundation for Parkinson's Research and Hillel: The Foundation for Jewish Campus Life. David graduated *summa cum laude* with distinction in all subjects from Cornell University in 1991, where he earned a B.A. from the College of Arts and Sciences.

Index